To Sam
very best wishes
from
[signature] Dec 1999

Making Sexual History

For my mother

Making Sexual History

Jeffrey Weeks

First published in 2000 by Polity Press in association with Blackwell Publishers Ltd.

Editorial office:
Polity Press
65 Bridge Street
Cambridge CB2 1UR, UK

Marketing and production:
Blackwell Publishers Ltd
108 Cowley Road
Oxford OX4 1JF, UK

Published in the USA by
Blackwell Publishers Inc.
Commerce Place
350 Main Street
Malden, MA 02148, USA

A catalogue record for this book is available from the British Library.

Library of Congress Cataloging–in–Publication Data

Weeks, Jeffrey, 1945–
  Making sexual history / Jeffrey Weeks.
    p. cm.
  Includes bibliographical references and index.
  ISBN 0–7456–2114–7 (acid-free paper).
  ISBN 0–7456–2115–5 (pbk :
acid-free paper)
    1. Sex—History. 2. Sex—Historiography. 3. Homosexuality—
History. 4. Homosexuality—Historiography. 5. Sexology—History.
I. Title.
HQ12.W44   2000
306.7'09—dc21   99–36411
                                                              CIP

Typeset in 10 on 12 pt Sabon
by Kolam Information Services Pvt Ltd, Pondicherry, India
Printed in Great Britain by T J International, Padstow, Cornwall

This book is printed on acid-free paper.

Contents

Preface and Acknowledgements

This book attempts two closely related tasks. First of all, it argues that in order to understand the world of sexuality we need to grasp that it is not made behind our backs, by Nature, History or Society. *We* are the makers of sexual history, in our everyday lives, in our life experiments, in the tangle between desire, responsibility, contingency and opportunity. We may not make it in circumstances entirely of our own choosing, but we have more choice than we often believe or seize. Secondly, in various essays, written over a number of years, it records my own efforts both to understand and to help to remake the history of sexuality.

Though the essays were written for different occasions, and varying audiences, I would suggest that they reveal a consistency of outlook, though a constantly developing rethinking of issues, which gives the collection a coherence and value beyond the contingencies of the first appearance of the chapters. The organizing theme is the relationship between writing about, and acting on, the history and social organization of sexuality: the process of making sexual history in an ever more complex world.

Part I is concerned with writers on sexuality, from Havelock Ellis to influential contemporaries. The persistent theme is less the truth or scientific validity of the topics these writers discuss than the social and political context in which they wrote, and the significance of their writings for shaping the meanings given to sex and intimacy. In an important sense, as we move through these writers, we can witness a major shift from an expert discourse to an activist discourse: from science to grassroots sexology.

Part II is more concerned with the historical and sociological rethinking of what sexuality is (a 'historic invention'), and the ways in which the erotic is being reinvented by the new sexual movements and day-to-day experiments in living. The impact of AIDS is a prominent theme, but so is the incremental change which has transformed personal lives.

Part III looks in more detail at recent examples of the everyday remaking of the sexual world: in the development of sexual communities, through the community-based response to HIV and AIDS, and in the emergence of 'families of choice'. The concluding chapter looks beyond the millennium, looming as I write, and argues that these grass-roots endeavours, everyday experiments in living, are both products and harbingers of profound changes in the opportunities open to us for living lives based on freedom, justice and choice rather than the harsh certainties of tradition. We live, I have argued elsewhere, in an age of uncertainty. That should not mean that we surrender to pessimism and despair. On the contrary, there are new opportunities to be grasped, new meanings to shape, better ways of making, and remaking, sexual history.

My debts to friends and colleagues over many years are too many to list here. The essays themselves testify to specific intellectual debts. I want to thank, however, all the editors and publishers who helped navigate the individual pieces to original publication, and who generously allowed me to republish here. I must thank Peter Aggleton, Chris McKevitt, Kay Parkinson and Austin Taylor-Laybourn, who were my research, and writing, colleagues on the 'Voluntary Sector Responses to HIV and AIDS' project, discussed in chapter 10. I owe Brian Heaphy and Catherine Donovan an immense debt for their friendship and collegiality in working on the 'Families of Choice' project, whose findings are outlined in Chapter 11. The British Economic and Social Research Council funded the research for both projects, and I am deeply grateful for their generosity and wisdom at a difficult time for funding sex-related research. My colleagues at South Bank University provided the usual academic distractions, but also a deep support, for which I am grateful. I owe especial thanks to Donna Thompson for her calm and deliberate administrative backing at all crucial times. Matthew Waites proved a loyal and thoughtful ally in helping me to make the final choice of these essays, and in helping me to make them suitable for publication here. I owe him many thanks.

Micky Burbidge, as always, has shown me the power, strength and durability of loyal friendship over many years, and I can only record my enduring gratitude. My partner, Mark McNestry, has lived with every moment of the construction of this book with patience, care, fortitude, and the ultimate compliment, trust. Its completion was momentarily delayed by the peculiar traumas and joys of a home move. I would not have missed that, or Mark's continuing devotion and support, for anything.

The introduction and chapter 12 are published here for the first time. Other chapters were originally published as follows:

'Havelock Ellis and the Politics of Sex Reform', first published in Sheila Rowbotham and Jeffrey Weeks, *Socialism and the New Life*, Pluto Press 1977.

'Mary McIntosh and the "Homosexual Role"', originally published as 'The "Homosexual Role" after 30 Years: An Appreciation of the Work of Mary McIntosh', *Sexualities*, 1(2), 1998, © Sage Publications 1998; republished with the permission of Sage Publications.

'Dennis Altman and the Politics of (Homo)Sexual Liberation', originally published as 'Introduction' to Dennis Altman, *Homosexual Oppression and Liberation*, new edition, New York University Press 1993; republished with the permission of the publishers.

'Guy Hocquenghem and *Homosexual Desire*', originally published as 'Preface' to Guy Hocquenghem, *Homosexual Desire*, Allison and Busby 1978, Duke University Press 1995.

'Foucault for Historians', originally published in *History Workshop Journal*, 14, Autumn 1982; republished with the permission of the HWJ Collective and Oxford University Press.

'Sexuality and History Revisited', originally published in Lynn Jamieson and Helen Corr (eds), *State, Private Life and Political Change*, Macmillan and St Martin's Press 1990; republished with the permission of the publishers.

'AIDS and the Regulation of Sexuality', originally published in Virginia Berridge and Philip Strong (eds), *AIDS and Contemporary History*, Cambridge University Press 1993; republished with the permission of the publishers.

'An Unfinished Revolution: Sexuality in the Twentieth Century', originally published in Victoria Harwood, David Oswell, Kay Parkinson and Anna Ward (eds), *Pleasure Principles: Politics, Sexuality and Ethics*, Lawrence and Wishart 1993; republished with the permission of the publishers.

'The Idea of a Sexual Community', first published in *Soundings*, 2, Spring 1996; republished with the permission of the editors and Lawrence and Wishart, the publishers.

'Community Responses to HIV and AIDS: The "De-Gaying" and "Re-Gaying" of AIDS', originally published in Jeffrey Weeks and Janet Holland (eds), *Sexual Cultures: Communities, Values and Intimacy*, Macmillan and St Martin's Press 1996; republished with the permission of the publishers.

'Everyday Experiments: Narratives of Non-Heterosexual Relationships', originally published in Elizabeth Silva and Carol Smart (eds), *The New Family?*, Sage Publications 1999; republished with the permission of the publishers.

Introduction: Making Sexual History

Who makes sexual history? A generation ago the question would have been absurd. It was taken for granted that the truths of sex were timeless. Attitudes, legal forms, religious injunctions, moral codes, literary expressions, subcultural patterns might change, but the substratum of erotic energy and gendered (as it was not then called) relationships remained locked into biological necessity, beyond the realms of history or social science. There was a world of social life, susceptible to understanding through learning the laws of society or of historical necessity; and there was the domain of the essential, graspable only through uncovering the laws of nature. As a result, historians and sociologists (the two categories I could myself identify with) left the quest for sexual knowledge to others: psychologists, mythologists, anthropologists, sexologists could delve, but my own disciplines largely stood aloof. Ken Plummer as late as the 1970s (Plummer 1975) noted the lamentable absence of a sustained sociology of sexuality, and I began my own work on the modern history of sexuality in Britain, what became *Sex, Politics and Society* (Weeks 1981/1989), with a similar sense that this was *terra incognita*.

Today that has all changed, in large part at first as a result of the efforts of self-proclaimed sexual dissidents: the new feminist and lesbian and gay scholarship led the way in politically charged interventions, recovering a lost or ignored history or experience, and inventing or reinventing the idea of women's history, lesbian and gay history and the like. More recently senior scholars from more traditional backgrounds have engaged seriously with the sexual (and of course many of the pioneering explorers are today themselves senior members of the academy). Now bookshops groan with shelves of books on the history, sociology, psychology, literature, philosophy, theory, theologies, practices and politics of sexuality. Publishers large and small have (more or less) profitable lists. Universities run courses. Many of us thrive on an extensive international conference circuit. There has been an unprecedented discursive revolution in writing about sexuality, gender and the body.

As I argue later in the book, writing about sexuality can be dangerous, but it is also constitutive: through the web of meaning we writers about the erotic weave in our intricate ways not only are beliefs and behaviours shaped, but the very definition of what sexuality is can be refined and then radically rethought. After Michel Foucault (1979) we have become accustomed to seeing 'sexuality' as an invented ensemble of related but disparate elements sometimes only contingently related to bodily needs or desires, and 'performed', as Judith Butler (1990, 1993) has suggested, in power-laden situations. After Plummer (1975, 1995) we have become aware of the impact of stigma in defining the boundaries of acceptability, and the impact of sexual 'stories' in both voicing and giving meaning to erotic activities. A vast literature on sexual identities, to which I myself have contributed (Weeks 1977/1990, 1985, 1991, 1995), has conclusively demonstrated the power of culture in giving definition to what or who we are, even as cultures of power are at last recognized as central to the construction, legitimization and delegitimization of patterns of sexual interaction. Now even the body and its pleasures, which Foucault saw as the last point of resistance to the controlling apparatus which delimited the erotic, are seen as part of a 'reflexive project' in which thoughts and meanings – even virtual reality – have as much weight as physiognomy and genetic imprinting (see Giddens 1991).

So we need to explore how sexual history is written because its contribution to how sexuality is lived is central. Hence my own preoccupation with theories of sexuality, and the construction, and contestation, of sexual knowledge, from Havelock Ellis to the present. Unless we can understand what they (we) were trying to do it becomes impossible, I believe, to understand fully the web in which we are entangled.

Yet most people live their sexual lives without a sense of history (or at least a detailed knowledge of the history of sexuality), and certainly without reading books on sexual history. Whatever the genuine theoretical breakthroughs of thinking of the erotic in terms of 'performativity', inventions, narratives or fictions (see Weeks 1995), we must always be aware that sexuality is lived as well as written about. The ultimate makers of sexual history do not dwell in the ivory towers of academe but on the ground, or perhaps, better, in the bedrooms or even at what AIDS researchers call the PSEs (public sex environments), negotiating their everyday lives as best they can in the circumstances in which they find themselves. The writers of sexual history must necessarily balance their theories with an understanding of practices, weighing their discursive analysis against an analysis of how discourse is lived.

Transformations

My own practice as a professional social scientist, grounded in a historical training and performing as a sociologist, dabbling in a host of other intellectual activities, but specializing in the sexual, has been tempered by my own practice as a sexual being and my wider socio-cultural belongings and political engagements and alignments. This nexus has demanded simultaneously a commitment to traditional canons of scholarly achievement and to the perceived truths of my experience. I have sought, in my own way, to be both a truth-teller and a yeah-sayer, to analyse and to tell my personal stories and preoccupations. My local, particular experience has not been purely individual, however, because I profoundly believe that personal life and macro-historical trends are inextricably combined. In the contingencies of everyday life we can see the impact of world-historical events; and through our understanding of the long-term shifts in social and economic transformation we may grasp the limits and possibilities of change in the sphere of the intimate. The changes in our own private lives are part of wider, collective transformations. The challenge lies in teasing out the hidden connections, making sense of what often seems incomprehensible, or merely idiosyncratic.

Of course, such thoughts were only latent in my mind when I began what has become, despite my original best intentions, a career in sexual studies, an intellectual sex-worker if you like. At the beginning of the 1970s I was completing a postgraduate study in political theory, an exploration of early twentieth-century socialist pluralist writings (the work of the British Guild Socialists largely), to which I gave the title 'The Search for Community'. The title seemed apt for that particular piece of research, but in a peculiar way it became a leitmotif in my subsequent intellectual career – and personal life. For it was another definition of community that grabbed me as I finished the study – the new idea of a gay community, condition for and product of the eruption of lesbian and gay activism after 1970. Working at the London School of Economics from October 1970, in my first academic research job, I soon got drawn into the London Gay Liberation Front, which had its first meetings there. It is not too extreme or exaggerated a description when I say that everything changed for me from then on: my personal life and commitments, my political engagement and eventually my intellectual trajectory and research agenda. It was, in Anthony Giddens's (1991) graphic phrase, a 'fateful moment' which forced a reordering of my personal narrative and the way I saw the world. I came out with a bump, and eventually harnessed my innate romanticism and latent utopianism to a new sense of what was possible. I assumed a new personal identity, found a new sense of belonging, and became committed to a new political project. And I began research on sexuality and sexual history.

Of course, though it seemed like – indeed was – a deeply personal experience, it was also a profound collective experience. Through a new social involvement, I began remaking my sense of self, but the new identity I embraced was the product of a transformation of historical possibility that we are still working through, though in quite different ways from those we anticipated in the early 1970s. With decent hindsight it is now possible to see that what I, and many others, lived through was the first burst of what has now become a firestorm of change that is literally changing the world.

My experiences then opened an ongoing conversation between academic knowledge, political and ethical commitments and personal life which has continued to this day. The essays in this book, written at various periods in response to research interests and ongoing changes, are a reflection of this continuing dialogue. Let me now, therefore, try to outline the main concerns of my own historical and sociological practice, the making of sexual history.

As I suggested earlier, we need to address two fundamental questions: how we conceptualize, and know, the sexual; and how we live it – 'make it' in every sense. This has shaped three preoccupations which have dominated my work, and provide the framework of this book: with the construction and reconstruction of sexual knowledge; with rethinking the history of sexuality; and with the everyday making of sexual history. In the rest of this chapter I shall attempt to explore each of these themes with reference to my own work, and in particular the essays in this book.

Reconstructing sexual knowledge

Sexuality emerged as a subject for serious study at the end of the nineteenth century, signalled most clearly by the development of a separate discipline devoted to it: sexology, the would-be science of desire (Weeks 1985). Havelock Ellis (see chapter 1) was one of its pioneers in the English-speaking world, and I became interested in him originally for two reasons. First, he was in his earlier life part of that circle of British socialists and radicals that in the 1880s began to try to link up the woman question and the problem of sexuality with wider questions of social and cultural transformation (a group I had first encountered when I began my postgraduate research in socialist theory). He was a participant in the Fellowship of the New Life out of which came both the Fabian Society and the first Labour prime minister, but which was originally concerned with 'the subordination of material things to spiritual' and 'the cultivation of a perfect character in each and all'. He was a close friend of the South African feminist Olive Schreiner, and became a hero to many other feminist leaders. He was a friend of the socialist propagandist and pioneering advocate of homosexual love, Edward Carpenter. Heterosexual himself, though with a minor sexual 'perversion' of his own, urolagnia (pleasure in urination), he married a lesbian, and with John Addington Symonds he wrote the first 'scientific' book on homosexuality, *Sexual Inversion*. There was interest enough here!

But I came to realize that Ellis represented more than simply a complex and fascinating life. He seemed to me to embody the influence of sexology on progressive thinking in the twentieth century. His theories on homosexuality, as an inborn inversion of the sexual instinct, his way of writing about the subject, with abundance of cross-cultural, even cross-species, examples, his cautious advocacy of decriminalization and of social toleration, seemed to epitomize the liberal approach that was dominant when I was first coming to terms with my own sexuality. His views on women, equal but different, sexual but needing to be 'kissed into love' by the more aggressive male, had also, in the post-war world, become hegemonic. I was fascinated, therefore, by this paradox: how a man who had come out of a radical milieu, not, other things being equal, all that different from the one I was involved in, could become the icon of a liberal sexual ideology that by the 1970s I was committed to opposing because of its drastic limitations. How could a perceived radical of the 1890s seem not only *passé* but positively reactionary by the 1970s?

From this sense of dislocation came an insight which structured much of my later work: that sexology not only attempted to understand the sexual world, but actually helped to shape it. This was clearly the case, it seemed to me, with regard to homosexuality. In defining the homosexual as a distinct type of person, Ellis was one of those who helped the twentieth century to believe that homosexuals were different from heterosexuals, that they were separate types of sexual being. I argued, then, that work such as Ellis's was a major element in the constitution of a separate homosexual category, which in turn has fundamentally shaped the identities of self-defined homosexual people, women and men, throughout the twentieth century. Subsequently, a number of feminist writers have gone further, in excoriating Ellis as the definer of female sexual subordination (Jeffreys 1985). Such was the power of the word.

Of course, the reality was rather more complex than this simple summary. Ellis did not invent a separate homosexual experience. He learnt of it from colleagues like Symonds and Carpenter, from case studies solicited by or anonymously sent to him, from friends – and from his wife. What he did was to give theoretical weight to the idea, in Foucault's (1979) phrase, that the homosexual belonged to a species. He gave expert credence to the dichotomization of heterosexuality and homosexuality.

Many self-identified homosexuals welcomed this (see Weeks and Porter 1998), and it has indeed become the fundamental framework for twentieth-century sexual categorizations, identities and politics. The obsessive contemporary searchers after the gay gene or gay brain can be seen as Ellis's and his confrères' spiritual heirs. So why did I – do I – find it problematic?

The first difficulty was that Ellis presents as true something that he was in part – with a number of others – inventing: the idea that sexuality can be understood in terms of neat categories and typologies. The research I was already undertaking for what became my book *Coming Out* (1977/ 1990) was making me aware that the late nineteenth century was doing something more than simply applying reason to understanding sexuality, and especially homosexuality. It was attempting to impose a particular meaning on it. Yet it was clear in Ellis's own work, and has become even clearer in the work of sexual theorists and investigators throughout the twentieth century, that the erotic always overflows the neat divisions that science simultaneously imposes. From Freud to Kinsey we can see the tensions between behaviour and identity, private desire and public morality, dreams and reality, sexuality as presented and sexuality as lived (Weeks 1985). Secondly, however important the sexological effort was in feeding into liberalizing efforts in the twentieth century (and despite his limitations I remain convinced that Ellis and his like were on the whole forces for good), we now needed to go beyond that in order to realize the hopes awakened by the new radical sexual politics of the early 1970s.

Mary McIntosh's essay on 'The Homosexual Role' provided an intellectual spur to my understanding of what was wrong with the liberal sexological tradition (see chapter 2). That tradition assumed that homosexuality was a condition which some people had and others did not. In a groundbreaking think piece published as early as 1968, McIntosh wondered why we did not ask a more difficult question: what were the historical circumstances that led us to believe that this was the case? As she was able to show, the assumption of a distinct condition obscured the gap between behaviour and category that Alfred Kinsey and comparative anthropology (and indeed sexologists like Ellis himself) abundantly demonstrated. It ignored the existence of varying transhistorical patterns for organizing same-sex activities. And most daringly of all, McIntosh was able to show that the concept of a separate historical existence for the people we call homosexuals was of comparatively recent origin, probably dating back no earlier than the late seventeenth century. This article opened up an agenda – almost ten years, be it noted, before Michel Foucault published a similar argument – which historians and social scientists, and indeed 'queer theorists', are still pursuing. It posed fundamental questions which still tease us: what are the sources of the heterosexual/homosexual binarism, and what are the effects of that dichotomy on structuring individual lives, and sexual history?

Following through the logic of the argument, I suggested that the recent history of homosexuality could best be interpreted as a complex process of definition and self-definition. On the one hand we could trace the social, cultural and political forces that shaped the creation of homosexuality as a minority, and generally socially execrated, experience: religion, the law, state activities, family ideologies, class consolidation, popular prejudice, the institutions of medicine, psychiatry, even sexology. On the other hand there were forces of resistance: individual struggles, subcultural developments, nascent organizations for homosexual rights.

In the heady days of the early 1970s it was these proto-gay 'movements of affirmation' that especially intrigued me, because they seemed the first tinklings of what became the chorus of self-assertion in the new international lesbian and gay movement. If as Dennis Altman asserted in his pioneering work of gay liberation theory, *Homosexual: Oppression and Liberation*, its aim was to welcome the end of the homosexual, and of course of the heterosexual – or to put it less polemically, to make the distinction socially meaningless – the road to it was through an affirmation of identity, a strengthening of community, and the political activity of lesbians and gays themselves (see chapter 3). The paradox that you can only get rid of oppressive dichotomies by affirming the subordinate form in order to challenge the hegemonic term is one that continues to haunt the radical agenda, and has led directly to an identity politics that is generally wedded to what differentiates us rather than what we have in common.

But a transgressive tradition has survived, most obviously alive in recent years in queer theory and politics. We can see the early expression of that not just in Altman's work but in a book from quite a different tradition, Guy Hocquenghem's essay on *Homosexual Desire* (see chapter 4). This was first published in France in 1972, almost contemporaneously with Altman's book, and I subsequently introduced it to an English audience in 1978. Its real significance, however, is that he sharply posed the issue in a way which has continued to be important: 'The problem is not so much homosexual desire as the fear of homosexuality.' Though expressed in the terms of post-1968 French intellectual delirium, the question he asks is actually similar to both McIntosh's and Altman's: why out of the flux of desires, which is neither homosexual nor heterosexual, do we insist on sharp categorizations? His answer, in terms of Oedipalization, anti-homosexual paranoia, the sublimated anus and all, might not excite everyone's enthusiasm, but it is clearly congruent with more recent concerns with the roots and forms of homophobia, the embedded nature of the heterosexual imperative, and sexual transgressiveness as a form of resistance. Despite its limitations, which are explored in my essay, it is perhaps not surprising that his book has recently been welcomed as a proto-queer intervention (see Marshall 1996; and Moon 1993).

From Ellis to McIntosh, Altman, Hocquenghem and the like we can trace, I would argue, a profound shift in the locus of sexual knowledge construction: from the scientific expert to the politicized grass roots. The fact that Ellis had radical roots and his own liberalizing agenda, and the new theorists were academics or intellectuals, does not obviate my main point: that whereas the pioneering sexologists were speaking for a scientific understanding of the erotic, the new sexual intellectuals were speaking from experience, from a sense of community involvement, and for a political-cultural project. In the new writing on sexuality from the early 1970s we can see the beginnings of what Steven Epstein (1996), with particular reference to HIV/AIDS, describes as 'credibility struggles' to determine who can legitimately speak the truth about sexuality. The generation since has seen a number of symbolic struggles over this, from the early zaps by gay liberationists of psychological conferences and dubious publications, through the battles to remove the definition of homosexuality as a disease from diagnostic manuals, to the heavy involvement of activists in defining the nature of HIV/AIDS and the burgeoning literature on sexual diversity – from s/m to transgender – written by practitioners and fellow travellers. Of course, there have always been popularizing writers on sexuality, and the scientific exploration of sexuality continues. Both have an important part to play in our growing understanding of the domain of sexuality. The argument I want to make is a different one. The significant shift is that those who were talked about in the pioneering works of the sexologists are now speaking openly for themselves, in a variety of voices, and are changing the nature of the debate. The history of sexuality can never be the same again.

Rethinking the history of sexuality

So far I have given little credit to the work of Michel Foucault, often seen as the source of the revolution in sexual thinking I have tried to describe. This is not because I undervalue him – on the contrary, Foucault has profoundly influenced me (see chapter 5). But chronologically and theoretically, the intellectual revolution was already well under way by the time he published his introductory essay on the history of sexuality (Foucault 1979). What his *History of Sexuality* did was to offer a wider theoretical context for understanding the development of modern sexual discourses, and to relate it to broader considerations of power as a way of constituting a history of the present: a map of the sexual battle-field. Of course, in many ways Foucault fundamentally challenged the easy ideology of early sexual radicalism, and especially the assumption that sexuality in and of itself could provide a challenge to the complex configurations of power. His critique of the psychoanalytic institution – invoking a 'confession' in order for individuals to become free within a framework that was wholly complicit with a long, and repressive, cul-tural tradition – offered a vital justification for deconstructing the dis-parate forms of power. Similarly, it was salutary to have spelled out for us that by working within the confines of historically constituted categories of sexuality we were in danger of remaining trapped within them. Most important, however, was his injunction to see sexuality as itself an historic-ally specific discursive formation, with effects in the real world, and therefore pointing the way for a historical project that explored the various forces that shaped and regulated sexual life.

This is what I sought to do in my book *Sex, Politics and Society* (Weeks 1981/1989), conceived before I encountered Foucault, but completed in full knowledge of Foucault's enterprise. The essay 'Sexuality and History Revisited' (chapter 6) is an attempt at a critical review of a post-Fou-cauldian understanding of sexual history. I suggest that what the new sexual history has achieved is three things:

1 There has been a recognition that sex can no longer be seen as locked into the natural. It is a legitimate subject of historical investigation. Seeing sexuality as a 'social construction' or 'historical invention' forces us to think beyond the boundaries of existing categories and to explore their historical production.
2 Deconstruction of sexuality prepares us for reconstruction: for understand-ing the historical present so that we can potentially intervene in it to change it.
3 In demonstrating the moral and sexual diversity of the past we may learn to come to terms with the diversity of the present.

This last injunction is all the more important when we consider the role of the unexpected. The new sexual history has taught us to try to understand the variety of social forces which shape sexuality. The sudden emergence of the AIDS crisis in the early 1980s forced all of us to re-evaluate the taken for granted: about sexual behaviour, the importance of relationships, the way we treat the vulnerable and sick, the role of expertise, the potentiality for other voices to intervene, and so on. But it also tested the validity of the theoretical protocols developed over the previous decade, and by and large did not find them wanting. In the vast increase in sex research unexpect-edly occasioned by the AIDS crisis, it is striking that many of the most controversial insights of the sexual writers of the 1970s – about the difference between behaviour and identity, for instance, and the possibility of collective changes of behaviour, as in the adoption of safer sex in the gay male community – were confirmed. The new sexual history offered a guide to further research and practice – as we had hoped when we first tried to formulate it. In 'AIDS and the Regulation of Sexuality' (chapter 7), which attempts to place our responses to HIV and AIDS in a complex history which frames our beliefs and behaviours, I try to put this hard-earned understanding into analytical operation.

The AIDS crisis also, however, cast a sharp new light on what I have called the 'Unfinished Revolution' in sexual attitudes (chapter 8). It revealed the difficulty our cultures have in coming to terms with sexual diversity. We acknowledge it, but find it difficult to live with it and accept it fully. In the 1980s, moreover, in the shadow of AIDS it was not sexual radicalism but the moral conservatism of the New Right that appeared to be seizing the initiative. Sexual radicalism seemed doomed to be locked either into the 'sex wars', a vituperative assertion of incompatible claims to right and justice amongst competing groups of self-declared radicals; or overwhelmed in the culture wars; or seeking salvation in returning to the fruitless search for origins and a natural justification of sexual difference and diversity in the genes or the brain. I became convinced that none of these offered viable ways forward. On the contrary, what we had to do was to articulate more clearly our values. If we believed that homosexuality offered a valid way of life, and a legitimate life choice, then why couldn't we just say that, instead of proving the unprovable: that gays constituted a natural born minority? If AIDS demonstrated the permeability of our identities, was it valid to stay trapped within them? If social constructionism demonstrated the power of definition, in what ways should we redefine the sexual? This is what I tried to address in my book *Invented Moralities* (1995), and 'An Unfinished Revolution' offers a background to this argument.

Making history

In fact, all around us we can see the rich development of everyday sexual values which belies the prophets of doom:

1 In the ideal of the sexual community embodied in the lesbian and gay community, we can see the growth of social capital, which made possible the response to the HIV/AIDS crisis (chapter 9).
2 In the community-based response to HIV/AIDS itself we can see the significance of grass-roots knowledge and creativity in making possible a

massive response, originally in the face of indifference or deliberate neglect, and then as a model of care and innovation in the complex response to the epidemic (chapter 10).

3   In the development of non-heterosexual created families, or 'families of choice', we observe networks of mutual care and support where key values of mutual respect, responsibility, care and love can be worked through in genuine 'experiments in living' based on new forms of intimacy, equality, mutual negotiation and choice (chapter 11).

Which brings us squarely to the present, and likely futures. In the 1980s, as writers began to perceive the *fin de millennium* looming under the shadow of AIDS and sexual reaction, a rash of gloomy prognostications began to appear about our sexual futures. In the countdown to the millennium a rise in apocalyptic thinking may indeed be inevitable, and we have not been short of prophets of that. A sense of an ending seemed to loom over many analyses, a sense of living at the edge of the world, enticed and repelled by panic culture and the pleasures and pains of catastrophe. Yet as the millennium strikes my sense is of a new mood. Yes, the culture wars continue, sex panics still rise and fall, fundamentalism grows. There are many areas of profound cultural uncertainty, and new dilemmas emerge and confuse: genetic engineering, embryological research, virtual sex, the boundaries between children and adults, the permeability but resilience of gender and sexual categories, sex tourism and exploitation – the list is potentially endless. But many of the old issues are already fading; what seemed impossible thirty years ago – like same-sex marriages – is now on the agenda everywhere in the west, in varying degrees. Even the threat of epidemic begins to fade as new therapies lengthen lives, and make it possible to see HIV/AIDS as a chronic but manageable disease. The sexual world changes. New issues arise. But what is surely new is the sense we have today that it does not do so behind our backs. We can intervene in the world of the erotic as we can in other social phenomena. The sexual is not an all-powering force beyond human control. Made in a complex history, it can be changed in and through history. Sexual history is not made somewhere out there, in Nature. It is made by us here, in our everyday lives. We all make sexual history.

Coda

These essays were written over a period of twenty years or so. They reveal (I trust) a continuous development in my own thinking about the nature of sexuality. It would be surprising, therefore, if they did not show both overlaps and contradictions. I have not sought to eliminate these, not least because their presence should uncover the hazards of attempting to write sexual history, and the changing circumstances in which we both write about and live sexuality. I have attempted to eliminate errors where they have stared me in the face, and have added additional observations, especially concerning subsequent interpretations, where I thought it appropriate and necessary. I have not ordered the chapters in the chronological order in which they were written, but tried to group them in what seemed to me a logical, analytical order to offer a kind of intellectual autobiography. The result, I hope, is a dialogue between my present and past selves, in a fashion which makes sense of what I have been trying to say over an extended period of work.

My own rereading of this work, however, suggests as much consistency as inconsistency in my arguments over a hectic twenty years. My interpretations of events may have subtly altered over time, but my broad preoccupations have been constant. Theoretically, I have been continuously concerned with the struggle to understand the ways in which what we call the sexual has been shaped in a complex history. I have never subscribed to the view that sexuality is simply the domain of nature, because the evidence is overwhelming that the sexual world is in constant flux. The physical acts may seem broadly the same across all cultures, all historic periods, but their meanings change all the time. A simple comparison of the nineteenth and twentieth centuries reveals this: my preoccupation with the history of homosexuality over the past century is more than simply a personal obsession. I believe it to be deeply revealing about the ways in which sexuality as a whole is shaped and reshaped. It is a marker for wider sexual change. Similarly, my analysis and reanalysis of the question of sexual identity which recurs throughout the essays may have roots in personal change, but it has been a focus of my writing because it is self-evident to me that identities are more than reflections of a deep natural instinct. They are the sites for the historical positioning of who and what we are, and want to become. They are made in history.

This is turn poses questions about how we conceive the relationship between past and present. I have avoided, I believe consistently, an unthinking progressivism, a sexual whiggism. I do not think the present is an automatic outcome of the past, that everything is for the best in all possible worlds. The real gains in openness about the erotic, in increasing toleration of diversity, in widening spaces for life experiments, have to be measured against the suffering that all too many people have been burdened by because of their personal struggles, the resilience of ignorance, prejudice and discrimination, the reality of epidemic, moral fundamentalism, and the timidity of politicians. The changes that have taken place have had to be fought for in ever-changing circumstances. In trying to understand this tangled skein we cannot rely on easy distinctions between the traditional and the modern, the modern and the postmodern. These terms are themselves contested, underlining the complexity of sexual history. To take one example, the rise of sexual fundamentalisms wedded to the renewal of traditional values is itself a product of late modernity, using advanced means of information technology to promote the values of an imagined past (Bhatt 1997). One of the themes that goes through the essays in this book is precisely that of the changing meaning of modernity. Havelock Ellis saw himself as the very essence of the modern. By the early 1970s he seemed part of the problem. Today, perhaps, it is easier to see that 'modernity' (to say nothing of 'postmodernity') is an ambiguous concept whose meaning depends on your value stance.

Politically, like everyone else's, my positions have shifted over time. I have no doubt shed some of my youthful utopianism. Time tempers euphoria. Experience hardens caution. Circumstances force new, hopefully more realistic, commitments. Yet my basic values, refined by lived experience, rendered more sophisticated, one hopes, through the intellectual trajectory, have remained steady. I believe in the necessity to question constantly the taken for granted, especially explanations which rely on unthinking genuflections to Nature, to broaden our understanding of the intricacies of the erotic, to respect diversity, and to explore the possibilities of different ways of being. The aim is not to develop a new set of truths about sexual history, but rather to challenge the assumption that there can be a final truth about sexuality.

So these essays are not definitive; they do not foreclose debate. On the contrary, I offer them here to open up debate, to continue the endless conversation about the meaning and place of sexuality in our history and culture.

References

Bhatt, Chetan (1997) *Liberation and Purity: Race, New Religious Movements and the Ethics of Postmodernity*, London: UCL Press.

Butler, Judith (1990) *Gender Trouble: Feminism and the Subversion of Identity*, New York and London: Routledge.

Butler, Judith (1993) *Bodies that Matter: On the Discursive Limits of Sex*, New York and London: Routledge.

Epstein, Steven (1996) *Impure Science: AIDS, Activism and the Politics of Knowledge*, Berkeley CA: University of California Press.

Foucault, Michel (1979) *The History of Sexuality, Volume 1: An Introduction*, Harmondsworth: Allen Lane.

Giddens, Anthony (1991) *Modernity and Self-Identity: Self, Society and the Late Modern Age*, Cambridge: Polity Press.

Jeffreys, Sheila (1985) *The Spinster and her Enemies: Feminism and Sexuality 1880–1930*, London: Routledge/Pandora.

Marshall, Bill (1996) *Guy Hocquenghem: Theorising the Gay Nation*, London: Pluto Press.

Moon, Michael (1993), 'New Introduction' to Guy Hocquenghem, *Homosexual Desire*, Durham NC and London: Duke University Press.

Plummer, Ken (1975) *Sexual Stigma: An Interactionist Account*, London: Routledge and Kegan Paul.

Plummer, Ken (1995) *Telling Sexual Stories: Power, Change and Social Worlds*, London: Routledge.

Weeks, Jeffrey (1977/1990) *Coming Out: Homosexual Politics in Britain from the Nineteenth Century to the Present*, London: Quartet.

Weeks, Jeffrey (1981/1989) *Sex, Politics and Society: The Regulation of Sexuality since 1800*, Harlow: Longman.

Weeks, Jeffrey (1985) *Sexuality and its Discontents: Meanings, Myths and Modern Sexualities*, London: Routledge.

Weeks, Jeffrey (1991) *Against Nature: Essays on History, Sexuality and Identity*, London: Rivers Oram Press.

Weeks, Jeffrey (1995) *Invented Moralities: Sexual Values in an Age of Uncertainty*, Cambridge: Polity Press.

Weeks, Jeffrey and Porter, Kevin (1998) *Between the Acts: Lives of Homosexual Men 1885–1967*, London: Rivers Oram Press.

PART I
Contested Knowledge: Writers on Sexuality

1

Havelock Ellis and the Politics of Sex-Reform

Early life and outlook

Havelock Ellis was the most influential of the late Victorian pioneers of sexual frankness. Like his friend, the socialist propagandist and sex-reformer Edward Carpenter (1844–1928), he sought to undermine the rigid and restrictive morality of what he defined as Victorianism, and to break through the taboos on free discussion. But where Carpenter's influence was largely through his lifestyle ('propaganda by deed') and personal following, Ellis's influence spread through the reception of his books. In his numerous publications on sex-psychology and morality he attempted to document the vast variety of sexual expression and reassert the importance of sex in the lives of individuals and in society. Today his major work, the multi-volumed *Studies in the Psychology of Sex* (largely completed by 1910, but still to this day not published in its entirety in Britain), seems a trifle old-fashioned, a diffidently elegant monument to past prejudice and ignorance. But to his contemporaries it often seemed daring, even outrageous. His close friend and ally, the American birth-control pioneer Margaret Sanger, confessed to feeling 'psychic indigestion' for weeks after struggling through its forest of detail on sexual variety. And to recent generations of admirers he has been seen as a 'sage of sex', a prophet of the Edwardian sexual revolution, the first of the 'yeah-sayers.' A creator, in other words, of modern ways of looking at sex.[1]

That the praises might seem a little extravagant when we look closely at his work is a measure of how far we have come in liberalizing sexual attitudes. But an examination of his life and work can still be of more than antiquarian interest. For his method of approach is still common amongst advocates of sexual reform. It is only now, under the impact of the sexual liberation movements, that we can properly begin to understand the strengths and weaknesses of his work. For above all, Ellis was a pioneer of those seemingly radical approaches to sex which were successfully integrated into the so-called 'permissive society' of the 1960s. His work is one of the springs from which the broad stream of sexual liberalism has flowed with apparent effortless ease. Today we can begin to see that the resulting approaches to sexual freedom are not enough: they have to be questioned and challenged before a truly radical perspective on sexual liberation can be realized.

Henry Havelock Ellis was born in 1859, the year of Charles Darwin's *Origin of Species*. He was born, that is, of a generation which, as George Bernard Shaw put it, 'began by hoping more from science than perhaps any generation ever hoped before'.[2] Ellis's outlook was moulded in this period of the triumph of Victorian science and the developing reaction against its implications.

He was the son of lower-middle-class parents living in the London suburb of Croydon. His father was a merchant sea captain, at home for only about three months a year, more a visitor than a constant presence. In his absence, Ellis's mother played the dominant role in the young boy's life. She was an ardent evangelical Christian, a convert at the age of seventeen, who vowed never to visit a theatre in her life, and kept to the promise. Despite this she seems to have been a humane influence and Ellis early sloughed off the more rigid aspects of her faith. He read avidly, and in his adolescence his reading of Renan's *Life of Jesus*, of Swinburne and of Shelley made him agnostic. But agnosticism was not an easy option then, and his emotional and intellectual development produced an inevitable personal crisis, one typical in the 1870s in his class and generation.

The crucial formative period for Ellis was his stay in Australia for several years from the age of sixteen. His father took him on what was intended as a voyage round the world, but he stopped off in Australia, where he became a teacher (and at the age of nineteen a headmaster) in the bush. Here, in almost total isolation, he began to experience conflicts in his awakening sexual life and simultaneously in his spiritual outlook. He experienced to the full the conflicts between his emotional longings, his guilt, his waning religion, and the dogmatic harshness of the Victorian ideologies of science, reduced to mechanical laws, outside human control. To the young Ellis the universe seemed a void, empty of all but money-making meaning.

This attitude, as he later wrote, was represented for him by David Friedrich Strauss's book *The Old Faith and the New*, a paean to Victorian science, published in 1872: 'I had the feeling that the universe was represented as a sort of factory filled by an inextricable web of wheels and looms and flying shuttles, in a deafening din.'[3] Neither a religion that was dead, nor a science that had been completely absorbed into the capitalist-utilitarian denial of life, gave a purpose to the young man's life. It was at this point that Ellis read, for the second time, a book by James Hinton, a former doctor and ear specialist turned writer on political, social, religious and sexual matters, entitled *Life in Nature*. Hinton had developed a philosophy of life based on a pantheistic faith in the goodness of nature, in the unity of man with his surroundings. The book now produced in Ellis what he later called a 'revelation':

> The clash in my inner life was due to what had come to seem to me the hopeless discrepancy of two different conceptions of the universe. On the one hand was the divine vision of life and beauty which for me had been associated with a religion I had lost. On the other was the scientific conception of an evolutionary world which might be marvellous in its mechanism but was completely alien to the individual soul, and quite inapt to attract love. The great revelation brought to me by Hinton ... was that these two conflicting attitudes are really but harmonious though different aspects of the same unity.[4]

The 'revelation' Ellis interpreted as a mystical experience. Though he henceforth rejected conventional religion, he was convinced that beyond the apparent gap between religion and science there was a basic unity and harmony to life. Although this now seems a typically Victorian semi-religious conversion, it provided Ellis with the inner strength with which he could confront the aridity of society, and offered a basis for his later philosophy. He became convinced that the meaning of life was a matter of individual perception; each person constructed for himself or herself a pattern of meaning, in effect a myth. The construction of this interpretation was an art, and much of his later philosophical writing was to be concerned with the depiction of this 'Art of Life'. The dance most perfectly represented for Ellis the form of life: a unity of pattern, rhythm, feeling and intellect. And, as if to underline it, his first best-seller, published when he was already in his sixties, was called *The Dance of Life*. Such a view of life was the complete opposite of a materialistic analysis, but balancing this was his belief that science, directed by a humanist outlook, could lay bare the truth of human nature. In particular, for the young Ellis, Hinton's belief that sexual freedom would bring in a new age of happiness helped turn Ellis towards the study of sexual behaviour. A further reading of Hinton persuaded Ellis that the way to fulfilling his ambition to construct a new view of sex was to train as a doctor, to learn the established conventions of medicine before he began to challenge them. With this new faith and new ambition Ellis returned to Britain in the spring of 1880.

During the next decade he successfully trained as a doctor, finally qualifying in 1889, though he practised only sporadically thereafter. And he began to develop and express the wide range of his interests through writing: about literature (he edited a pioneering series of un-expurgated editions of English plays called 'The Mermaid' series), science (he began editing the influential 'Contemporary Science' series of books), religion, philosophy, travel and politics. Above all, he entered in the early 1880s the heady world of radical political, moral and philosophical discussion that was emerging with the socialist revival. He met Hinton's family, who helped him through his medical training. Through his work on the radical journal *Today* he met H. M. Hyndman, the founder of the marxist Social Democratic Federation, and other early marxists. Through the Progressive Association of which he was secretary in the early 1880s, he became friendly with Eleanor Marx, and her lover Edward Aveling (translator of *Capital*). In the Fellowship of the New Life, of which he was a founder member, he established a close friendship with Edward Carpenter and other pioneering socialists. Above all, he began in the 1880s the two central emotional relationships of his early life, first with Olive Schreiner, and later with Edith Lees, who was secretary of the Fellowship's community house after Ellis had drifted away from the group, and whom he married. These contacts and personal relationships nourished his intellectual development and helped produce an outlook which could be defined in the fluid context of the 1880s as both socialist and feminist. In his first book *The New Spirit*, published in 1889, Ellis described what he saw as the 'spiritual awakening' of the age.[5] The chief elements of this were first, the growth of science; secondly, the rise of the women's movement; and thirdly, the march of democracy, demanding education and a 'reasonable organisation of life'. These elements became central parts of his outlook.

Nevertheless, in a conventional sense Ellis was never a political activist. In the early 1880s he acted as secretary to various discussion groups. Later, as a well-known writer, he worked with various organizations which aimed to promote more enlightened attitudes to sexual matters, such as the British Society for the Study of Sex Psychology, and he became in the 1920s a distinguished sponsor of the World Congress for Sex Reform. He gave his support to campaigns for birth control and abortion, and, towards the end of his life, for voluntary euthanasia. But he was acutely shy, and never became deeply involved in public activity. His membership of an organization or committee was always more nominal than real. His abiding interest was in exploring personal relationships and ethical concepts rather than in organizing political campaigns.

This interest can be seen in the socialist organizations he was involved with in the early 1880s. The Progressive Association cultivated a tone of ethical uplift; for it Ellis edited a book of *Hymns to Progress* which had a distinctly inspirational quality. He wrote a hymn which sums up the spirit:

> Onward, brothers, march still onward,
> March still onward hand in hand;
> Till ye see at last Man's Kingdom
> Till ye reach the Promised Land.[6]

But it was the Fellowship of the New Life which most clearly represented Ellis's attitudes. He was one of its founders in the winter of 1883, and he helped draw up its constitution. According to this the Fellowship was to be based on the 'subordination of material things to spiritual', and aimed at 'the cultivation of a perfect character in each and all'. Through discussion, simple living, manual labour and religious communion, members hoped to lay the basis of a new life.[7] In early 1884, however, a split developed. Shaw, a leading protagonist, wrote later, 'Certain members of that circle ... [felt] that the revolution would have to wait an unreasonably long time if postponed until they personally attained perfection.'[8] The dissidents split to form the Fabian Society, while the Fellowship followed its more individualistic path: 'one to sit among the dandelions, the other to organise the docks'.[9] Ellis stayed with the Fellowship (though with less and less involvement); its emphasis on the personal and spiritual suited his temperament better than the 'practical' and social engineering outlook of the Fabians. Nevertheless, in later years, his views can be loosely described as Fabian.

Ellis was familiar with many marxist ideas, but his socialism owed little to Marx and even less to the working class. In his book *The Task of Social Hygiene*, published in 1912, he rejected the revolutionary socialism of what he called the 'dogmatically systematic school of Karl Marx', and saw it, paradoxically on the eve of its greatest achievement, as a fading dream.[10] Given the organization of English marxism under Hyndman, with its rigid determinism, so like the mechanical materialism that Ellis had early on rejected, and particularly its hostility to personal issues and feminism, this is not surprising. Instead he accepted the Fabian belief in the inevitable and gradual triumph of 'socialism' through the growth of large organizations and state control. However, this was for him but a means to an end. He advised the Fellowship in 1890 that we must 'socialise what we call our physical life in order that we may attain greater freedom for what we call our spiritual life.'[11] And as the utopian hopes for a rapid and total change nourished in socialist circles in the 1880s receded as the 1890s opened, Ellis, like many others, adopted a more cautious tone and a political outlook which combined gradualism with individual self-cultivation. Like other late nineteenth-century radicals such as G. B. Shaw he found an inspiration in the work of the Norwegian playwright, Ibsen, whom he helped introduce to an English audience. In particular, he expressed his agreement with Ibsen's belief that the day of 'mere external revolutions' has passed, and that the only revolution now possible was the 'revolution of the human spirit'.[12]

Ellis was, with his brand of socialism, close to that 'humanist' ethical revolt against capitalism which has been a central strand in British radical thought in the absence of a developed historical materialism. Basic to it is the concept of a human essence, a true human nature, conceived of as basically good, whose full expression is thwarted and denied by 'civilisation' (as Carpenter called it), 'commercialism', or more straightforwardly, capitalism. In Ellis's view the 'essence' seems to have come close to being human biological make-up, which had been distorted by capitalism and private property. Ellis's work here enters the whole debate about the nature of individuals, their relationship to society, and to the wider debate of 'nature' versus 'nurture'. Nowhere does Ellis more clearly reveal himself as a child of the age of Darwin. For an earlier age nature might seem vile and evil; but Ellis argued that 'It must be among our chief ethical rules to see that we build the lofty structures of human society on the sure and simple foundations of man's organism.'[13]

Ellis shared with Carpenter and others a belief in the innate possibilities for good of human biological nature: with him romanticism marries nineteenth-century scientific optimism in anticipation of a new enlightenment. But this is a central paradox of Ellis's work. The assumption that individual behaviour is an expression of inherent biological drives rather than of social processes tends today to be a hallmark of reactionary thought. For Ellis, however, it was the starting point of his radicalism. In this paradox lies the key to grasping Ellis's ambivalent position: he attempted to advance progressive arguments by methods which had an inbuilt limitation. For if social characteristics were given by nature there were limits beyond which social reform could not go. And it further suggested that change, to be successful, had to be gradual rather than radical, for it was constrained by inherent biological imperatives.

These biological assumptions come out very clearly in his study of *The Criminal* where, following Lombroso, he details the innate criminality of certain types of people; and in his work on 'genius', published in 1904, where he explores the inherent qualities in the limited number of people who reveal it. The implications of both these works are highly conservative, and have been largely discredited in the past half century, certainly among most liberals and radicals. But biological models of sexuality and sex roles have been much more persistent.

It was with relation to sexual affairs, Ellis believed, that 'man's organism' was most severely distorted by ancient prejudice and ignorance. With typical Fabian optimism he saw the traditional social problems – of religion and of 'labour' – as being on the road to solution. The sexual problem was for Ellis the outstanding remaining problem of the nineteenth century. After generations of war, revolution and counter-revolution in the twentieth century, Ellis's optimism seems misplaced. It is, however, the crucial context for understanding his approach to sex reform. In the first revelation in the Australian bush he had envisaged himself as transforming attitudes to sexuality. By the 1890s he was more cautious; the work he now began to execute had a propagandist and educational tone, designed to produce long-term changes in attitudes. His most typical method was to assume an agreement in his audience and, as he admitted, be 'quietly matter of fact in statements that at the time were outrageous'.[14] His aim was to begin to chip away the poison of the ages to allow men and women's real sexuality to emerge. It was with this approach that he began to produce his *Studies* and related works.

Politics of homosexuality

For Ellis, two areas of sex-psychology in particular needed exploration. The first was the question of sexual variations, what had, in western culture at least, traditionally been seen as 'sins' or 'perversions'. Homosexuality was the major example of these. The second area was the question of the relative social roles of men and women.

The first part of Ellis's *Studies* to appear was that dealing with homosexuality, *Sexual Inversion*, which was finally published in England in 1897. The troubles it immediately confronted clearly reveal the difficulties involved in discussing not only homosexuality but any sexual matter which did not conform to official stereotypes. It is therefore important to examine Ellis's treatment of homosexuality at some length.

It was Ellis's boast that he was one of the first to produce a major study of sex-psychology which dealt with the 'normal' manifestations of sex as opposed, for example, to the work of the Austrian Richard Krafft-Ebing, whose massive *Psychopathia Sexualis* details sex in all its varieties, as a 'nauseous disease'.[15] On the surface, therefore, it seems surprising that Ellis chose to open with a work on homosexuality. But the paradox is only a superficial one. He believed, indeed, that the so-called 'abnormal' manifestations of sex were often merely variations of the 'normal' mechanisms of sex, and that there was only a difference of degree between them. It is in this light, for instance, that Alfred Kinsey in his researches into sexual behaviour after the Second World War was able to recognize Ellis and Edward Carpenter as spiritual forebears, though he criticized them for lack of empirical accuracy. Equally important, Ellis recognized that of all the so-called 'deviations' homosexuality was closest in emotional terms to accepted heterosexuality, in that it provided the basis for close personal and sexual relations, just as heterosexuality did. Given this, the taboos against it seemed all the more dubious and Ellis recognized that an understanding of homosexuality was essential to the understanding of sexuality generally.

It was not until the last few decades of the nineteenth century that any attempt was made to conceptualize homosexuality as such. The pioneering work of homosexual rights campaigners, such as the German Karl Heinrich Ulrichs (1825–95), found only a muted response in Britain. Traditionally, homosexuality had not been distinguished legally or morally from other forms of non-procreative sex. Legal prohibitions in Britain up to the mid-century had not identified a separate homosexual crime but had punished sodomy, the 'crime against nature', indifferently, regardless of whether between man and man, woman and man, or man and beast. Lesbianism as such was not recognized at all. Moreover, both in medical opinion and in the works of the social purity movement, homosexuality was little differentiated from masturbation, which, by inducing precocity of physical sensation, opened the gates to wickedness and 'lead inevitably to those terrors of unnatural vice which belong to disease not nature'.[16] It was the concept of homosexuality as a disease or mental illness which first grabbed the attention of 'medical authorities', who could then conceptualize homosexuality as a characteristic sign of individual mental derangement, derived from morbid ancestors or from corruption. Krafft-Ebing brought this trend to its peak by seeing homosexual behaviour as a fundamental sign of 'degeneration' and product of 'vice' working on 'tainted' individuals.[17] When Ellis first approached the subject there was no specific vocabulary in English for homosexuals separate from that of sin or disease – he was the first to use the word 'homosexuality', and to popularize the terms 'sexual inversion' and 'invert'. And there was little empirical data of a neutral sort; not a single British case, unconnected with the asylum or the prison, had ever been recorded.[18]

But what made his work more than a theoretical effort but rather a political one was the new state of the law and public opinion. The death penalty for buggery – which had long fallen into disuse – had been abolished in 1861, but this was the prelude not to liberalization but to a tightening of the laws against homosexuality. By a clause of the 1885

Criminal Law Amendment Act all sexual activities between men short of buggery were declared to be acts of 'gross indecency' punishable by up to two years' hard labour.

This Act, originally intended to raise the age of consent for girls to sixteen, and hence help control the 'white slave trade', was part of a series of measures passed in the late nineteenth century which had the effect of sharpening the division between 'legitimate' sex (sex between husband and wife within the family) and 'illegitimate' sex (sex which threatened the emotional stability of the family, and the socially sanctioned sexual roles of men and women). Homosexuality was seen as posing a threat to stable sexual relations within the bourgeois family, which was increasingly regarded as an essential buttress to social stability. Not surprisingly the late nineteenth century saw a distinct sharpening of social hostility towards homosexuality. The immediate result of the 1885 Act was a series of highly publicized court cases, which dramatized and accentuated the new mood. For homosexuals it meant an increased threat of social ostracism, a high incidence of blackmail, the threat of prison. In this furnace a modern homosexual identity was born.

Though not himself homosexual, Ellis had more than a theoretical interest in homosexuality from the start. He had, for instance, close friendships with homosexuals, such as Edward Carpenter; and above all his own wife, Edith, was lesbian. It has also been suggested that Ellis's own form of sexual variation, what he called 'urolagnia' or 'undinism' – his sexual delight in seeing women urinate – made him more aware of the variety or 'naturalness' of sexual drives and the folly of trying to deny or obliterate them. But actually Ellis showed a relative indifference to the subject until the early 1890s. His book *The New Spirit* (1889) had contained a powerful essay on Walt Whitman, a strong influence on the ideas of personal liberation propagated by Carpenter and others, and had even compared him to Jesus Christ, which naturally shocked the bourgeois reviewers. But he passed over Whitman's theme of male comradeship, with its strong homosexual undertones, in relative silence.[19]

Nevertheless, the references had been enough to stir John Addington Symonds, a poet and critic, to write to Ellis, delicately broaching the subject of homosexuality; and by mid-1892, after a tentative correspondence, they had agreed to collaborate on a study of 'sexual inversion'.[20]

Symonds himself was homosexual and had been exploring the new European theories concerning 'inversion' since the 1860s. He had already written for private circulation two pamphlets, *A Problem in Greek Ethics* and *A Problem in Modern Ethics*, concerning homosexuality in the ancient and modern world, and had conducted an extensive correspondence with Walt Whitman, culminating in a famous (and disingenuous) denial by the latter of his homosexuality. When he read Ellis's Whitman essay Symonds had at first felt that here was a sympathetic soul (something that he was always searching for); but their correspondence shows the development of a literary and intellectual rather than a personal relationship. The collaboration by letter – they never met – had a powerful impact on Ellis's views. He broadly agreed to work on the scientific aspects of the book, while Symonds contributed some case histories and historical notes. The aim was clearly propagandist as well as 'scientific'.

Ellis explained in a letter to Edward Carpenter the complex of aims behind the joint effort:

> I have been independently attracted to it partly through realising how widespread it is, partly through realising also, how outrageously severe the law is in this country (compared with others) and how easily the law can touch a perfectly beautiful form of inversion. We want to obtain sympathetic recognition for sexual inversion . . . to clear away many vulgar errors – preparing the way if possible for a change in the law.

He concluded by stating that both he and Symonds were determined to put their own names to the book. Indeed, Symonds had insisted on this.[21]

But the political and social scene changed considerably between the conception of the book and its completion. The 1890s saw the evaporation of many of the millenarian hopes which had dominated the small socialist groups in the 1880s. The 1895 trial and downfall of Oscar Wilde, aesthete, utopian socialist and homosexual, symbolized for many the 'return of the philistines', the crushing of the more radical hopes of the 1880s for rapid and total change, and of the prospect of any swift changes in attitudes to sexuality. It particularly made the publication of a book on 'sexual inversion' a perilous matter.

Symonds died in 1893, but Ellis went ahead with the preparation of the book under joint authorship. A German edition appeared in 1896 and was favourably received in the medical press. Symonds had always spoken of the hazards of 'speaking out' on the 'great matter', and his *Memoirs*, written to reveal his attitudes and experience, and designed to educate the public opinion, had been suppressed after his death by his family; they remained under restriction in the London Library until 1976. Now, in the wake of the Wilde trial, the family panicked, and with the English edition already in print. Symonds's literary executor, Horatio Brown, bought up the whole issue of *Sexual Inversion*. Ellis was forced to agree to expunge all references to Symonds. But in attempting to bring out a new edition Ellis was faced with accumulating difficulties.

He had very cautiously attempted to have the book published as a medical treatise, preferring to work in accepted channels rather than risk confronting morality directly, but even this encountered strong opposition from the authorities. A friend of Ellis's, Dr Hack Tuke, whom Symonds had already judged 'unscientifically prejudiced to the last degree', had warned against publication, despite Ellis's protestations that it was for a specialist audience, by saying that there were 'always the compositors' who might be corrupted.[22] None of the orthodox medical publishers would take the book. As a result, more or less in desperation, Ellis accepted the offer of one Roland de Villiers, apparently a liberal-minded independent publisher, to produce the English edition. Ellis seems to have naïvely been taken in by de Villiers, who was clearly less interested in the educational value of the work than in its commercial possibilities. Moreover, it later became apparent that he was a notorious confidence trickster, wanted by the police on the Continent and in Britain. With these inauspicious auguries, the second edition of the book, this time without Symonds's name on the title page, appeared in 1897. And almost immediately the book was drawn into an unexpected court case.

The book received a favourable response from the Legitimation League, a small society dedicated to sex-reform, and in particular to advocating changes in the law relating to illegitimacy. Its magazine the *Adult* was published by de Villiers, and through him the Society came to display the book in its offices. Unfortunately for Ellis, Scotland Yard was keeping a close watch on the League, convinced it was the haunt of anarchists, then currently the terror of respectable London. The police obviously felt that a book on *Sexual Inversion* would provide a convenient hammer with which to crush the society.[23]

The secretary of the League, George Bedborough, was arrested, and eventually brought to trial in October 1898, for selling 'a certain lewd, wicked, bawdy, scandalous libel', namely Ellis's *Sexual Inversion*. Ellis himself was not charged nor indeed was the book itself on trial as such. A Free Press Defence Committee was established to defend free speech. Its membership reads like a roll-call of the political and literary left – Hyndman, Shaw, Carpenter, Belfort Bax, Grant Allen, George Moore, and the weather seemed set fair for a vigorous battle. But the case ended in anticlimax. Bedborough, under strong police pressure, was persuaded to plead guilty and was bound over. This had the effect of preventing anyone giving evidence on the book's merits. Ellis himself was never called to the stand, and the book, completely undefended, was labelled scandalous and obscene.

The case had important effects. In the first place Ellis determined that future editions of his *Studies* would not be published in Britain. Thereafter they were printed in America, and to this day no full British edition of Ellis's most important work has appeared. In the second place, the police achieved a double victory: they crushed the Legitimation League as a supposed 'haunt of anarchists'; and they had effectively banned *Sexual Inversion* without even trying it on its merits (subsequently too they caught up with the publisher, de Villiers).

The case confirmed Ellis in his belief in the difficulties of changing attitudes. The 'crusade' he had vigorously advocated in his early work became more a subtle tilt at outrageous attitudes. He justified his caution in a famous pamphlet: 'The pursuit of the martyr's crown is not favourable to the critical and dispassionate investigation of complicated problems. I must leave to others the task of obtaining the reasonable freedom that I am unable to obtain.'[24]

Nevertheless, even this limited aim had its effect. The prosecution had in one major way been counter-productive: it publicized the book. As a result hundreds of homosexual men and women wrote to Ellis with their problems, their life histories, information and views. Many of these he was able to reassure; others he referred to Carpenter and other homosexual friends. Many of his correspondents found their way, as examples, into his books. Given the conspiracy of silence this was a major achievement. As Ellis said of the Wilde trial, publicity appeared 'to have generally contributed to give definiteness and selfconsciousness to the manifestations of homosexuality, and to have aroused inverts to take up a definite attitude'.[25]

Similarly, Ellis's work, like Carpenter's at the same time, greatly contributed to the sense of a homosexual self-consciousness that becomes increasingly apparent from the 1890s. The contents of the book thus had a great impact on the ways in which homosexuals were labelled in the next generation or so; and the book is a crucial contribution to liberal views of homosexuality.

'Anomalies'

The aim of *Sexual Inversion* was to present a case for homosexuality, and its moral tone and method were the models for the later volumes of Ellis's *Studies* that dealt with sexual variations. The two principles he employed were a form of cultural relativism as applied to moral attitudes, and biological determinism as applied to essential sexual characteristics.

The first principle was useful in demonstrating the potentially transient nature of Victorian attitudes. By piecing together the anthropological, historical, religious and literary evidence that was available he attempted to demonstrate its common incidence: among animals (thus suggesting its 'natural' base to a generation gradually getting used to the idea that we were descended from the lower animals); amongst primitive peoples and in ancient civilization; amongst famous literary and artistic figures; and in all social classes. His conclusion, written into his approach, was that homosexuality had always and everywhere existed; and in many cultures, indeed, it had been tolerated and even socially valued. Even in his own culture, he detected marked differences of attitudes between classes, with the working class relatively indifferent in attitude to the so-called 'perversions'.

Ellis's approach is still the most common amongst liberals in attempting to understand homosexuality: by collating all the available data, the aim is to show that it is not a product of particular national vices or periods of social decay, but a common and recurrent part of human sexuality. This is an important element in liberating our ideas of homosexuality. But in Ellis's case (and in that of most of his successors) it stopped there. No attempt was made to explore why forms of homosexuality were accepted in some cultures and abhorred in others, and the only hints he gave as to why homosexuals were oppressed in contemporary society were vague references to the survival of religious taboos. Ellis's approach is basically descriptive: the deeper roots are left unexplored.

Ellis was above all a naturalist, interested in recording 'facts' about human nature rather than judging them, or placing them into a coherent historical framework. It is said that his method was to collect information on a topic in an envelope until he had enough to write an article or piece on it. The result of this was to place a huge emphasis on what he regarded as the basic truth about homosexuality, its biological roots.

This was the second major element in Ellis's approach. The 'scientific' investigation of inversion was of recent date, and had developed in two distinct directions: one emphasizing the acquired nature of homosexuality, the other its biological roots. The 'acquired' school had the disadvantage for reformers that it saw inversion as a vicious acquired *corruption*, evidence of national or personal decline. It pointed more to a moralistic clamp-down than to liberalization. One of Ellis's case studies recounted that he first learnt of inversion in a class of 'medical jurisprudence', when it was classed with other non-normal acts as 'manifestations of the criminal depravity of ordinary or insane people'. The correspondent commented: 'To a student, beginning to be acutely conscious that his sexual nature differed from that of his fellows nothing could be more perplexing and disturbing.'[26] Biological arguments had the advantage of challenging this perplexity.

Ellis, like Krafft-Ebing, was prepared to accept that some homosexual predilections were acquired, and in the final revised version of *Sexual Inversion* he made a distinction between 'homosexuality', which he defined as any sexual and physical relation between people of the same sex, and 'inversion', which was defined as a congenital condition. This implied that some people might indeed be 'corrupted' into homosexuality, and he was later to write in a typically liberal way that it was the task of a sound social hygiene to make it difficult to acquire 'homosexual perversity'.[27] This opened up moral chasms and confusions that Ellis was never able to face. In the work of later would-be reformers in the 1950s and 1960s it led to some peculiar distinctions between 'inversion', which, was regarded as 'natural', and therefore unavoidable and tolerable, and 'perversion', which was vice adopted by weak natures and therefore had to be condemned.[28]

Both 'inverts' and 'perverts' did the same things in bed, however, and the distinction relied on purely arbitrary judgements as to whether the homosexuality was inherent or acquired. And of course it implied that homosexual behaviour was only acceptable if it was involuntary and could not be suppressed. Havelock Ellis dodged this spongy ground by concentrating his arguments on congenital 'inversion'. This placed him in the main line of campaigners for homosexual rights, from Ulrichs through Edward Carpenter to the great German reformer, Magnus Hirschfeld (once fancifully called the 'Einstein of sex'); but distinctly apart from the work on sexuality that Freud was beginning at about the same time.

Havelock Ellis was deeply rooted in theories of the biological origins of human behaviour. His book, *The Criminal*, published in 1889, had been greatly influenced by notions of innate criminality derived from the Italian writer Lombroso. The book, though dated, has an uncanny prevision of arguments current in the 1950s and 1960s, and still important today, that crime was essentially an abnormality, which could be treated like other illnesses. Several pieces of evidence convinced Ellis (he allowed himself to be easily convinced) that 'inversion' was similarly innate in homosexuals, and that most cases of acquired homosexuality on closer examination would reveal a retarded emergence of congenital tendencies. First, he observed the 'strong impetus' in inverts which enabled them to defy conventional disapproval. This suggested to Ellis a drive which could only be examined as a fundamental element of the sexual instinct. Secondly, he noted the commonness of inversion in the same families, which again suggested to him its inherited nature. Finally, he observed its early appearance in most inverts. In his case histories, for instance, the average age of first same-sex attraction seems to be about nine. For Ellis this ruled out in most cases the possibility of environmental influences.

These are tenuous arguments which do not in the least rule out other explanations. But they had the propagandist advantage of allowing Ellis to reject current theories of 'degeneration', for a drive which was natural and spontaneous, he argued, could not simultaneously be a manifestation of a morbid disease.[29]

He took pains, therefore, to find a form of words describing homo-sexuality which did not suggest sickness, and the process can be traced in his correspondence with Symonds. Symonds originally felt that Ellis was too inclined to stick to 'neuropathical' explanations. Ellis countered this by suggesting that 'inversion' could best be seen as a technical 'abnormal-ity', a congenital turning inwards of the sex drive, and away from the opposite sex. He rejected Carpenter's description of homosexuals as an 'intermediate sex', or 'third sex', feeling that it merely crystallized into a metaphor the superficial appearances. Struggling to escape the notion of sickness he suggested that perhaps 'inversion' could best be described as an 'anomaly', or a 'sport of nature'. Symonds was not so keen on 'sport' and suggested instead an analogy with colour blindness, which was a harmless variation. Ellis, in return, felt that even this might appear a deficiency, and suggested a comparison with colour-hearing, the ability to associate sounds with particular colours.[30] In this terminology inver-sion seemed less a disadvantage than a harmless quirk of nature.

He backed this up by carefully challenging certain stereotypes of homosexual behaviour, and even hinting at the moral excellence of 'inverts'. He particularly questioned the association of buggery with homosexuality, suggesting it was rare. The taboos against sodomy were still severe. Oscar Wilde had brought his disastrous court case against the Marquess of Queensbury after being accused of having 'posed as a sodomite' – 'posing' was enough! As Edward Carpenter put it, the law inhibited homosexual love by linking it with 'gross sensuality', and, like Carpenter and Magnus Hirschfeld in Germany, Ellis deliberately played down this aspect for fear of jeopardizing his reform aims.[31] This is a good example of the way in which Ellis was willing to temper his arguments (and tamper with the evidence) to get a foothold for reform. In the same way he attempted to challenge stereotypes of homosexual appearance. He denied, for instance, that most homosexual men were 'effeminate'; and he regarded transvestism as an essentially heterosexual phenomenon. Ellis was striving, in other words, to stress that 'inverts' were essentially 'ordinary' people in all but their sexual behaviour. This had the positive effect, on the one hand, of allowing him to challenge conventional misconceptions. For example, he denied that in homo-sexual relationships one person was always active, physically and emotionally, the other passive: 'Between men at all events, this is very frequently not the case, and the invert can not tell if he feels like a man or a woman.'[32]

This is an important point for it challenges the assumption, still cur-rent, that homosexuals must pattern their relations on the stereotyped models of traditional male/female relations. But on the other hand, it had the danger, and one which sexual liberals have rarely avoided, of imposing new standards of behaviour for the supposed 'deviant' which may be as restrictive, if more subtly so, as the old; it offers, for example, the possibility of being accepted as homosexual as long as you are suitably 'masculine' in appearance and manner. Such an approach does not, in the end, challenge assumptions but helps to reinforce them.

Ellis was anxious, above all, to suggest the respectability of most homosexuals. He went to great lengths, for instance, to demonstrate that homosexuality was frequently associated with intellectual and artistic distinction. Some thirty pages of *Sexual Inversion* are devoted to homosexuals of note, including Erasmus, Michelangelo. Christopher Marlowe, Francis Bacon, Oscar Wilde, Walt Whitman, Sappho. Even here he showed a form of 'political tact': he carefully omitted names (like Shakespeare's) that might prove too controversial, and thus obscure his case. Again he established the pattern of later writers on the subject by bolstering up his case with long lists of distinguished names. The method unfortunately smacks strongly of tokenism, as if fame could give credence to behaviour, and leaves a slightly patronizing air behind.

Of much more significance were the case histories he gathered, some forty in all. They demonstrated much more effectively the moral, personal and intellectual quality of homosexual people, though he never went to the lengths of Carpenter, who tended to see the 'intermediate sex' as morally superior. The case histories, often selected as he said from 'friends' (amongst them his wife, Carpenter and Symonds), were central to his argument. They were carefully selected (and in some cases doctored) to put them in the most favourable light possible. Just as earlier case histories, in Krafft-Ebing's work for instance, were biased towards sickness, so Ellis's were biased towards health. They illustrated the major part of his argument: the strength of homosexual feeling; its ineradicability despite moral repression; its wide distribution (interestingly the working-class 'inverts' cited seemed to accept their homosexuality more easily than those from the professional class); its lack of pathological forms; the absence of effeminacy, and the variety of sexual expression. The great majority of people cited found themselves fully able to accept their inversion. Those who did not nevertheless emerged as towers of moral strength.

If homosexuality was not a medical problem, then there was no necessity for a 'cure'. Ellis briefly discussed various methods of 'cure' – particularly hypnotism and psychoanalysis – and found them wanting. The various disorders often associated with homosexuality, he felt, were more often associated with society's attitudes than with the sexual orientation itself.[33] And this pointed to the necessity of changing the law. The arguments he put forward (influenced in the first place by J. A. Symonds's essays) questioned whether the law had a right to intervene in private

behaviour; questioned the effectiveness of the law in catching homosexuals, or in stopping homosexual behaviour; recognized the encouragement the law gave to blackmail; and pointed to the general absurdity
of a law which made 'gross indecency' (usually mutual masturbation
between men) illegal while masturbation itself was not a penal offence.
He concluded that the law should only concern itself with preventing
violence and protecting the young and public order: 'Whatever laws are
laid down beyond this must be left to the individuals themselves, to the
moralists, and to social opinion.'[34]

These were exactly the arguments put forward some sixty years later in
the liberal campaign to change the law relating to homosexuality in
England and Wales in the wake of the Wolfenden Report. The whole
force of *Sexual Inversion*, its tempered tone, its often muted evidence,
was directed to this end.

The type of case Ellis argued has had a long history among reformers.
Three elements have been central: first, the argument that homosexuality
is characteristic of a fixed minority, and is incurable: second, the argument that reforming efforts should be directed towards changing the law
so that this minority may live in peace: thirdly, the belief that such reform
would only come about by a long period of public education. Few people
until very recently argued for more than this. Indeed, even the abolition
of penalties against homosexuality in Russia after the Bolshevik Revolution did not go beyond this (the direct influence there being the similar
work of Magnus Hirschfeld).

But though liberal sexual ideology 'tolerates' homosexuality it always
begins with the assumption that homosexual behaviour has to be
explained as a deviation from a norm of sexual behaviour. What has to
be tolerated in this view is an 'abnormality', however gently this is stated.
Ellis, despite his efforts to find a relatively neutral form of words, was no
exception to this. He stressed the impossibility of getting 'social opinion'
to accept homosexuality and found it difficult therefore to advise a
reluctant homosexual to 'set himself in violent opposition' to his society.
There was, in his view, a need for a reluctant acquiescence in the moral
views of society, and much the best result for the homosexual would be
attained: 'When, while retaining his own ideas, or inner instincts, he
resolves to forgo alike the attempt to become normal and the attempt
to secure the grosser gratification of his abnormal desires.'[35]

Ellis's scepticism about the possibility of radical changes in attitudes
stemmed from deeper roots than simple caution. Fundamentally, he was
trapped within the conservatism that his biological theories dictated.

His attitude to lesbianism is particularly relevant here. He claimed that
his work gave special attention to female homosexuality, and by comparison with his predecessors this may well be the case. There is, for

instance, a complete dearth of references to lesbianism in Krafft-Ebing's *Psychopathia Sexualis*. Ellis was, as a matter of course, as prepared to defend publicly the rights of lesbians as he was those of male homosexuals. His wife, Edith Ellis, was lesbian, a fact which became quite well known. A lecture tour of the USA by Edith had reached the headlines of the Chicago press when she defended lesbian relations. In the 1920s Ellis defended Radclyffe Hall's lesbian novel, *The Well of Loneliness*, and contributed a preface to it. He stated that his *Sexual Inversion* had, from its first edition, given special attention to lesbianism. Nevertheless, only one chapter of *Sexual Inversion* is entirely concerned with lesbianism and only six case histories are properly described. References to it in later volumes of his *Studies* are similarly spare. Two immediate explanations occur. First, there was possibly an element of personal embarrassment, given Edith's own lesbianism. Secondly, there was a great absence of easily obtainable information. There was no visible subculture in Britain for lesbians until later in the twentieth century, unlike the situation for male homosexuals. And lesbianism was not illegal – largely because it was scarcely recognized – so there were few spectacular court cases and no compelling reason for a political campaign on the question. There is, however, a curiosity in Ellis's approach. While he went to considerable lengths to stress that male homosexuals were *not* effeminate, he stresses that lesbians *were* inclined to be masculine. He believed the use of the dildo was common, and played down the importance of clitoral sexuality.[36]

Beyond this was his conviction that 'masculinity' and 'femininity' were qualities which were based on deep biological differences. In this view, male sexuality was basically active: female was essentially passive and responsive to the male's. If this was the case lesbianism, which asserts the autonomy of female sexuality, could only be explained by Ellis as a deeply rooted element of masculinity in the woman. As a result Ellis did not seem able to challenge existing stereotypes of lesbian behaviour.

Today, it is increasingly recognized that the sexual organs a person is born with do not in themselves predetermine either sexual behaviour or social roles. These are learnt, in the family and in society at large. This concept offers a fundamental challenge to theories which rely solely on biological concepts of behaviour.

Ellis, in fact, flirted with certain ideas which restated an original bisexual constitution in every individual. As an idea, it dated back to ancient Greece, and perhaps earlier, but it was just at this period, in the late nineteenth and early twentieth centuries, that the notion became the subject of scientific investigation. European writers like Wilhelm Fleiss, Otto Weininger and Freud made it a central part of their theories. It is potentially radical because it does open up the possibility that roles are socially moulded rather than dictated by nature.

Ellis was at one with these writers in recognizing that both sexes had elements of intersexuality, recessive characteristics of the opposite sex. But he fundamentally disagreed with Freud over how this should be interpreted. He felt that Freud's theory of the Oedipus complex suggested that bisexuality ought to be regarded as the basic state, so that homosexuality arose through the suppression of the heterosexual element. This opened up the possibility of similarly regarding heterosexuality as the product of the suppression of homosexual elements. Ellis recognized the dangers of this for his concept of the congenital basis of sexual behaviour:

> If a man becomes attracted to his own sex simply because the fact or image of such attraction is brought before him, then we are bound to believe that a man becomes attracted to the opposite sex only because the fact or image of such attraction is brought before him. Such a theory is unworkable.[37]

If he were to accept Freud's views then he would have to accept that the 'most fundamental' human instinct could equally well be adapted to 'sterility' as to propagation of the race. Such a view, Ellis believed, would not fit into any 'rational biological scheme'.

Ellis followed Magnus Hirschfeld in emphasizing the role of congenital influences. The discovery at the beginning of the twentieth century of the importance of hormones in determining male/female characteristics provided an apparently 'scientific' basis for an explanation. Ellis believed that each child was born with an equal number of sex-determining factors of either sex. Sexual difference emerged when one set of these elements asserted themselves over the other in the course of development, so that homosexuality arose because of an imbalance of the 'correct' elements. For Ellis, then, sexual differences were based on physiological differences which emerged more or less spontaneously, being rooted in the individual heredity.

Ellis regarded this disagreement with Freud as of central importance, and it coloured their relationship. Freud, in later debates with Hirschfeld's followers in Germany, was to concede in the 1920s that certain elements of homosexuality might be congenital, and Ellis, as we have seen, conceded the possibility of environmental influences. But at stake was the larger issue of the extent to which external influences could influence emotional and sexual patterns. Freud's theories at least left open the possibility that historical changes might alter sexual behaviour and sexual roles. Ellis, wedded to biological theories, remained more sceptical.

Ellis's work on homosexuality was not strikingly original in method or content. *Sexual Inversion* is essentially a work of synthesis, much influenced by Hirschfeld's researches, particularly on the importance of hormones, and on transvestism. Moreover, in comparison with later volumes of his *Studies* it is thinner, in detail and vigour, a fact underlined by his later revision of the first editions. But its form is the central fact about it: Ellis was arguing a case which history has made not less but more pressing. This must be noted at the same time as we criticize its conceptual inadequacies.

The laws of nature

There were two, ultimately contradictory, elements in Ellis's work. First, he attempted to stress the value and importance of sex in people's lives and the pleasure that could be got from it. From James Hinton he had learnt the dynamic nature of sexuality, influencing many varied aspects of a person's behaviour. Like Freud he was a pioneer in stressing the existence of childhood sexuality, though he felt that Freud exaggerated its closeness to adult sex. And, again with Freud, he traced the sexual origins of many apparently disparate phenomena, such as hysteria. Although Ellis was unable to accept the revolutionary implications of many of Freud's bolder theories, believing he was too sweeping in his generalizations, seeing as universal what was culturally specific, he shared with him a common aim – to widen the acceptable definitions of sexuality – and as a result, despite their ambiguous intellectual dialogue, their work is to a large extent complementary.

To Ellis's mind sexuality was not something to be regarded with horror. It was a powerful force which suffused and enhanced the whole of life. 'Auto-erotism', which formed the subject of the second volume of his *Studies* was, Ellis believed, its prime symptom.

'Auto-erotism', a term Ellis coined, he defined as the sexual energy of a person automatically generated throughout life, and manifesting itself without any definite external stimulation. Its typical manifestation was orgasm during sleep and involuntary emissions, though it also included erotic daydreams, narcissism and hysteria. In opposition to conventional restrictiveness, Ellis felt it wiser to recognize the inevitability of these sexual manifestations and their relative harmlessness. He recommended the avoidance of both excessive indulgence and excessive horror.

Ellis stressed what most people had always recognized in practice, that sex could be enjoyed, and did not just serve the utilitarian function of procreation. So just as Ellis gave cautious approval to the most public form of non-utilitarian sex – homosexuality – so he did to the most private – masturbation – which had been subject to ferocious taboos in the nineteenth century, and to which had been ascribed all sorts of physical and mental enfeeblement. He demonstrated that there was no evidence linking masturbation with any serious mental or physical disorder, and he pointed to its enormous prevalence. Even more striking was his view that it was particularly prevalent – indeed even more common – amongst women than men.

Ellis was not quite able to bring himself to give an absolute *carte blanche* to masturbation. Like Freud, who believed it well into the 1920s, Ellis felt that there were harmful side-effects. He could not entirely free himself of the myth that sex was a drain on a person's productive energies. Moreover, he felt that excessive masturbation in youth might leave a person incapable of associating sexuality with love. But at least he attempted to remove the spurious medical gloss from it.[38]

In the same way he examined other non-reproductive forms of sex and sex-related behaviour, particularly in a supplementary volume of his *Studies*, published in 1927. Coprophilia, undinism, sadism and masochism, frotage, kleptomania, narcissism, necrophilia and many others: all were examined with dispassionate interest, with a wealth of cross-cultural evidence detailing their incidence. In the supplementary volume he also examined at length the nature of transvestism, or cross-dressing, developing the brief references in *Sexual Inversion*.[39] He followed Hirschfeld in seeing it as a largely heterosexual phenomenon, only remotely connected to homosexuality, and quite separate in origin. With his passion as a 'naturalist' Ellis refused either to condone or to condemn: these things existed, and they were only harmful when another individual was hurt. In the relationship of the male and female, Ellis argued, all varieties of sexual activities were allowable. He showed that other cultures had sanctioned various forms of coitus, and that fellatio, cunnilingus, buggery, all played a useful preliminary role in sexual behaviour. Typically, however, Ellis saw these only as aspects of sexual foreplay, not activities valid in themselves. They became 'abnormal', he believed, when they substituted themselves for the 'real aims of sexuality' – the act by which the race is propagated.[40]

This brings us to the second element of Ellis's attitudes. For he sought to relate all the so-called sexual 'anomalies' to a single process, rooted in the biological make-up of men and women. And in so doing, his work increasingly sought to confirm, rather than challenge, the conventional interpretations of male and female sexual roles.

The process which gave coherence to sexuality Ellis called 'courtship'. Courtship was rooted in the most primitive acts of the animal world, the sexual conquest of the female of the species by the male. It was the process in which sexual excitement was built up in the partners, arousing the mechanisms which bring about orgasm (Ellis called them 'tumescence' and 'detumescence'). All the so-called 'perversions' were actually distortions. Ellis believed, of this activity.[41] So for instance, sadism was just an exaggeration of the pain-causing inherent in the sexual act, while transvestism ('sexo-aesthetic inversion') was a product of an exaggerated identification with the object of one's sexual attraction. In other words, Ellis was suggesting a 'continuum' between 'normal' and 'abnormal' phenomena, and this idea has been of major importance in modern works on sexual theory (e.g. the work of Alfred Kinsey). But the essential element in 'courtship' for Ellis was the *male* wooing the *female* for the sake of procreation, and in this formulation Ellis was already undermining his acceptance of 'anomalies'. For the two central strands of conventional attitudes remained: first, that the male was the initiator of sex, and the woman was receptive; second, that the chief justification of sexual activity was procreation, the act of perpetuating 'the race'. These came together in his attitude to women and their role.

Ellis's work belonged to a tradition which expected significant changes for women to come about only through enlarging the sphere in which their sex-determined characteristics could flourish. And in some ways this did involve an advance in the supposedly 'scientific' definition of womanhood. Ellis rejected for example that element of nineteenth-century ideology which attempted to deny female sexuality altogether. William Acton, whom Ellis took to be the typical representative of the Victorian 'double standard', presented an image of male sexuality as forceful, direct and uncontrollable, while female sexuality was not recognized as existing, 'a vile aspersion'.[42] Common sense, let alone theory, told Ellis that this was little more than a myth, one he believed peculiar to the nineteenth century, and to a few western countries (Britain, Germany, Italy). Ellis believed that a woman had a right to have her sexuality satisfied and typically he argued that there was a biological justification for a woman enjoying sex: sexual excitement in women was essential to combat sterility. Moreover, he recognized that mutual sexual satisfaction was not automatic; it was a technique, which could be learned and by the male at that.[43] Female indifference or frigidity lay not in the woman but often in the male's inadequacies.

But on the other hand Ellis had very fixed concepts of male and female sexuality. He saw the male's as 'open and aggressive', and to his mind this was so obvious that a special investigation of it was unnecessary. It was woman's sexuality that was problematical, because through it the race was propagated.[44] A large part of Ellis's work is thus concerned with female sexuality; it is both a landmark in the study of sexuality, and an indication of how persistent sexual stereotypes were.

He defined a woman's sexuality as essentially secondary, responsive to that of a man. The male must generally take the initiative in sexual matters. His role in courting the female is, through displaying his energy (which Ellis saw as the characteristic of men) and skill, to capture the female and arouse her to an emotional condition by which she surrenders sexually to him. 'The female responds to the stimulation of the male at the right moment just as the tree responds to the stimulation of the warmest days in spring.'

He believed that the sex life of the woman was largely conditioned by the sex life of the man, so that while a youth spontaneously becomes a man, the woman 'must be kissed into a woman'. The woman attracts by her beauty, while the man attracts by his strength, physical or mental.[45]

Ellis detected a particular characteristic of woman called 'modesty', which was so prevalent that it amounted to almost the chief secondary characteristic of woman. It was the element of female refusal, which safeguarded her, and at the same time aroused the male. The apparent passivity of the female was, Ellis believed, essential to the full success of courtship. He made it clear that attitudes to modesty have changed throughout history. He cites the Turkish prostitutes who were more concerned with covering their faces than their organs, and the Tahitians seen by Captain Cook who did not mind copulating in public but would never dine together. But though the forms of modesty might change, the fact of it was a characteristic part of femininity.[46]

Ellis is clearly reading into 'nature' the social forms of masculine and feminine behaviour that he observed around him: the male is active, initiatory; the female passive, responsive. He is surrendering to the positivist delusion of confusing the surface appearance of things with their real potentiality. Both the existence of lesbianism and that of female masturbation, which he acknowledged, demonstrate the actual auto-nomy of female sexuality. Any 'passivity' that may be observed is more the product of social conditioning than of 'nature'. On the basis of his ahistorical description, however, Ellis builds his theory of the different social roles that men and women should play.

In his book *Man and Woman* (first published in 1893, and among the most frequently republished of his books) Ellis examines what he called the secondary and tertiary characteristics of men and women. His con-clusion is that there is in nature a 'cosmic conservatism', a natural harmony, which had become: 'as nearly perfect as possible, and every inaptitude is compensated by some compensatory aptitude'.

For a just society, therefore, each sex must follow 'the laws of its own nature'. For Ellis the fundamental truth of natural life was that the two sexes were separately defined in evolution only as a method of favouring reproduction, and this could only partially be over-ridden.

Nature therefore sanctified the social roles that men and women inhab-ited: 'woman breeds and tends; man provides; it remains so even when the spheres tend to overlap'.[47]

There was, Ellis believed, an organic basis for the separate social spheres. For associated with the woman's *biological* capacity to produce children were fundamental 'feminine' characteristics: not only modesty, but affectability, sympathy, maternal instincts, devotion, emotional receptivity. These were essential to woman's sphere. And accompanying these advantages were compensating disadvantages: biological barriers to women performing satisfactorily in competition with men in their sphere. Amongst these were the biological imperatives of motherhood, and the debilitating effects of menstruation.[48]

Nature therefore defined a woman's true sphere as motherhood, the supreme position which life had to offer. In a particularly devastating phrase Ellis wrote that women's brains are 'in a certain sense ... in their wombs', and when he speaks of pregnancy as a woman's destiny his language becomes extraordinarily elevated: the woman is 'lifted above the level of ordinary humanity to become the casket of an inestimable jewel'.

While the male's task as defined by nature is to 'forage abroad' and 'stand on guard' in the antechamber of the family, the female's is to care for the children and the husband.[49]

In his *Origins of the Family* Engels had argued that the subordination of women was a result of the historical developments which gave eco-nomic dominance to men through the development of private property. Even in the working-class family, which was propertyless, the husband, because of his direct involvement in social production, had economic dominance over the wife: in the working-class family, Engels wrote, the man was the bourgeois. Engels concluded that the precondition for woman's equality with man was her economic liberation through direct involvement in social labour, which would only be fully achieved in a socialist society. Only on the basis of economic equality could individual sex-love between the woman and the man flourish, the woman be released from her enslavement in the house, and child care and house-work be socialized.

Though Ellis never appears to mention Engels's work (it was not published in English until the early twentieth century) he must have been familiar with the main lines of its arguments. He had, in the 1880s, reviewed August Bebel's book on *Women and Socialism* and he himself argued that morality had hitherto been based on private property, as particularly revealed in the workings of the English divorce laws, where 'the infidelity of the wife was a serious crime against property'.[50] But against Engels's advocacy of economic equality based on female integration into the workforce, Ellis argued for a *moral* equality based on the separation of roles.

Ellis increasingly believed that the women's movement had gone in the wrong direction in demanding for women equal opportunity with men in industry and the professions (particularly the latter: it was mainly middle-class women who made the demand). By 1912 he was highly critical of the tactics and aims of the suffragettes of the Women's Social and Political Union (WSPU). Although he recognized the importance of the vote, and the crucial role the WSPU had played in energizing the women's movement, he criticized them for sectarianism, narrowness of aim, increased conventionality and a tendency to 'morbid emotionalism'.[51] Many feminists tended to agree with him that law reform was not enough. Emma Goldman, for one, shared many of his complaints and was influenced by his ideas. As an alternative Ellis believed that feminists should follow the German movement in stressing the question of motherhood.

Ellis's views were deeply influenced at this time by the work of the Swedish feminist Ellen Key, whose works, *The Century of the Child, The Women's Movement* and *Love and Marriage*, he helped to introduce to an English-speaking public. She argued essentially that women did need free scope for their activities, so that in this sense early feminist aspirations were justified. But the real need was not to wrest away from men tasks that men might be better able to fulfil, but for women to play their part in that field of creative life which was peculiarly their own. As a result, Ellen Key believed that the highest human unit was 'triune': father, mother and child, with marriage becoming the central point of life.[52]

This involved the social recognition and elevation of motherhood, and Ellis took up this point. At present, he believed, motherhood was without dignity: the vitality of mothers was crushed; there was widespread ignorance about sexuality and childbirth; the care and protection of the pregnant woman and the young child were ignored. To combat this the mother must become the dominant parent – he assigned her, for instance, the central role in sex education – and must be fully trained for her role. He even appears to approve of Ellen Key's notion that each woman should do a year's compulsory service in housekeeping.[53] He argued, therefore, for a confirmation of the woman's traditional sphere, with state help to make it function more efficiently.

The radical emphasis of the modern women's liberation movement has been the challenge to the identification of womanhood with housekeeping and child-rearing, which serves not the interest of women but the sexual division of labour under capitalism. Ellis worked within the existing preconceptions and argued that women should withdraw from social labour. This would be easier, he stated, for working-class women than for professional. The fact that working-class women usually had to work to maintain a minimum standard of life seems to have escaped him. But to compensate Ellis believed that the state must take a greater part in aiding and regulating motherhood.

Ellis saw in the liberal reforms of the years before 1914 evidence of the growing recognition of the importance of motherhood and the care of the child. The setting up of child guidance clinics, school meals, schemes for the 'endowment of motherhood', the compulsory registration of births, were in fact important steps forward, and did help to improve the lot of working-class mothers. But if they are just seen as well-intentioned liberal reforms their true significance is lost. The new emphasis on the social role of motherhood must be placed in a wider context. The Boer War (1898–1902) had demonstrated the appalling physical condition of working-class recruits into the British army. The 1904 report of an inter-departmental committee on physical conditions headed by General Maurice had caused a great furore in the ruling class, and a conviction that the stock of the imperial race was endangered. As Ellis put it: 'The State needs healthy men and women, and by any negligence in attending to this need it ... dangerously impairs its efficiency in the world.'

Healthy mothers and children were needed to breed an imperial race capable of competing in the new era of imperialist rivalries. And this was the rationale behind the 'national efficiency' campaigns launched by a motley bunch of right-wing Tories, Liberals and Fabians in the aftermath of the Boer War. Ellis saw the liberal reforms, and particularly the 1908 Notification of Births Act, as the 'national inauguration of a scheme for the betterment of the race', and as a triumph for 'national efficiency'. Many of these reforms Ellis had in fact anticipated in a short book entitled *The Nationalisation of Health* published in 1892.

As one would expect, military metaphors abounded at this period. Ellis quotes with approval Ellen Key's phrase that: 'as a general rule the woman who refuses motherhood in order to serve humanity, is like a soldier who prepares himself on the eve of battle for the forthcoming struggle by opening his veins'.[54]

The theme of social betterment becomes increasingly dominant in Ellis's work. He advocated that every *healthy* woman should at least once in her life exercise her supreme function in the interests of the race. Moreover, in opposition to the socialist tradition which theoretically at least favoured the socialization of housework and child-rearing, he believed that the rearing of the child would best be served by each mother being responsible for the individual upbringing of the child. This was in keeping, as he saw it, with both the aptitudes of the mother, and the best interests of healthy childhood.

Ellis's growing concern with 'the future of the race' inevitably brought him into sympathy with the eugenics movement. This movement had a considerable impact in the early decades of the twentieth century, and it provided Ellis with an ideology which offered a new outlook on social improvements. If, as he argued, the reproduction of the species was the supreme aim of life, then it was here that social reform should concentrate.

Eugenics was a theory of improving the human stock by selective breeding. Essentially utopian in outlook, it believed that the identification of inborn characteristics would make possible the elimination of the weakly and the unfit. Ellis defined it as: 'The scientific study of all the agencies by which the human race may be improved, and the effort to give practical effect to those agencies by conscious and deliberate action in favour of better breeding.'[55]

In its origins in the late nineteenth century, eugenics theories had been seized on by reformers of a pre-marxist outlook who saw in its ideas a useful supplement to social reform. But in its emphasis on innate characteristics as opposed to environmental influences it fitted in more usefully with the ideas of conservatives opposed to social change. In England the chief theorist was Francis Galton, whose general outlook was archconservative. His work became generally known from about 1905–6, in the wake of the panic over 'racial suicide', and he was the inspirer of the Eugenics Education Society founded in 1908.

Ellis's interest was longstanding. He mentioned Galton's work in his essay on 'Women and Socialism' as early as 1884, and had even criticized Galton for what he called his timidity over the 'central problem', that of control of population.[56] From the early 1900s, however, it became the key element of continuity in his sexual studies. His book *Sex in Relation to Society*, which sums up his *Studies*, climaxes on two themes: 'The Art of Love' and the 'Science of Procreation'. He makes it clear that they must be interdependent, one the condition of the other.

Ellis believed that 'eugenics' was the ultimate stage of the movement for social reform. Hitherto, the social reform movement had concentrated on improving the environment. This was important, but not enough. It was now necessary to purify 'the stream of life' at its source, and to concentrate on the 'point of procreation'.[57] To his mind eugenics represented the highest point which social reform had reached.

The supreme danger of all eugenics arguments is that they are filtered through the dominant sectors of society. It is they who decide whether the population is too large or small, which part of it is superior or inferior, which people have to limit their procreation. And inevitably, the eugenics movement was linked with ideas of racial superiority. Much of the debate in the pre-First World War period was over the declining birth rate and over whether it was the 'best class' which was declining most rapidly. The 'best class' in this terminology was the upper class and even Ellis, who regarded such questions as 'hazardous', felt constrained to accept that it was generally so. In his book *A Study of British Genius*, he noted that the vast majority of the population (the working class and women) produced the least amount of genius, and concluded that 'genius' revealed a high degree of heredity. With regard to the more mundane level of life, the criterion which Ellis used was 'fitness' – mental or physical. It followed that generally the least fit were those from lower-class families where conditions and facilities were bad. The question of improving the conditions and opportunities of life thus became inextricably involved with questions of class and of control of reproduction, and the ideals of socialism became confused with the mechanisms of state control.

Ellis's confusions were common in the socialist movement. Eugenics in some ways rushed in to fill the gap in socialist theories over sexual matters so that: 'particularly on the question of racial and ethnic differences, the left did not offer an especially enlightened leadership'.[58]

Karl Pearson, who was Galton's closest disciple, and certainly called himself a socialist at that period, wrote in 1885: 'If child-bearing women must be intellectually handicapped, then the penalty to be paid for race predominance is the subjection of women.'

The work of Galton and Pearson greatly influenced other socialists. H. G. Wells, who was present at an exposition of eugenics by Galton, had a rush of blood to the head and advocated the 'sterilisation of failures', while Sidney Webb felt that unless the decline in the birth rate was arrested the nation would fall to the Irish and the Jews.[59]

These writers were closer to social imperialism than to revolutionary socialism. But even the more radical writers succumbed. Eden Paul, a member of the ILP and later a member of the Communist Party, worried over eugenics before 1914, and wrote: 'Unless the socialist is a eugenicist as well, the socialist state will speedily perish from racial degradation.'[60]

Eden Paul believed that the ability to earn a minimum wage must be the condition of the right to become a parent. Behind this was the conviction, even amongst socialists, that distinction could be made between the 'deserving' and the 'undeserving' poor.

One of the major rationales of 'neo-Malthusian' ideas was that, by limiting the growth of the population of the unfit poor, they would help solve the problem of chronic unemployment, which seemed to many a product of nature rather than of capitalism. Marx had long ago punctured the bubble of Malthusian myths but they survived, even among socialists despairing of rapid social change. Moreover, such was the predominance of social-Darwinist ideas that few people would have questioned, before the racialist terrors of the 1920s and 1930s, that some people were innately better endowed than others.

Many of the early proponents of eugenics equated it with a new religion. Galton called for a 'Jehad' – a Holy War – to be declared on the survival of ancient dysgenic customs, and urged that eugenics – 'a virile creed' – should become a 'religious tenet' of the future. In the same fashion Ellen Key believed that men and women would eventually devote the same religious fervour to propagating the race as Christians devoted to the salvation of souls.[61]

Ellis on the other hand adopted a slightly more measured position. He rejected what he called eugenic fanaticism, and he denied that it was eugenicist to speak of one race being better than another. He preferred, he said, to speak of the 'human race', and to speak of 'quality' of person rather than 'quantity'. Moreover, he believed that knowledge was not yet sufficient to justify a *positive* eugenics: breeding of the best. It was only possible to develop a *negative* eugenics, designed to eliminate the unfit, by which he seems to have meant the 'feeble-minded'. And he rejected compulsion, so though he favoured health tests before marriage, the encouragement of the best classes to marry, and the sterilization of the unfit, he believed that this would only come about through education, not direction. In accord, therefore, with the whole trend of his work, he believed the first necessity was to create a new enthusiasm for health and moral awareness in matters relating to reproduction.

Ellis believed that it was women who should be the focus for the education. And he saw two 'practical' ways in which eugenics ideas would spread: through the development of a 'sense of sexual responsibility' in men and women; and through the development of effective contraception (including abortion, of which he was a pioneer advocate). In practice both involved the 'autonomous authority' of women: 'The State has no more right than the individual to ravish a woman against her will.'[62] Nevertheless, of course, the whole point of Ellis's arguments was to confirm women in their exclusive child-bearing role. Ellis recognized the necessity of women controlling their own sexuality but this was theoretically and practically hampered by a prior commitment to the sort of social role women should perform.

A subtle change in terminology reveals the dangers. Margaret Sanger, the American feminist, had coined the phrase 'birth control', and this suggested the liberating possibilities in the development of contraception. The name of Marie Stopes's society which campaigned for birth control after the First World War added another element: Society for Constructive Birth Control and *Racial Progress*. By the 1930s the emphasis had shifted again: to 'population control' and 'family planning'. The radical possibilities of contraception depended then, as now, on the existence of a radical women's movement which recognized the central importance of women regulating their own fertility. The disappearance of such a women's movement in the 1920s and 1930s subordinated the campaigns for birth control to the demands of class society and the ideology of 'stable middle-class families'. The idea of reproductive self-determination had become swamped in the social control of contraception. Ellis, who continued to assert the primacy of eugenics into the 1930s, was himself chiefly concerned with the problem of 'control' rather than of a woman's right of free choice.[63]

One example of this was a distinct hardening of Ellis's attitude to the role of the family. In his early writings, Ellis emerged as a critic of the Victorian family and marriage system. The legal system of monogamy, he argued, was a product of class society, and the development of private property. He likened contemporary marriage to prostitution, in that it subordinated the wife to the authority and whim of the man. In some ways, he felt, the prostitute was better off: more rapes had occurred in marriage than outside it. He therefore favoured reform of marriage, and both in his life and in his early work he advocated what he (and Edith Ellis) called a 'companionate', or ethical union of two people in which the equal rights of both partners would be respected. His own marriage strove to follow this model. He and Edith lived apart for large parts of the year, attempted to enjoy their separate incomes, and both had emotional and sexual entanglements outside the marriage, while remaining emotionally loyal and open with one another. Ellis argued strongly that the state had the right to intervene in marriage laws only where children were involved and in order to safeguard the child. But of course this was the crux. For in his social ideas the family came to assume an increasing importance, as he became more deeply involved in eugenics. And as was typical in his work he accepted the view that monogamy was 'natural', rooted in the biology of men and women. By the 1930s the emphasis on the importance of marriage in cementing a monogamous union had become more pronounced. In his textbook, *Psychology of Sex*, first published in 1933, the emphasis on the need for love between partners is still clear. But now he cautiously advises against rash marriages, or cross-cultural or cross-religious matches, because of the danger of incompatibility. And he stresses the importance of medical examinations, and of mutual knowledge of each other's anatomy and physiology as well as feelings, for 'Marriage is much more than a sexual relationship.'[64]

It was, in fact, in his eyes, the key to social policy, for it was through the family that the future of the human race could be ensured. As in much else of his work Ellis's ideas prefigured many of the arguments which have become the ideological glue of the welfare state. Ellis's views on marriage and motherhood found their realization in the idea of family allowances, the state supporting the family in the interests of healthy childhood and social stability. And his advocacy of reformed marriages, with equal rights for both partners, found its its outcome later in ideas of the 'Symmetrical Family'.[65] By an apparent paradox, the writer who had first achieved notoriety as an advocate of sexual freedom ended his career as the liberal advocate of a reformed family, where social roles are cemented rather than questioned.

Middle ways

Ellis once advised Margaret Sanger to follow a middle road in challenging authority. It was a middle road that Ellis travelled in his advocacy of sex-reform, and as a result many of his views have now become commonplace. Unlike his near contemporary Sigmund Freud, he left behind no clear theoretical heritage, no school of devoted followers, no sustained effort to found a new science of sexology as Freud attempted to found a science of psychoanalysis. The content of Ellis's major work, *Studies in the Psychology of Sex*, now seems empirically dated and theoretically weak compared to the imaginative flights of a Freud.

Nevertheless, an analysis of Ellis's work does reveal a great deal about the nature, strengths and weaknesses of the pathmakers in sexual frankness. For he attempted to sum up and give coherence to the various reforming attitudes that were in the air. In his writings we can see the effort needed to break out of the Victorian taboos; and the scars that the struggle left behind.

In the first place it is important to recognize Ellis's role as an *ideologist*. The purpose of his works was to change attitudes and to create a new view of the role of sex in individual lives and in society. He set out to rationalize sexual theory, and in doing so helped lay down the foundations of a 'liberal' ideology of sex. The essence of this was a greater toleration of sexual variations; a desire to relax the rigid moral code; and an emphasis on the 'joys of sex'. Its weakness was its inability to ask *why* societies have continued to control sexuality and persecute sexual minorities throughout the ages; and as a result its eventual absorption into dominant value structures.

Secondly, and perhaps his most real and lasting achievement, he was a pioneer in bringing together and categorizing information on the different types of sexual experience. Even this, to us apparently elementary, task shocked his contemporaries. It was, however, an essential preliminary to any rational study of sexuality. From it stemmed two central strands in his approach: the acceptance of the biological roots of sexual variations – particularly homosexuality; and the use of evidence from other cultures to underline his argument that morals were not unchanging or unchangeable, but were in constant evolution. The *Studies* are a pot-pourri of details about the enormous variety of sexual experiences through different times and climes.

Thirdly, he recognized that the question of the social roles of the two sexes was of paramount importance in the new century, particularly because of the influence of the women's movement. He therefore attempted to suggest guidelines for more humane and equal sexual and social relations and behaviour. The particular form these guidelines took now seems among the most reactionary aspects of his work – particularly his view of woman's role – and reveals clearly the ways in which he was trapped within the stereotyped images that he inherited. And yet, for a long period, his preoccupations were shared by all progressive tendencies, including revolutionary socialists.

But to grasp fully Ellis's impact we must also look at the way he was viewed by his contemporaries. Margaret Sanger spoke of the tremendous sense of excitement she felt when she first encountered Ellis, and this seems to have been a common response. Conservative leaders of the women's movement shunned his overt support in case his reputation damaged the cause, while radicals such as Stella Browne, Emma Goldman and Margaret Sanger saw him as a giant who: 'beyond any other person, has been able to clarify the question of sex and free it from the smudginess connected with it from the beginning of Christianity, raise it from the dark cellar, set it on a higher plain'.[66]

Ellis provided a rationale for sex reform which, inadequate as it now appears, was a major achievement for his time. It is this which justifies placing Ellis as one of the pioneer sexual enlighteners of the twentieth century.

Note

This essay was originally twinned with one by Sheila Rowbotham on Edward Carpenter in a book we wrote together, *Socialism and the New Life* (London: Pluto Press, 1977). It was written without our being granted access to the family papers, pending the completion of the authorized biography of Ellis, by Phyllis Grosskurth. This account was subsequently published as *Havelock Ellis: A Biography* (London: Allen Lane, 1980). Vincent Brome also published his biography, written much earlier, with some access to private papers, but held up because of wrangles with the Ellis heirs, after I completed the essay: *Havelock Ellis: Philosopher of Sex* (London: Routledge and Kegan Paul, 1979). Since then various books have thrown new light on Ellis's work. A full discussion of his relationship with Olive Schreiner can be found in Ruth First and Ann Scott, *Olive Schreiner: A Biography* (London: André Deutsch, 1980). John Addington Symonds's memoir, mentioned above, has been edited by Phillis Grosskurth and published as *The Memoirs of John Addington Symonds* (New York: Random

House, 1984). The private papers, including extensive correspondence, are now available at the British Library in London. Alongside these contributions to scholarship concerning Ellis's life and work, a radical feminist polemical tradition critical of Ellis has developed: see, for example, Sheila Jeffreys, *The Spinster and her Enemies* (London: Routledge/ Pandora, 1985). My own most recent thoughts on Ellis may be found in the entry on him I have written for *The New Dictionary of National Biography* (Oxford University Press: forthcoming).

Despite all these efforts, I see nothing to distance myself radically from in the approach and conclusions I offer in my essay. My critique of the liberal tradition may be less arduous now than it was in the mid-1970s, tempered as it has been by the difficulty of transforming attitudes and changing laws, and by the potent challenge to liberalism offered in the 1980s by the rise of the New Right. But I stand by my basic argument: Ellis was a pioneer who wrote a large part of the script for twentieth-century concepts and attitudes. To understand where we are now, we still need to understand the complexities and ambiguities of our inheritance. In particular, the idea that sexual variations are 'conditions' which need explanation and justification has had a long provenance, which only began to be challenged in the late 1960s under the impact of radically changing political and cultural circumstances. The essay on Mary McIntosh which follows (chapter 2) demonstrates the resilience of many of the theories on sexuality which Ellis helped put into circulation.

References

1   Margaret Sanger is quoted in Arthur Calder-Marshall, *Havelock Ellis*, London, Rupert Hart-Davis 1959, p. 154. Other comments come from Samuel Hynes, *The Edwardian Turn of Mind*, Princeton NJ, Princeton University Press 1968, pp. 171, 149; E. H. Brecher, *The Sex Researchers*, London, André Deutsch 1971, and Paul A. Robinson. 'Havelock Ellis and Modern Sexual Theory', *Salamagundi*, No. 21, Winter 1973. This is the best modern discussion of Ellis's sexual ideas. It is the basis for the section on Ellis in Paul Robinson. *The Modernisation of Sex*, London, Elek 1976. For works on his life, see Calder-Marshall's biography; and Isaac Goldberg, *Havelock Ellis*, London, Constable 1926: Ellis's autobiography, *My Life*, London, Heinemann 1940, is very revealing. The biographical details in this article come from these works.

2   Hynes, *The Edwardian Turn of Mind*, p. 132.

3   Havelock Ellis, *The Dance of Life*, London, Constable 1923, p. 204.

4   Ellis, *My Life*, 1967 edn, pp. 130–1. For further details of Ellis's ideas, see Robert Sprich. 'The World as Beauty', *Man and Society*, No. 14, Winter 1973–4.

5   Havelock Ellis, *The New Spirit*, London, G. Bell & Sons 1889, pp. 6, 9, 13.

6   Goldberg, *Havelock Ellis*, p. 99.

7   See W. H. G. Armytage, *Heavens Below: Utopian Experiments in England, 1560–1960*, London, Routledge & Kegan Paul 1961, p. 331ff.

8   G. B. Shaw, *Fabian Tract*, No. 41, quoted in Calder-Marshall, *Havelock Ellis*, p. 87.

9   Quoted in Armytage, *Heavens Below*, p. 332.

10   Havelock Ellis, *The Task of Social Hygiene*, London, Constable 1912, p. 389.

11   Armytage, *Heavens Below*, p. 332.

12   See, for example, Havelock Ellis, 'Women and Socialism', *Today*, Vol. 2. July–December 1884, p. 363.

13   Ellis, *The New Spirit*, p. 9.

14   Ellis, *The New Spirit*, 4th edn, London, Constable 1926, p. viii. He wrote in the General Preface to the 1st edition of *Sexual Inversion*, p. v: 'As a youth, I had hoped to settle problems for those who came after: now I am quite content if I do little more than state them.' He cites the question of sex – to which he significantly adds 'the racial question' – as the outstanding problem of the day in this same preface, p. x.

15   See Brecher, *The Sex Researchers*, for details.

16   Dr Elizabeth Blackwell, *The Human Element in Sex*, London, J. and A. Churchill 1884, p. 32.

17   See R. Krafft-Ebing, *Psychopathia Sexualis*, trans. of 7th edn, London, F. A. Davis & Co. 1892, pp. 288–9. Krafft-Ebing's work was to have a long history and influence. It was still the basic sex manual for the girls in Mary McCarthy's novel *The Group*, set in the 1930s.

18   Ellis, *Sexual Inversion*, 1897 edn. p. xix. *Sexual Inversion* was later republished in a fuller and revised form as vol. 2, part 2, of *Studies in the Psychology of Sex*, New York, Random House 1936, 4 vols. All references, except when otherwise stated, are to this final edition of the *Studies*. More details regarding nineteenth-century attitudes can be found in Jeffrey Weeks '"Sins and Diseases": Some Notes on Homosexuality in the Nineteenth Century', *History Workshop Journal*, No. 1, Spring 1976.

19   See Ellis, *The New Spirit*; see also Ellis, *My Life*, p. 263.

20   See H. M. Scheuller and R. L. Peters (eds), *The Letters of John Addington Symonds*, vol. III, 1885–93, Detroit, 1969, L. 1791, 6 May 1890; L. 1984 and L. 1996, June–July 1895. For biographical details see Phyllis Grosskurth, *John Addington Symonds*, London, Constable 1964.

21   Ellis to Carpenter, 17 December 1892. (Letter in Edward Carpenter Collection, Sheffield City Libraries.)

22   For Symonds's comment see *Letters*, L. 1996, p. 710. Tuke was probably so hostile because his own son, a minor artist, was himself notoriously homosexual.

23   The fullest study of the case can be found in A. Calder-Marshall, *Lewd, Blasphemous and Obscene*, London, Hutchinson 1972, p. 193ff.

24   Quoted in Calder-Marshall, *Lewd, Blasphemous and Obscene*, p. 218.

25   Ellis, *Sexual Inversion*, p. 352.

26   Ibid., p. 105.

27   Ibid., pp. 1, 325.

28   See, for example, D. S. Bailey, *Homosexuality and the Western Christian Tradition*, London, Longman, Green & Co. 1955, p. ix.

29   Ellis, *Sexual Inversion*, pp. 59, 82–4, 301. He noted in a later book, *Psychology of Sex*, London, Heinemann 1946, p. 198, that only 8 per cent of observed inverts were 'morbid'!

30   *Letters*, Symonds to Edward Carpenter, L. 2039, 29 September 1892, and L. 2070, 29 December 1892; Symonds to Ellis, L. 1996, 7 July 1892; *Sexual Inversion*, p. 317ff; *Psychology of Sex*, p. 194ff.

31   Edward Carpenter, *The Intermediate Sex*, London, George Allen & Unwin 1908, p. 19.
32   Ellis, *Sexual Inversion*, p. 283.
33   Ibid., p. 325ff, 338; Ellis, *Psychology of Sex*, p. 212ff.
34   Ellis, *Sexual Inversion*, pp. 349ff, 354.
35   Ellis, *Psychology of Sex*, 1946, p. 217.
36   See, for example, Ellis, *Sexual Inversion*, pp. 203–4, 251, 257, 258, 261. Paul Robinson makes a similar point in his article, cited in n. 1 above.
37   Ellis, *Sexual Inversion*, p. 304. For documentation on the relationship between Ellis and Freud, see Vincent Brome, 'Sigmund Freud and Havelock Ellis', *Encounter*, No. 66, March 1959. Ellis's dialogue with Freud can be seen in all the *Studies*, but particularly in the supplementary volume on *Eonism*. See also Ellis, *Psychology of Sex*. This has a restatement of the importance of hormonal differences between the sexes. For Hirschfeld's views on this, which influenced Ellis, see M. Hirschfeld, *Sexual Anomalies and Perversions*, London, Encyclopaedic Press 1952. Freud discusses the connection between bisexuality and inversion in *Three Essays on the Theory of Sexuality*, London, Imago 1949, p. 143 (first published 1905). In 1915 he had added a significant footnote which read: 'Psychoanalytical research is most decidedly opposed to any attempt at separating off homosexuals from the rest of mankind as a group of special character.'
38   Ellis, *Autoerotism: Studies*, vol. 1, part 1, pp. 164ff, 244–6. See also Robinson, 'Havelock Ellis and Modern Sexual Theory', p. 37.
39   Ellis, *Eonism and other Supplementary Studies: Studies*, vol. 3, part 2.
40   Ellis, *Sex in Relation to Society: Studies*, vol. 4, p. 536ff.
41   See Ellis, *Love and Pain*, and *Analysis of the Sexual Impulse: Studies*, vol. 1, part 2.
42   Quoted in *Psychology of Sex*, London, Heinemann 1946, p. 287.
43   Ellis, *Sex in Relation to Society*, pp. 536, 577.
44   Ellis, *The Sexual Impulse in Women: Studies*, vol. 1, part 2, p. 189.
45   *Studies*, vol. 1, part 2, pp. 24, 69.
46   There is a good discussion of this in Brecher, *The Sex Researchers*.
47   See Ellis, *Sex in Relation to Society*, p. 75; *Man and Woman*, London, Contemporary Science Series, Walter Scott 1894, pp. 440, 448. There were eight editions of this work up to 1934.
48   Ellis, *Sex in Relation to Society*, p. 415; *Man and Woman*, p. 447ff.
49   Ellis, *Studies*, vol. 3, part 1 (Preface), p. vi; *The Psychic State in Pregnancy: Studies*, vol. 3, part 1, p. 206; *Sex in Relation to Society*, pp. 2–3.
50   Ellis, *Sex in Relation to Society*, p. 375.
51   Ellis, *The Task of Social Hygiene*, p. 75.
52   Ibid., p. 100ff.
53   Ellis, *Sex in Relation to Society*, pp. 2, 32.
54   Ibid., pp. 588, 20, 29, 587.
55   Ellis, *The Task of Social Hygiene*, p. 28. A good account of the Eugenics Movement can be found in Linda Gordon, 'The Politics of Population', *Radical America*, Vol. 8, No. 4, July–August 1974.
56   See Ellis, 'Women and Socialism', in *The Task of Social Hygiene*, p. 363.
57   Ellis, *Sex in Relation to Society*, p. 582.
58   Gordon, 'The Politics of Population', pp. 72–3.

59 B. Semmel, 'Karl Pearson: Socialist and Darwinist', *British Journal of Sociology*, Vol. ix, No. 2, June 1958, pp. 119, 122.
60 Quoted in Ellis, *On Life and Sex*, London, Heinemann 1948, p. 11.
61 Quotation from Galton from Semmel, 'Karl Peauson', p. 119. References to Key are in Ellis, *Sex in Relation to Society*, pp. 580–1.
62 Ellis, *Sex in Relation to Society*, p. 586.
63 For details of the general change, see Gordon, 'The Politics of Population', p. 62ff. For Ellis, see 'The Control of Population', in *More Essays of Love and Virtue*, London, Constable 1931.
64 Ellis, *Psychology of Sex*, p. 231. For earlier views, see Ellis, *Sex in Relation to Society*, pp. 80, 363ff; Ellis, *The Task of Social Hygiene*, p. 102. See also Ellis, 'The Renovation of the Family', in *More Essays of Love and Virtue*. Ellis's dialogue and correspondence with the anthropologist Bronislau Malinowski are key elements in the development of his views on marriage, monogamy and the family.
65 M. D. Young and P. Willmott, *The Symmetrical Family*, London, Institute of Community Studies 1973.
66 Margaret Sanger, *An Autobiography*, London, Victor Gollancz 1939, p. 132.

2

Mary McIntosh and the 'Homosexual Role'

By way of introduction

The American feminist writer Gayle Rubin (Rubin and Butler, 1994: 82) recently deplored the tendency in contemporary writings about sexuality to 'erase' its theoretical origins. This usually takes the form of privileging the work of Michel Foucault (1979) as the fount and origin of the currently dominant approach, which emphasizes the historical, contextual nature of the sexual, and which for shorthand is generally known as social constructionism (see, for example, Dynes, 1990). Like Rubin, I remain astonished at 'How quickly people forget even recent history, and how much they are willing to project current attitudes back as a fictive chronological sequence' (p. 82). It is frustrating for those of us who have been toiling in this particular vineyard since the turn of the 1960s and 1970s to have our early efforts in understanding sexuality in general, and homosexuality in particular, refracted back to us through post-Foucauldian abstractions (and I say that as someone who has been deeply influenced by Foucault's work), and then taken up as if the ideas are freshly minted. I am struck, for example, by the reception of queer theorists such as Eve Sedgwick (1985, 1990) and Judith Butler (1990, 1993) in recent writing about the body and sexuality (especially in literary studies) in the Anglo-Saxon world, when, to this perhaps jaundiced eye, they are not saying anything fundamentally different from what some of us have been trying to say for twenty-five years or so, inspired in large part by a reading of Mary McIntosh's 'The Homosexual Role' (1981), which was first published in 1968.[1]

Despite efforts at theoretical effacement, however, the almost canonical status of that article is, in fact, quite well documented. Its influence can be traced in a range of historical studies since the mid-1970s (e.g. Trumbach, 1977; Weeks, 1977). It has been frequently anthologized, especially in readers in lesbian and gay studies (for example, Plummer, 1981; Stein, 1990). And it has been seen by some of the most astute contributors to the debates on the social construction of sexuality as a founding document. As Greenberg (1988: 5) put it, Mary McIntosh 'pointed the way in a path breaking article...that proposed to consider homosexuality as a social role whose origin and changing content could be studied historically'. Yet I cannot help feeling that its real significance has been generally missed, even in such an encomium, and that is what I want to try to indicate in this paper.

McIntosh herself remarked in the article that it dealt with 'only one small aspect of the sociology of homosexuality' (1981: 43), and that is of course true. Compared to the tomes that preceded it and those that in a flood followed it and now pour off the press in probably the greatest discursive explosion in the history of sexuality, it is a deliberately modest and low-key paper: relatively short (about 6000 words), based not so much on original research as on a careful rereading of often familiar sources, politically cautious in the sense that its main tone is one of declared sociological objectivity (it even has tables, derived from Kinsey), and published originally in an influential but not particularly high-profile American journal, *Social Problems*. Its major impact did not emerge for several years, when it was taken up by a number of the activists and proto-academics associated with gay liberation. Many of its specific suggestions or interpretations have, inevitably, been challenged by later scholarship, and McIntosh has herself acknowledged a number of lacunae in its approach (1981: Postscript). McIntosh herself has published little since that explicitly follows up her original insights about homosexuality (but see McIntosh, 1992, 1993), and even the term 'homosexual role' now seems time bound, and has largely gone out of fashion, despite its galvanizing impact in the 1970s.

The importance of the work is not that it is a definitive statement, but that it asks what was at the time a new question: not, as had been traditional from the late nineteenth century, what are the causes of homosexuality, but rather, why are we so concerned with seeing homosexuality as a condition that has causes? And in tackling that new question, McIntosh proposed an approach which opened up a new research agenda: through seeing homosexuals 'as a social category, rather than a medical or psychiatric one'. Only in this way, she suggests, can the right questions be asked, and new answers proposed.

For someone like myself, originally trained as a historian, and a historian of ideas, but keen to understand the social context of ruling concepts, politically active in the gay movement from 1970, and wanting to understand why it had emerged then, and not earlier, and what its implications were for my sense of self and being in the world, that was a radical reformulation of the question of homosexuality. It offered a distinction between homosexual behaviour, universal in its manifestations, across time and cultures, and the specific historical and social forms in which it was organized. It invited us to uncover the complex mechanisms through which specific forms of organization ('roles') had developed; but also, and this is often ignored, asked us to consider the disjunction between lived sexual behaviour and the adoption of specific roles: not all people who had homosexual sex saw themselves as homosexual. So Greenberg's formulation, however flattering to McInstosh's work, seems to me to get it slightly wrong: it is not the case that homosexuality should always be seen as related to role; rather the question ultimately posed is why do certain categorizations of homosexuality emerge in certain cultures and not in others; and what are the effects of such categorizations both on those who accept them, and on those who do not, even if they are behaviourally homosexual? That is a historical and sociological question; it is, ultimately, also a political question. For if homosexuality cannot be seen as existing in a timeless configuration, and contemporary forms have traceable historical roots, then attitudes, beliefs and social and cultural patterns can and will change again, not simply as a reflex to structural change but through human action. And of course the dramatic changes of the past thirty years, largely brought about by lesbian and gay activism, in which Mary McIntosh has herself played an important part, offer proof positive of the prescience of her basic argument.

I now summarize briefly the main arguments of 'The Homosexual Role', and then go on to analyse the significance of its organizing themes.

McIntosh begins the article by suggesting that homosexuality is commonly seen as 'a condition characterizing certain persons in the way that birthplace or deformity might characterize them' (1981: 30). The problem with this way of seeing homosexuality, she argues, is twofold. First, if homosexuality is a condition, then people either have it, or do not. All the evidence, however, suggests that this leads to spurious distinctions between people. For example, 'in terms of behaviour, the polarization between the heterosexual man and the homosexual man is far from complete in our society' (p. 43) – an interesting pre-echo of a point made many years later by writers such as Eve Sedgwick (1990), and pretty much part of our common-sense understanding today, but clearly not in the 1960s, despite the impact of Alfred Kinsey. Second, the assumption that homosexuality is a condition leads to a preoccupation with aetiology – with the causes of homosexuality. Yet, McIntosh argues, the evidence on this is as 'sadly inconclusive' at the time of writing as it was when Havelock Ellis first wrote on the subject in the 1890s – and, one might add, as it is today, despite the best efforts to discover the gay gene or gay brain. And the reason for this, McIntosh goes on, is clear: the wrong question is being asked. 'One might as well try to trace the aetiology of "committee chairmanship" or "Seventh Day Adventism" as of "homosexuality".'

It is important to note here, though I come back to its significance later, that the idea that homosexuality was a condition was the guiding assumption of the British 'Wolfenden Report' in 1957 (Wolfenden, 1957), which had advocated partial decriminalization of male homosexuality, and subsequently shaped the campaigns, reaching their height when McIntosh was writing the article, which led to the reform of the law in England and Wales in 1967 (see Weeks, 1977). Against this approach, McIntosh offered the perspectives of comparative sociology, which allows us to see that the conception of homosexuality as a condition is itself a possible object of study. This conception, she argues, and the behaviour it supports, act as a mechanism of social control in a society which condemns homosexuality and sees homosexuality as a social problem.

The practice of the social labelling of homosexuals as having a deviant condition operates as a mechanism of control in two ways:

1 It helps to provide a clear-cut threshold between permissible and forbidden behaviour, preventing drift into deviant behaviour by creating the likelihood that a small step will lead to a total fall into a deviant role.
2 It serves to segregate the deviants from others, thus containing deviant practices within a relatively narrow group.

McIntosh sums up the effect of this graphically: 'The creation of a specialized, despised and punished role of homosexual keeps the bulk of society pure in rather the same way that the similar treatment of some kinds of criminal keeps the rest of society law-abiding' (1981: 32).

Instead of trying to fit the manifestations of homosexuality into a fixed definition of a condition, McIntosh suggests an alternative approach: 'It is proposed that the homosexual should be seen as playing a social role rather than as having a condition' (p. 33). To back this up, McIntosh then proceeds to locate homosexuality in a comparative and historical framework. First, based largely on the Human Relations Area Files (via Ford and Beach, 1952), McIntosh traces the evidence for different patterns of homosexual life in other cultures, and detects two broad forms: those societies which condone intergenerational sex as part of the rites of passage to (male) adulthood, linked to a distinction between active and passive masculine behaviour (as in certain tribal cultures, or the classical Greek model); and certain cultures which sanction a form of institutionalized cross-gender role, the most famous example of which is the berdache among some Native American tribes.

Second, McIntosh goes on to trace the development of the homosexual role in Britain, concluding that by the end of the seventeenth century, a distinctive male role was emerging, linked to the development of subcultural forms in London.

Finally, using Kinsey et al. (1948), McIntosh makes a critical distinction between the widespread nature of homosexual behaviour and the homosexual role, proposing that 'Homosexual behaviour should be studied independently of social roles, if the connection between the two is to be revealed' (1981: 39) – an injunction, I have to say, that has until recently been largely ignored.

So much for a necessarily brief and crude summary of a tightly argued and suggestive article. More important for an evaluation of its significance are the key themes underlying it. I suggest that these can best be seen in terms of three sets of oppositions latent in the piece: (1) between, most obviously, behaviour and category; (2) between pre-modern and modern forms of the organization of homosexuality; and (3) between heterosexuality and homosexuality. I now look at these in turn.

Homosexual behaviour and homosexual category

The most crucial distinction is between behaviour and category. Few today would question that such a distinction exists – though some doubtless would want to argue that behaviour is largely essence not fully realized in consciousness. The problem is how we understand the significance of the distinction. This was the nub of what became known during the 1980s as the essentialist/social constructionist controversy – a long-term and ultimately tedious debate, largely, alas, confined to lesbian and gay studies despite its wider implications (see Stein, 1990), which petered out under the weight of its own exhaustion as much as found a final resolution. It was, nevertheless, a critical debate, which I once tried to sum up in the following terms:

> [essentialism] is a method which attempts to explain the properties of a complex whole by reference to a supposed inner truth or essence, the assumption 'that in all sexological matters there must be a single, basic, uniform pattern ordained by nature itself' ... Against such an approach I

shall argue that the meanings we give to 'sexuality' are socially organized, sustained by a variety of languages which seek to tell us what sex is, what it ought to be – and what it could be.

(Weeks, 1986: 15–16)

McIntosh's ostensible targets were the sexologists, psychologists and the like who defined the homosexual condition as a fixed set of characteristics. A hidden target was the leaders of the homophile movement who justified law reform on the grounds that homosexuality was a given attribute, which deserved toleration or even pity rather than moral censure or prison. The problem with this critique, however, as McIntosh acknowledged, was that many self-defined homosexuals wanted to feel they had a condition, or in subsequent formulations, had an identity which was not only related to but derived from their sexual characteristics and desires. It legitimizes membership of an out group without forcing participants to reject 'the norms of society' (1981: 33). So a critique of essentialism could also be conceived of as an attack on the very idea of a homosexual identity – which is why gay critics became so fervid and overheated at the arguments of social constructionism, seeing it as a fundamental challenge to their hard-won gains, and the claim to recognition as a legitimate minority group. Especially in a rights-based culture like the US, the claim of lesbian and gay activism to recognized minority status may be boosted by the latest fashionable theories of the gay gene or the gay brain (Rose, 1996), forgetting, of course, that as in the 1930s, the idea of a genetic disposition towards homosexuality can as easily lead to attempts at genetic engineering, or worst, to eliminate it as to legislative reform to legitimize it.

By their nature, then, constructionist views were less likely to be politically appealing than the pleasing simplicities of essentialism. Yet they have had enormous political impact, especially for those anxious to understand homosexuality in a wider socio-political framework; and have been the main stimulus to research on homosexuality by lesbians and gays themselves since the early 1970s – precisely because a distinction between behaviour and category forces us to try to ask crucial questions about anthropological, historical, sociological, psychological and even literary evidence. There seem to me two important caveats to be made.

First, the distinction between behaviour and category does not necessarily require us to ignore questions of aetiology; it merely suspends them as irrelevant to the question of the social organization of sexuality. Ken Plummer, at an early stage of the debate about social construction, implicitly made this point when he wondered in *Sexual Stigma* (Plummer, 1975) whether indeed there might be a 'deep structure' to sexuality –

which did not stop him going on to analyse the processes of identity formation and stigmatization. Foucault himself remained agnostic: 'On this question I have absolutely nothing to say' (cited in Halperin, 1995: 4). One might have views, but that does not alter the most important question. The really interesting issue is not whether there is a biological or psychological propensity that distinguishes those who are sexually attracted to people of the same gender from those who are not – that can safely be left to those who want to cut up brains, explore DNA, or count angels on the point of a needle. More fundamental are the meanings these propensities acquire, however or whyever they occur, the social categorizations that attempt to demarcate the boundaries of meanings, and their effect on collective attitudes and individual sense of self. This fairly obvious point has been largely ignored by those who define themselves as essentialist, and even by those who do not. David Halperin, for example, though lauded or execrated, depending on your taste, as a high priest of social constructionism (see Halperin, 1990), and a devotee of Foucault, once admitted that if he were shown conclusive proof of the genetically determined nature of homosexuality, he would have to revise all his historical theories (see Epstein, 1990). But this is nonsense. Halperin's interpretation of the sexuality of the classical world may or may not be historically accurate; but it does not depend one iota on whether homosexuality is inherent or acquired. It is a fairly banal point to make, but it still seems important to make it: social categorizations have effects in the real world, whether or not they are direct reflections of inherent qualities and drives, whether or not their genealogies can be traced in a murky history of power and resistance.

For this reason the little side debate over whether essentialists are 'realists' while constructionists are 'nominalists', started by the American historian John Boswell (1990), whilst no doubt intellectually stimulating, is pretty irrelevant to the wider issue. Mary McIntosh has in fact been described as an arch-nominalist (Weinrich, 1990) – even though her explanation of the homosexual role in Britain is pretty clearly, if implicitly, related to material developments, especially the clear link suggested between urban growth and subcultural evolution, and her general philosophical framework has been marxist.

The second caveat to be made is that the value of the argument in 'The Homosexual Role' does not depend ultimately on the validity of the variants of role theory – as some fervently aggressive critics of McIntosh's argument seem to suggest (see, for example, Murray, 1996; see also the obsessive search for homosexual roles in various cultures in Whitam and Mathy, 1986). The references in the original article suggest a certain eclecticism about the concept of role, citing Parsons, Lemert and Goffman, veering between functionalism and dramaturgy; and McIntosh herself has suggested that her use of labelling theory to sustain the concept of an execrated role was somewhat 'mechanical' (1981: 'Postscript', 45). But as McIntosh explicitly states, the use of the word 'role' was ultimately a form of shorthand: 'It refers not only to a cultural conception or a set of ideas but also to a complex of institutional arrangements which depend on and reinforce these ideas' (1981: 38).

For this reason I do not think it is particularly useful to argue over the validity or invalidity of the term. Rather, its real importance is that it defined an issue that required exploration. The concept suggests a social and historical space shaped by a galaxy of contending forces, not a linear development. These forces, McIntosh suggests, include the defining power of all forms of heterosexual activity, courtship and marriage, as well as specific labelling processes – gossip, ridicule, psychiatric diagnosis, criminal convictions, and the groups and networks of the homosexual subculture. There is an obvious research agenda here, which can be traced in many subsequent works. It also has to be said that this way of stating the problem is not a million miles from Foucault's later formulation in terms of a triplet linkage of discourse/power/resistance (Foucault, 1979). McIntosh and Foucault come from different theoretical traditions, but they home in on the same problem. For both, the category of the homosexual is constructed in relation to other constructions; it is, in more contemporary formulations, relational.

Terms such as 'constructionism' and 'roles', I would argue, are in the end no more than heuristic devices to identify and understand a problem in studying sexuality in general and homosexuality in particular. It is transparently obvious that the forms of behaviour, identity, institutional arrangements, regulation, beliefs, ideologies, even the various definitions of what we call only for convenience the 'sexual', vary enormously through time and across cultures and subcultures. Yet we apparently need to believe that as things are so they have always been, rooted in our essential natures (the 'truth of our being'). A major objective of historical and social scientific study of the erotic over the past twenty years or so has been to problematize the taken for granted, to denaturalize sexuality in order to understand its human dimensions and the coils of power in which it is entwined, how it is shaped in and by history. The historicization of the idea of the homosexual condition by McIntosh is an excellent pioneering example of this.

The suggestion that psychologists and psychiatrists have not been objective scientists of desire, dispassionate seekers after the truth of the body, decoders of the laws of nature, as the sexological tradition proclaimed, but on the contrary 'diagnostic agents in the process of social labelling' (McIntosh, 1981: 33), opens up a set of questions about the emergence of sexology and related disciplines, their constitutive role in categorizing sexual patterns, their impact on legal processes, and their effect on individual lives, which have resulted in a host of detailed studies (Weeks, 1977, 1986) on the medicalization of homosexuality. Foucault's *The History of Sexuality* (1979) is often seen, misleadingly, as the *locus classicus* of approaches that attribute the emergence of the homosexual category in the nineteenth century to medicalization. But the agenda on this was already set by McIntosh, as was the question of the impact of would-be medical definitions on individual lives. And as recent work has suggested, recognition of the significance of medicalization in constituting the homosexual category – a prolonged, contradictory and contested process with no single agent determining it – is not the same as saying that homosexual existence was created by it. On the contrary, it is clear that medical definitions were in large part a response to efforts to regulate subcultural developments, as well as the institutional imperialism of the new professions (for example, see Silverstolpe, 1987).

The complex relationship between societal categorization, whether through medicine, legal processes, religion or various informal processes, on the one hand, and the formation of subjectivities and identities on the other hand, has in fact been the key focus of writing about homosexuality since the mid-1970s. I myself, clearly directly influenced by McIntosh, suggested (Weeks, 1977) that the recent history of homosexuality could best be seen as the effect of a complex process of definition and self-definition. On the one hand, we need to understand the classifying and categorizing processes which have shaped our concepts of homosexuality – the law, medicine, religion, patterns of stigmatization, formal and informal patterns of social regulation. On the other hand, we must also understand the level of individual and collective reception of, and battle with, these classifications and categorizations: power *and* resistance. The best historical work has attempted to hold these two levels together, though inevitably, the stick has been bent one way or the other, depending on the biases or inclinations of the authors concerned, and sometimes the stick has snapped altogether under the strain, leading either to sociological determinism (you are what society dictates) or extreme voluntarism (you can be anything you want): neither is true (see Vance, 1989).

The best work has been more carefully nuanced. This is clearest if we look at the main focus of lesbian and gay studies until recently, the emphasis on identity, and the relationship between identity and community – between sense of being and social world. The most illuminating studies – summed up in George Chauncey's superb work of historical reconstruction, *Gay New York* (Chauncey, 1994) – has demonstrated the complex interplay of elements that shape subjectivities. Chauncey's reconstruction of the class configurations of emerging categories of fairy, wolf, trade, invert, queer, gay, illustrates the intricacies of labelling, identity invention, social networking and regulation in a vibrant and living way. The main lesson I would draw from work such as this – and this is at the heart of the project of historicizing sexuality – is that pre-existing identities do not make communities or social worlds; they are shaped in and through those evolving social worlds (Weeks, 1995). Not surprisingly, some of the most interesting work has attempted to explore the subcultures, networks, urban spaces or even rural idylls that provided the space, the conditions of possibility, for the emergence of distinctive homosexual identities.

As Bech (1997) has argued, there is a danger in over-concentrating on consciousness – expectations, attitudes, ideas, perceptions, discourses, labels, roles and identities – at the expense of the conditions of life. For Bech, homosexuality is a way of being, a form of existence, in which other elements are equally vital: moods and recognition, ways of experience, dreams and languages, forms of behaviour and expression, the existence of social worlds, life spaces. But that, I would suggest, is not incompatible with the line pursued in 'The Homosexual Role'.

McIntosh's suggestion that the late seventeenth century saw the emergence of a subcultural context for a distinctive homosexual role in England has been enormously influential. Her rediscovery of the London mollies' clubs has been the starting point of numerous historical excavations (for example, Trumbach, 1977; Norton, 1992). Alan Bray's influential study of *Homosexuality in Renaissance England* (Bray, 1982) began as an attempt to refute McIntosh (and myself), but shows pretty conclusively that the idea of 'the homosexual' did indeed not exist in the sixteenth and seventeenth centuries, and closes with the emergence of the mollies' clubs at the beginning of the eighteenth century, the birth of something akin to the modern homosexual, precisely McIntosh's starting point. Of course, there is now plentiful work which attempts to show that subcultures and identities existed before the late seventeenth century – for example, in the early Christian world (Boswell, 1980), or in other parts of Europe (see essays in Herdt, 1994) – just as there have been scholars who have argued that we cannot really talk about homosexual identities until the late nineteenth or even mid-twentieth centuries (see essays in Plummer, 1981). There is no need here to enter that argument one way or another. The really important point is that we cannot talk about identities (and their complex relationship to social categorizations) any more without a sense of their historical and social context. Identities are made in history not in nature (compare Hacking, 1990).

However, the nature of those identities has been contested fiercely. The emphasis in the early stage of the social constructionist debate on 'the making of *the* modern homosexual' (Plummer, 1981) was problematized in the very moment of its articulation. To start with, much of the early historical work had concentrated overwhelmingly on men, and not women. This was partly a reflection of who was doing the research and writing. It was partly because, as McIntosh put it (1968): 'the notion of a separate homosexual role is much less well developed in women than it is for men, and so too are the attendant techniques of social control and the deviant subculture and organization' (1981: 42).

But there was a more fundamental reason, that McIntosh outlined in her most sustained discussion of lesbianism to date (1993), when she noted that feminists and lesbians have used social constructionism quite differently in their historical and theoretical productions. Women have tended to trace the evolution of lesbianism in relation to the asymmetries of heterosexuality, and the power of men to define – for example, Smith-Rosenberg (1985), Faderman (1981). For men, on the other hand, 'gender has lurked in the wings' (McIntosh, 1993: 40), rarely marching fully armed onto the stage. This is an important point, which I take up later. The issue here is the insight that the history of homosexuality cannot possibly be a history of a single homogeneous entity, because the very notion of homosexuality is dependent on at the very least a binary notion of gender. Without binarism, the concepts of homosexuality and hetero-sexuality could not possibly exist – though what we call 'homosexual behaviour' no doubt does.

But gender is of course only one of the categorical and hierarchically ordered divisions that shape our sexual identities. Race is another. Rather bizarrely, some of the critics of social constructionism have complained that its advocates have assumed that only homosexuality is constructed (see Dynes, 1990). In fact, McIntosh in 1968 was already drawing a comparison between the social labelling of homosexuality and the social labelling of racial difference (McIntosh, 1981: 32). This may not have been immediately taken up over-enthusiastically by the first generation of lesbian and gay constructionists, but by the 1980s there was no doubt that the idea of a single modern gay identity had to be severely revised, largely because of a growing recognition of the diversity of possible sexualized identities. Now there were 'modern homosexualities':

In scarcely a quarter of a century, same-sex experiences in the western world have been ruptured from the simplified, unified, distorting, often medical, frequently criminal, always devalued categories of the past. Instead, they have increasingly become a diverse array of relational, gendered, erotic, political, social, and spiritual experiences, difficult to tame and capture with restrictive and divisive labels. Criss-crossing their way through class, gender, and ethnicity, a stream of emerging

identities, new experiences, political practices, and ways of living together
have been firmly placed on the political agendas of the future.

(Plummer, 1992: xiv)

In other words, the category that McIntosh was anxious we should
explore has become categories. Roles, neat slots into which people
could be expected to fit as a response to the bidding of the agents of
social control, have become performances (Butler, 1990), masquerades
(Garber, 1992) and fictions (Weeks, 1995). Identities which once seemed
categoric are now seen as fluid, relational, hybrid: we are not quite
today what we were yesterday, or will be tomorrow. Identities have
become narratives, built out of stories we tell each other in the various
interpretive communities to which we belong (Plummer, 1995). And
there are so many stories, most of which refuse to fit into the neat
pigeon-holes that history (whose history?) has written for us. The homosexual, as Plummer argues, is now 'both rigid scientific discovery and
diverse signifier of potential, plurality, polymorphousness' (Plummer,
1992: 13).

McIntosh asked us to concentrate on category, not condition, and this
has now to a large extent been done. She also, and for a long time this
was forgotten, asked that we explore behaviour, the myriad ways in
which sexuality is experienced outside category, role, identity, and this
too is now being done. The efforescence of studies of what, for want of a
less ideological word, we call homosexuality, in other cultures, tribal,
Islamic, southern, has put our western preoccupations into a comparative framework, not diminishing our experience, but enhancing our
sense of the diversity of the sexual (Herdt, 1994). And this comparative
framework has also, at last, been used in our own societies, to highlight
the difficulty of subsuming behaviour within a confining definition of
condition. McIntosh used Kinsey to this end. Much more recently,
stimulated largely by the AIDS tragedy, a series of studies has shown
the disjunction between behaviour and identity. Attempts to categorize
the non-identity, non-gay forms – such as the emergence of the clumsy
label 'men who have sex with men' (MSN, MESMEN) in the late
1980s to describe the complex forms of sexual interaction among
men, falling outside the easy signifier of 'gay' (see, for example, Prout
and Deverell, 1995) – illustrate the enduring paradox of sexual
taxonomies and categories. Without them experience, behaviour, desire,
are in danger of being obscured. With them we are in danger of forgetting
the ambivalence and ambiguity of sexual lives. Yet however we try to
deal with the flux of sexualities, we can never again believe that homosexuality is simply a condition which some people have, and others
do not.

The pre-modern and the modern

The premise of 'The Homosexual Role' is that the concept of a homosexual condition is a product of specific, if not easily specified, historical and social conditions. But if it is indeed the case that 'modernity brought with it distinctive new forms' (Plummer, 1992: 13) then new questions arise; not least, what came before?

One of the early attractions of the first volume of Foucault's *The History of Sexuality* was precisely that it both offered an account of the birth of the modern homosexual, and put that into a broader historical framework, by proposing the famous – if by no means new (see Weeks, 1977) – contrast between sodomy and homosexuality: 'as defined by the ancient civil or canonical codes, sodomy was a category of forbidden acts; their perpetrator was nothing more than the juridical subject of them ... The sodomite had been a temporary aberration; the homosexual was now a species' (Foucault, 1979: 43).

Several historians have now chased the sodomite down many highways and byways, and we have a good picture of the intricacies of the sexual order in pre-modern times (Herdt, 1994: Part 1). On one level we can characterize the difference as between acts (which may or may not have been, according to our understanding, homosexual, for sodomy applied to heterosex as well), and identities and ways of being in the world. But in saying that we should not assume that a world without rigidly dichotomized homosexual and heterosexual identities is the same as one without significant categorizations; it is simply that the categorizations – between sinner and saved, libertine and respectable, or whatever – were different from our own. So to understand the non-modern we have to understand the principles of the dominant moral order. Religion was clearly one highly influential principle of organization – and the last (published) volumes of Foucault's *History* (1985, 1986) are an attempt to look at the classical and early medieval roots of Christian moral preoccupations around the body and truth. But in 'The Homosexual Role' McIntosh had also suggested two other regulating elements, whose relation to religion are ambivalent, to say the least: between adults and non-adults (as in the intergenerational sex which denoted the passage from childhood to adulthood in some tribal and pre-modern societies), and between the genders (as the case of the berdache suggests, where it is clearly necessary, in McIntosh's account, for you to be either male or female, or intermediary between two sexes). For some writers these have been seen as the keys to understanding homosexuality in pre-modern times. Historians have traced the evolution of patterns of homosexual life which have shifted from intergenerational ordering, through categorization around gender and class, to recognizably modern forms of egalitarian relationships (for a historical perspective see Trumbach, 1989).

There is in all this, as Plummer (1992) has argued, a sort of neo-evolutionism, a form of whiggism which sees the American lesbian and gay as the pinnacle of social development, and the very model for the rest of the world. Leaving aside that, there are two points that need to be made here. First, it strikingly builds on McIntosh's model, rewriting the comparative sociology as evolutionary history. McIntosh's own version of history was necessarily brief, but to a significant extent it prefigured this subsequent work, both in its approach and in its detail. The second point is equally important. Once the concept of the homosexual is problematized, what is being studied tends to dissolve, making an isolated history of homosexuality itself problematic (despite foolhardy attempts at writing them). One index of that is the difficulty of finding either a noun or an adjective to act as a guide through the historical material, and the need for circumlocutions to avoid the culturally specific terms such as 'the homosexual', 'homosexuality' or 'gay'.

Already within a decade of the McIntosh essay appearing, it was becoming very clear that to understand homosexuality we had to understand the construction of sexuality as a whole – hence the appeal of Foucault's own introductory essay on *The History of Sexuality* to many of us interested in exploring the history of homosexuality. If the homosexual condition was an invention of history, so too was heterosexuality and 'sexuality' itself, constituted in large part from a complexity of relations: between men and women, adults and children, the family and the social, as well as the 'perverse implantation'. One fact was becoming increasingly clear: understanding heterosexuality was the key to understanding homosexuality.

Heterosexuality and homosexuality

Social constructionism, Carole Vance (1989) remarked in the late 1980s, has paid little attention to the construction of heterosexuality. Although this is no longer entirely true (Katz, 1995), it is the case that the deconstruction of the category of heterosexuality has not been the central concern of writers on homosexuality until fairly recently. Although the relational nature of the homosexual/heterosexual divide – one cannot exist without the other – has been implicit in most lesbian and gay scholarship, the main focus of exploration has been elsewhere. Even the most fervent lesbian feminist scourges of heterosexism have in practice concentrated on exploring the lesbian continuum rather than tracing the evolution of the heterosexual imperative; while those feminist writers who have sought to excoriate male sexual violence and domination as constitutive of compulsory heterosexuality, such as MacKinnon (1987), Dworkin (1987) and Jeffreys (1990), have tended to see gay men as exemplars of misogyny, and lesbians as the privileged bearers of feminism, without any sense of the history of homosexuality, or of sexuality in general.

'The Homosexual Role', as McIntosh subsequently admitted, tended to take heterosexuality for granted, a tendency underlined by the deviance perspective. As McIntosh said in her 1981 Postscript: 'I now think that what needs to be understood is heterosexuality and that you can't understand homosexuality without locating it in sexuality in general' (p. 46).

Of course, sexuality in general is not a domain of easy pluralism, where homosexuality and heterosexuality sleep easily side by side. It is structured in dominance, where heterosexuality is privileged, and that privilege is essentially male oriented. Throughout McIntosh's writings on sexuality we can see a concern with the dominant structures. In the 1981 Postscript McIntosh comments on the taken-for-granted nature of masculinity, while later she shows the power of the ideology of 'male sexual needs' in shaping responses to prostitution. Although never in danger of succumbing to the fantasies of separatist feminism, and certainly not endorsing the anti-porn campaigns of some feminists, her developed view was that the privileging of heterosexuality was about male power over women (1993: 33).

To put it another way, while most feminist and gay male writing, though from different starting assumptions, has tended to see the binarism of heterosexuality/homosexuality as the conflict between two more or less homogeneous categories, McIntosh as a feminist has become increasingly concerned to see both categories as sites of conflict in which masculinity is the dominant term. So when McIntosh argues (1992: 162ff) that social constructionism is vital for understanding heterosexuality, we also have to understand that it is simultaneously central to understanding male power – though not in a straightforward or simple way. She rejects the idea that patriarchy is a 'seamless social whole', without contradictions: 'we need a theory of the social construction of sexuality that is somewhere between what might be called the "liberal" view that it lies outside the social altogether and the "totalitarian" view that it is a determinate aspect of a homogeneous social whole' (1992: 162).

So pornography is not the essence of male power, requiring censorship. It is, on the contrary, the repository of all the unacceptable and repressed desires of men – even if these are only fantasies about sexual expression outside marriage. As in her earliest writings on homosexuality, McIntosh is anxious to see the ordering of sexuality as a result of various processes, of which familial, heterosexualized ideology and practice are a critical crucible (see Barrett and McIntosh, 1982). The logic of this is to concentrate less on homosexuality as such, and more on the emergence of the binary relationship of heterosexuality and homosexuality.

Ironically, much the most influential work on the heterosexual/homosexual relationship in recent years has not come from within the sociological tradition with which McIntosh is most closely aligned but from within poststructuralist, deconstructionist and queer literary studies, of which the ruling deity is Eve Kosovsky Sedgwick. As she put it in her influential book, *Between Men: English Literature and Male Homosocial Desire* (1985), Sedgwick's work is an attempt to understand the moments of change by 'working on historical questions through the reading of literature' (p. 137). More specifically, her intention is to read chosen texts for what they reveal of the play of gender and sexual conflict in the key period for contemporary consciousness, the late nineteenth century. Whereas history and sociology have characteristically attempted to produce order and pattern out of the chaos of events, the main feature, I would argue, of the Sedgwick school is to show the conflict and disorder under the appearance of consistency and uniformity. The texts are read as sites of gender and sexual contestation, and therefore of power and resistance, in the Victorian period.

Two points can be drawn from this study. First, Sedgwick clearly relates the discourse of male homosociality and homosexuality to the elaboration of heterosexual norms and the reordering of male power, thus breaking decisively with any attempt at minoritizing homosexual history, and aligning herself closely with the project opened up by McIntosh twenty years earlier. Second, she emphasizes that the preoccupation with whether homosexuality is the experience of a minority or a universal tendency is itself an explosive element in late nineteenth-century literature and twentieth-century sexualities (Sedgwick, 1990). It matters less whether either is true, and more that both are the focus of anxiety in the shaping of modern sexual and gender relations. They represent the poles of anxiety around which homophobia and homosexual panic revolve.

Where homophobia and homosexual panic are the particular focus of Sedgwick's *Epistemology of the Closet* (1990), Jonathan Dollimore in *Sexual Dissidence* (1991) looks at the other side of the equation, the manifestations of the perverse, from 'Augustine to Wilde, Freud to Foucault', the other of sexual order and moral consciousness, and the permanent reminder of the arbitrariness of social norms and sexual cultures. The perverse is the worm at the centre of the normal, giving rise to sexual and cultural dissidence and a transgressive ethic, which constantly works to unsettle binarism and to suggest alternatives.

These texts of 'queer theory' are on the surface a long journey away from the sociological objectivity espoused by McIntosh in 'The Homosexual Role'. As I have already suggested, that essay was itself highly political in its implications, and became retrospectively more so following the emergence of gay liberation. The three oppositions implicit in the original essay suggest the inadequacies at best and dangers at worse of isolating the experience of homosexuality from its wider historical and social context, of minoritizing it. When, a few years after the publication of 'The Homosexual Role', Dennis Altman (1993[1971]), in a founding text of gay politics, looked forward to 'the end of the homosexual' (and of course, the end of the heterosexual), he was building on foundations already laid down. And in the transgressive politics of the gay liberation movement, there was a weapon with which the binarism could be challenged.

But the logic of gay politics as it developed over the next twenty years was less towards the challenge to categories and much more to their reification as a proto-ethnic gay identity solidified (Epstein, 1990). The queer theory that emerged at the end of the 1980s, especially in the US (see Warner, 1993), in many ways harked back to the earlier gay liberation inspiration, and was in large part a reaction to the recategorization of sexual dissidence.

I have suggested elsewhere that most social movements embody two moments: the moment of citizenship and the moment of transgression (Weeks, 1995). The first argues for inclusion in the social order; the second fundamentally challenges it. In one sense, 'The Homosexual Role' is shaped by a moment of citizenship. In the 1981 Postscript McIntosh describes the circumstances which shaped its political tact:

> I remember writing a letter to the Homosexual Law Reform Society at one stage, supporting the cause in general, but saying that I had lots of reservations about the nature of the arguments they were putting forward because I could not really accept the view that homosexuality was a sickness. And they wrote back and said that they had a lot of sympathy with my position but at that time they had to use the arguments that were suited to the moment. I quite understood that; in fact, I was doing some work on Parson's theory of legitimation, and I wrote a seminar paper around that time about types of legitimation in which I compared the type of legitimation that the gay world adopts with the type of legitimation that the homophile movement adopts. It argues that the homophile movement had to seek what Parsons calls 'total legitimation', that is legitimation in terms of the general value system; whereas what the gay world does is to

seek legitimation in terms of the sub-culture and simply say 'we don't care what the rest think about us, in terms of our subculture being gay is ok'.

(McIntosh, 1981: 44–5)

The needs of the political moment required that radicalism be muted – a dilemma that has returned many times in subsequent history. Of course, in the process, the claim to full citizenship is itself muted. This is the challenge that radical sexual dissidence takes up. The moment of transgression, in which the whole social order is symbolically challenged, is actually necessary, it seems, to achieve citizenship.

This is the attraction of queer theory and queer politics: they provide a theoretical justification for transgression, and practices of sexual dissidence and subversion which challenge the symbolic order. So in her critique of anti-porn feminism, McIntosh (1992) argues that the task of anti-porn campaigners was not to ally with the moral right but to be subversive of the forms of heteronormativity. In a subsequent essay on queer politics (1993) she argues that lesbian politics had underplayed transgression, and from this perspective the queer challenge was a powerful one. At the same time it was important that queer theory 'should not forget that the heteronormality in terms of which we are defined as others is a highly gendered one, so that our otherness and the forms of meanings of our dissidence are also gendered' (McIntosh, 1993: 47).

This is an important emphasis, but it conceals a more pointed criticism that could be made. By putting the heterosexual/homosexual binarism at the heart of their analysis, queer theorists are in danger of displacing all other social contradictions from serious consideration, and of forgetting in the process Foucault's injunctions about the dispersed nature of power (see Mort, 1994). From homosexuality being at the frozen margins of power, it is now in danger of becoming the beating heart.

Mary McIntosh's more nuanced approach is characteristic of an engaged sociologist who has always been conscious of the complexities of the political as well as the hazards and intricacies of the social. But it is characteristic also of someone whose values, in an age of postmodernist uncertainty, remain defiantly feminist and humanist, for whom feminism is in fact a liberatory project rooted in humanism (1993). Sexual dissidence for McIntosh is clearly part of a wider political project.

Conclusion

I would argue that the sexual radicalism of McIntosh's most recent essays is fully congruent with 'The Homosexual Role' essay, despite the passing of some thirty years. At both periods there is a concern with 'deminoritizing' the homosexual experience, of letting it escape from the narrow confines of a historically specific categorization. There is a political undercurrent to the analysis then and now which belies the calmness of sociological objectivity. There is a continuing recognition of the need to contextualize homosexuality within a broader sociological and historical framework. What is, of course, different, is the radically changed historical context: thirty years of feminism and of lesbian and gay politics have placed squarely on the agenda insights, approaches and analytical tools which could only be hinted at, and then in the safe confines of an American academic journal, in 1968.

The transformed cultural and political worlds in turn have made other things possible. Between 1968 and the early 1990s, McIntosh wrote little about homosexuality; her work went in other directions, into explorations of crime, prostitution, the family. But there is, I would suggest, a strong unifying element throughout this work: a willingness to challenge the taken-for-granted naturalness of our social institutions. As Michèle Barrett and Mary McIntosh put it in their book, *The Anti-Social Family* (1982): 'Considerable social effort is put into defining the boundaries of the "natural" and in decrying things that fall outside them – be it incest, celibacy or homosexuality...It is in the realm of gender, sexuality, marriage that we are collectively most seduced by appeals to the natural' (p. 27).

The ultimate significance of 'The Homosexual Role' essay, I would suggest, was that it persuaded many of us that in trying to understand the historic marginalization and stigmatization of homosexuality it was better to follow Mary McIntosh (and paraphrase Mae West) in grasping that 'nature had nothing to do with it' (Katz, 1983) than to pursue the will-o'-the-wisp of the causes of homosexuality. But we also learned that it was important not to stop at analysis. As Barrett and McIntosh put it in concluding their deconstruction of the naturalness of the family:

> It is the belief that kinship, love and having nice things together are naturally and inevitably bound up together that makes it hard to imagine a world in which 'family' plays little part. This mythologised unity must be picked apart, strand by strand, so that we can understand its power and meet the needs of each of the separate elements more fully. In part this can be done by analysis and discussion...But it must also be done by experiments in new ways of living and by political campaigns to transform not the family – but the society that needs it.
>
> *(Barrett and McIntosh, 1982: 159)*

For many of us, a first reading of 'The Homosexual Role' carried the same twin imperatives: to analyse the sexual order more effectively in order to change things more decisively. That is not a bad epitaph for a shortish essay published in academic obscurity in 1968.

Note

1 Mary McIntosh, 'The Homosexual Role', *Social Problems* 16(2): 182–92, republished in Plummer, 1981, with a Postscript. All quotations are from the 1981 version.

References

Altman, D. (1993[1971]) *Homosexual: Oppression and Liberation.* New York: New York University Press.

Altman, D., Vance, C., Vicinus, M., Weeks, J. et al. (1989) *Homosexuality, Which Homosexuality?* London: GMP.

Barrett, M. and McIntosh, M. (1982) *The Anti-social Family.* London: Verso.

Bech, H. (1997) *When Men Meet: Homosexuality and Modernity.* Cambridge: Polity Press.

Boswell, J. (1980) *Christianity, Social Tolerance, and Homosexuality: Gay People in Western Europe from the Beginning of the Christian Era to the Fourteenth Century.* Chicago IL: University of Chicago Press.

Boswell, J. (1990) 'Categories, Experience and Sexuality', in E. Stein (ed.) *Forms of Desire: Sexual Orientation and the Social Constructionist Controversy,* pp. 133–73. New York: Garland.

Bray, A. (1982) *Homosexuality in Renaissance England.* London: GMP.

Butler, J. (1990) *Gender Trouble: Feminism and the Subversion of Identity.* New York: Routledge.

Butler, J. (1993) *Bodies that Matter: On the Discursive Limits of Sex.* New York: Routledge.

Chauncey, G. (1994) *Gay New York: Gender, Urban Culture and the Making of the Gay Male World 1890–1940.* New York: Basic Books.

Dollimore, J. (1991) *Sexual Dissidence: Augustine to Wilde, Freud to Foucault.* Oxford: Oxford University Press.

Dworkin, A. (1987) *Intercourse.* New York: Free Press.

Dynes, W. R. (1990) 'Wrestling with the Social Boa Constructor', in E. Stein (ed.) *Forms of Desire: Sexual Orientation and the Social Constructionist Controversy,* pp. 209–38. New York: Garland.

Epstein, S. (1990) 'Gay Politics, Ethnic Identity', in E. Stein (ed.) *Forms of Desire: Sexual Orientation and the Social Constructionist Controversy,* pp. 239–93. New York: Garland.

Faderman, L. (1981) *Surpassing the Love of Men.* London: Junction Books.

Ford, C. S. and Beach, F. (1952) *Patterns of Sexual Behaviour.* London: Methuen.

Foucault, M. (1979) *The History of Sexuality, Vol. 1: An Introduction.* London: Allen Lane.

Foucault, M. (1985) *The History of Sexuality, Vol. 2: The Use of Pleasure.* London: Viking.

Foucault, M. (1986) *The History of Sexuality, Vol. 3: The Care of the Self.* London: Viking.

Garber, M. (1993) *Vested Interests: Cross-Dressing and Cultural Anxiety.* New York: Routledge.

Greenberg, D. E. (1988) *The Construction of Homosexuality.* Chicago IL: University of Chicago Press.

Hacking, I. (1990) 'Making up People', in E. Stein (ed.) *Forms of Desire: Sexual Orientation and the Social Constructionist Controversy*, pp. 69–88. New York: Garland.

Halperin, D. (1990) *One Hundred Years of Homosexuality, and Other Essays on Greek Love.* New York: Routledge.

Halperin, D. (1995) *Saint Foucault: Towards a Gay Hagiography.* Oxford: Oxford University Press.

Herdt, G., ed. (1994) *Third Sex, Third Gender: Beyond Sexual Dimorphism in Culture and History.* New York: Zone Books.

Jeffreys, S. (1990) *Anticlimax: A Feminist Perspective on the Sexual Revolution.* London: Women's Press.

Katz, J. N. (1983) *Gay/Lesbian Almanac: A New Documentary.* New York: Harper & Row.

Katz, J. (1995) *The Invention of Heterosexuality.* New York: Dutton.

Kinsey, A. C., Pomeroy, W. B. and Martin, C. E. (1948) *Sexual Behavior in the Human Male.* Philadelphia PA: W. B. Saunders.

McIntosh, M. (1981) 'The Homosexual Role' and 'Postscript', in K. Plummer (ed.) *The Making of the Modern Homosexual*, pp. 30–49. London: Hutchinson.

McIntosh, M. (1992) 'Liberalism and the Contradictions of Sexual Politics', in L. Segal and M. McIntosh (eds) *Sex Exposed: Sexuality and the Pornography Debate*, pp. 155–68. London: Virago.

McIntosh, M. (1993) 'Queer Theory and the War of the Sexes', in J. Bristow and A. Wilson (eds) *Activating Theory: Lesbian, Gay, Bisexual Theory*, pp. 30–52. London: Lawrence and Wishart.

MacKinnon, C. A. (1987) *Feminism Unmodified: Discourses on Life and Law.* Cambridge MA: Harvard University Press.

Mort, F. (1994) 'Essentialism Revisited? Identity Politics and Late Twentieth-Century Discourses of Homosexuality', in J. Weeks (ed.) *The Lesser Evil and the Greater Good: The Theory and Politics of Social Diversity*, pp. 201–21. London: Rivers Oram Press.

Murray, S. O. (1996) '"The Homosexual Role" and Lesbigay Roles', in *American Gay*, pp. 143–66. Chicago IL: University of Chicago Press.

Norton, R. (1992) *Mother Clap's Molly House.* London: GMP.

Plummer, K. (1975) *Sexual Stigma: An Interactionist Account.* London: Routledge & Kegan Paul.

Plummer, K. ed. (1981) *The Making of the Modern Homosexual.* London: Hutchinson.

Plummer, K. (1992) *Modern Homosexualities: Fragments of Lesbian and Gay Experience.* London: Routledge.

Plummer, K. (1995) *Telling Sexual Stories: Power, Change and Social Worlds.* London: Routledge.

Prout, A. and Deverell, K. (1995) *Working with Diversity: Evaluating the MESMAC Project.* London: Health Education Authority.

Rose, H. (1996) 'Gay Brains, Gay Genes and Feminist Science Theory', in J. Weeks and J. Holland (eds) *Sexual Cultures: Communities, Values and Intimacy*, pp. 53–72. Basingstoke: Macmillan.

Rubin, G. and Butler, J. (1994) 'Sexual Traffic', *Differences* 6 (2 and 3): 62–99.

Sedgwick, E. K. (1985) *Between Men: English Literature and Male Homosocial Desire*. New York: Columbia University Press.

Sedgwick, E. K. (1990) *Epistemology of the Closet*. Berkeley CA: University of California Press.

Silverstolpe, F. (1987) 'Benkert was Not a Doctor: On the Non-Medical Origin of the Homosexual Category', paper given at the 'Homosexuality, Which Homosexuality?' International Scientific Conference on Gay and Lesbian Studies, Amsterdam.

Smith-Rosenberg, C. (1985) *Disorderly Conduct: Visions of Gender in Victorian America*. New York: Oxford University Press.

Stein, E., ed. (1990) *Forms of Desire: Sexual Orientation and the Social Constructionist Controversy*. New York: Garland.

Trumbach, R. (1977) 'London's Sodomites: Homosexual Behavior and Western Culture in the 18th Century', *Journal of Social History* 11(1): 1–33.

Trumbach, R. (1989) 'Gender and Homosexual Role in Modern Western Culture', in D. Altman, C. Vance, M. Vicinus, J. Weeks et al. (eds) *Homosexuality, Which Homosexuality?*, pp. 149–69. London: GMP.

Vance, C. S. (1989) 'Social Construction Theory: Problems in the History of Sexuality', in D. Altman, C. Vance, M. Vicinus, J. Weeks et al. (eds) *Homosexuality, Which Homosexuality?*, pp. 13–34. London: GMP.

Warner, M., ed. (1993) *Fear of a Queer Planet: Queer Politics and Social Theory*. Minneapolis: University of Minnesota Press.

Weeks, J. (1977) *Coming Out: Homosexual Politics in Britain from the Nineteenth Century to the Present*. London: Quartet.

Weeks, J. (1986) *Sexuality*. Chichester: Ellis Horwood/Tavistock.

Weeks, J. (1995) *Invented Moralities: Sexual Values in an Age of Uncertainty*. Cambridge: Polity Press.

Weinrich, J. (1990) 'Reality or Social Construction?', in E. Stein (ed.) *Forms of Desire: Sexual Orientation and the Social Constructionist Controversy*, pp. 175–208. New York: Garland.

Whitam, F. L. and Mathy, R. M. (1986) *Male Homosexuality in Four Societies*. New York: Praeger.

Wolfenden, Sir J. (1957) *Report of the Committee on Homosexual Offences and Prostitution*. London: Her Majesty's Stationery Office, Cmnd. 247.

3

Dennis Altman and the Politics of (Homo)Sexual Liberation

Most books lag behind change, describing to their readers a world they already know. Some fortunate books anticipate change, capturing a moment and pushing it forward into a hitherto unimagined future. Dennis Altman's *Homosexual: Oppression and Liberation* is one of these lucky books, and nearly thirty years after its first publication in 1971, I can pick it up now and marvel at its success at distilling a unique historical moment, and in anticipating key features of a future we now live.

The book is, of course, pre-eminently a product of its time – its assumptions, hopes, fears, style and language (do radicals anywhere still have 'rap-sessions'?) It could not be anything else, and that is part of its attraction to a new generation of readers. But what is striking is how many of the ideas in this book, despite an infinitely less generous cultural climate, and in the shadow of a devastating epidemic that no one could have foreseen, are still relevant, indeed being acted out in a new wave of lesbian and gay activism, and refined and developed in what is increasingly being termed 'queer theory'. Here, of course, the cheeky ironies of history tweak Dennis Altman's tail: one of the tasks of the book was to refuse the opprobrious label of 'queer'. He quotes a phrase of the early 1970s: 'chick equals nigger equals queer'. For Altman's generation, which is also mine, it was essential to reject a language ('queer', 'fag' and so forth) which execrated and marginalized us. The book is, in part, about forging a new language of homosexual politics; the language shaped then in the context of a new movement is now being reconstructed to meet new demands. But the constant need to do so is again part of the message of this book. The terrain of sexual politics, like all politics, constantly shifts, demanding new definitions and redefinitions. But in doing that necessary work we should not forget the context in which the terms of the debate were set. The republication of this book, then, is more than a pious homage to a pioneer; it is an essential part of understanding the history we are living and making.

The fundamental context of *Homosexual: Oppression and Liberation* was the emergence of the gay liberation movement in the United States in 1969. Although the movement itself is not discussed explicitly until chapter 4 of the book, it is the founding experience that gives the book meaning. As Dennis Altman remarks in the Introduction to the book, 'the best social analysis grows out of personal experience', and it was the living of the experience of the new movement that shaped his arguments. The title, though chosen by the publishers rather than the author, sums up rather well the trajectory of the book. *Homosexual* harks back to the traditional, clinical description. It is a come-on to an audience unfamiliar with the new arguments, new language. But the second terms, *Oppression* and *Liberation*, point forward to a new world of politics. The idea that homosexual people were opressed, not only individually but as a group or category of human beings, was new to the vast majority of us in the 1960s, though anticipated in some earlier, European as well as American literature and sexual politics. The idea that homosexuals, acting collectively, could transform the conditions of their individual and social lives, that we could be 'liberated', was transformative; in the language of the time, 'revolutionary'.

Unless you lived through the experience, it is difficult now to recapture fully the impact of those heady early days of gay liberation. Edmund White, in his novel, *The Beautiful Room Is Empty*, has his characters describe the Stonewall riots of June 1969, the symbolic beginning of gay liberation, as 'our Bastille Day...the turning point of our lives'; and although few experienced those riots, many thousands were indelibly affected by their aftermath, in all their confused glory. I have described some of that confusion and glory in my own first solo book, *Coming Out: Homosexual Politics in Britain from the Nineteenth Century to the Present* (1977/1990).

I have to say that as a student in Britain at the time, just about to start my first job as a teacher, I was completely ignorant of the riots. So were the vast majority of American people. As White's narrator says, 'we couldn't find a single mention in the press' of this turning point. I was sceptical of the garbled reports of the new movement carried in the

British media over the next year. I remember a jokey item on the BBC's premier radio news programme about a gay march, and shuddered with horror. That could never happen here, thank God! It was not until the London Gay Liberation Front was started in October 1970, at the London School of Economics where I was then working, that I felt any real interest. I went along to a meeting nervously, especially as I was on home ground. I was ready to leave at the first opportunity, but stayed, went back the next week, and the next, and the rest, if not history, is certainly my history. My politics, my personal relationships, my living arrangements, my personal appearance, even my career: all were challenged and transformed by those early days, and their impact and influence are still with me as I write. Many of my current intellectual and political preoccupations, like a background radiation, can be traced back to those early moments, a sort of 'big bang' of my adult life, and though many of my ideas have changed, my basic commitments have not.

But what someone like myself, a young academic, trained as a historian of ideas, lacked was precisely a systematic presentation of the ideas of gay liberation. I needed a map. My own attitude toward my gayness had been formed from a rag-bag of sources in the 1960s: a barely articulated resistance to the psychologizing of the standard textbooks of the period; reading between the lines of writers like Christopher Isherwood and Angus Wilson; and the essays (especially *The Fire Next Time*) and novels of James Baldwin. Baldwin was probably the single most important influence on me prior to gay liberation. I read *Giovanni's Room* while going for a university interview in 1964, my first time away from home on my own; I devoured *Another Country* when I came to London as a student later that year. I recognized myself in these books, and excitedly wrote about it to a school friend, quoting chunks of *Another Country*. For his reply I received the burned remains of my letter, with the scribbled comment that he never wanted to read such disgusting things again; this from the instigator of my earliest, confused sexual experimentations. I had no language to take the argument further, except that of an individualist appeal to the truth of my own needs and desires.

The rhetoric of gay liberation began to provide me with a wider rationale for 'coming out', a heady brew of liberationist aspirations, and a new affirmation of collective belonging. The leaflets and early journals of gay liberation began to seep through to London from the United States, passed from hand to hand or occasionally obtainable in the more radical bookshops. The new feminist texts, most famously from Kate Millett, Shulamith Firestone and Germaine Greer, began to fill my bookshelves, though few mentioned homosexuality except in passing. A framework for a new sexual politics was emerging, through practical experience in demonstrations, zaps, consciousness-raising groups, 'functional groups', as we called them, such as the Counter-Psychiatry Group, and in informal networks for discussion, and gradually, for writing: articles, manifestos, pamphlets. But what we needed was a framework that would pull all these experiences together, giving them a theoretical structure and some sense of history, which in turn could feed back into practice.

Dennis's Altman's book was the first full-scale work to try to do that. It must have been mid-1972 before I heard of it (unusually for me, I did not write the date in the copy I bought then and have before me now), and eagerly sought out a copy, a photographic reproduction of the first American edition, with an Author's Note on the inside cover pointing out a few minor typographical errors. I can't say it changed my life in the way reading Baldwin or going to my first GLF meeting did. It did something rather different, and of lasting importance: it helped make sense of the helter-skelter experiences and readings of the previous, hectic eighteen months. It helped give shape to a host of inchoate ideas. It started many intellectual hares running, some in quite different directions from those the author at that stage might have intended. I read it at precisely the moment that I was preparing myself to write about sexuality: I published my first effort on the theme later that year, an article entitled 'Ideas of Gay Liberation'. The book provided a good part of the map I needed. I have not taken all the pathways it indicated, and I have tried to construct maps of my own since. But this book helped point me in a direction from which I have not fundamentally erred ever since.

I refer to my own experiences here not because they were special but because they were, I believe, representative. Relatively few of us probably read the book when it first appeared. Most people picked up the ideas it synthesized and circulated more informally. But the point that needs underlining is that I, and many others, were picking up these ideas in Britain, in continental Europe, in Australasia, as well as in North America. Gay liberation may have taken on many different national guises, but several of its key elements have had an international significance. Here was an Australian political scientist writing about what seemed a quintessentially American phenomenon, and soon finding that its impact was also back at home, and throughout the developed world. Dennis Altman has proved since then that he is an ideal interpreter and translator, equally at home intellectually in Australia, North America, Europe, and most recently Southeast Asia. The internationalism of his commitments and activities is perhaps the most impressive thing about his career as a whole, and it is already latent in this book.

I want now to pick out three strands in *Homosexual: Oppression and Liberation* which seem to me to be of enduring importance: the emphasis on identity; the relationship between community and social movement;

and Altman's still controversial looking forward to the 'end of the homosexual'.

The book's central concern, Altman writes in his Introduction, is the 'question of identity'. It has also been the central concern of all subsequent lesbian and gay literature and politics. Coming out, the public assertion and affirmation of one's homosexuality, of identity, was at once the most simple and the most fundamental activity of the new sexual politics of the 1970s. Of course, there were many 'known' homosexuals before 1969, and many of them had made brave political and personal statements. But think of some of the consequences, just for some of the homosexual writers Altman respects and refers to in the book. Gore Vidal's first novel, explicit for the time (the late 1940s), had all but ruined his career before it had barely begun; Christopher Isherwood had gone into exile, and literary silence for a while, rather than endure the hypocrisies of England; James Baldwin had to endure the vituperations of his fellow blacks, convinced he had sold out to white faggotry. But for Altman's generation, writing as a gay person became for the first time not merely desirable, but a necessity, even if coming out was, as he says, a 'long and painful process'.

A new emphasis had entered the discourse of identity: an awareness of the historical and social factors that had shaped attitudes toward and inhibited the expression of homosexuality. 'To be a homosexual in our society', writes Altman, echoing Erving Goffman's discussion of 'spoiled identities', 'is to be constantly aware that one bears a stigma.' The task of the new identity-politics (though that term was only to be articulated fully a decade after this book first appeared) was to understand why homosexuals were stigmatized, or to put it in another, more political, way, why homosexuals were oppressed; and how to fight that oppression.

Oppression, the 'denial of identity', could take three forms: persecution, discrimination or tolerance. Of these, in the ostensibly permissive climate of the early 1970s, the most common was liberal tolerance, 'annihilation by blandness' in Christopher Isherwood's phrase. Here we can see the influence of another of Altman's mentors, Herbert Marcuse, whose emphasis on 'repressive desublimation', the controlled deregulation of sexuality in order to bind individuals ever more tightly to the system with chains of gold, had a powerful, if in retrospect short-lived, influence on 1960s radicals. In a cultural climate like that of the 1980s and early 1990s, tolerance does not, perhaps, seem such a bad thing as it might have done earlier. But the real point that Altman was making still rings true: there is a form of toleration which lives with difference without fully validating it; the sort of tolerance which says 'what a pity you are homosexual, but we still love you'. Altman's case was that this form of liberal pity was as unacceptable, and as damaging to self-pride, as the more overt forms of hatred of homosexuality. It fell far short of full acceptance.

Altman's arguments, then, asserted the validity of homosexuality in its own terms, and in particular its importance for a resolute and affirmative sense of self and of belonging, that is for identity. This offered a major break with traditional writings about homosexuality, which in effect had seen it as a symptom of failed identification, that is failure to be a normal, heterosexual person. Instead, Altman was asserting, on the contrary, that in a world of diverse sexualities, there was no intrinsic difference between heterosexuality and homosexuality. The imperative towards heterosexuality was a cultural, not an essential or inherent, phenomenon, and homosexual identities had been formed in part through resistance to that imperative.

Here Altman was broaching, though not yet explicitly developing, what was to become the central theoretical issue in lesbian and gay politics: were homosexuals a distinct minority, characterized by a more or less inherent attraction to their own sex, or was the category of homosexual a historical and social invention, formed in specific historical conditions, and likely to disappear as conditions changed? As the book unfolds, it is the latter position which is developed, and here it looks forward to the most creative historical, sociological and literary work of the next twenty years. The reference points are clearly there. In particular, there are the references to Mary McIntosh's groundbreaking article of 1968, 'The Homosexual Role', which argued that what was required was not an explanation of the homosexual condition, but an understanding of how homosexuality came to be seen as a defining condition of some people and not others in the first place (see chapter 2, above). This opened up immensely creative paths of historical investigation, to be followed through in the next few years by writers such as Michel Foucault, Jonathan Katz, John D'Emilio, Randolph Trumbach, Carroll Smith-Rosenberg, Lillian Faderman and many others, including myself. But Altman uses other sources as well, especially those from the Freudian left, such as Marcuse, who questioned the fixity of the heterosexual norm.

I'll take up some of the implications of the constructionist position below. The important issue to note here is that the stress on a positive gay identity in Altman's usage becomes more than an assertion of self; it is also, and crucially, a political stance. It both questions the naturalness and fixity of the heterosexual norm, and affirms the positive value of homosexuality as a way of life. Within that framework, there are limitations. The emphasis is overwhelmingly on male gayness; lesbianism is apologetically minimized. The different meanings of identity for lesbians, which later lesbian scholars such as Lillian Faderman, Carroll Smith-Rosenberg and Martha Vicinus were to clarify, are missed, as Altman has acknowledged in subsequent writings. Other controversial topics, such as the s/m culture that was already developing, are mentioned as transient products of a hostile environment. The main comparison is not with the feminist movement, which seems most obvious now, but with the black movement, and not the civil rights movement but new militants such as the Black Panthers.

From the perspective of twenty years later this may seem a little strange, but it does reflect very accurately the mood of the early 1970s, when the political identification of the new gay movement was less with its own homophile predecessors (who were often reviled for their 'liberalism') than with that amorphous, and as it turned out ephemeral, thing called 'the movement', the would-be revolutionary mobilization which had arisen in America in the wake of opposition to the Vietnam War and the rise of black militancy. For Altman's generation of activists, the oppression of homosexuality could not be seen as an isolated remnant of old prejudices. 'The oppression of homosexuals', he writes, 'is part of the general repression of sexuality, and our liberation can only come as part of a total revolution in social attitudes.'

This brings me to the second significant strand in Altman's book, the emphasis on a gay *movement* and on its complex relationship to the idea of 'community'. A movement committed to radical political militancy was the indispensable prerequisite for achieving lesbian and gay liberation, and in the developing divide between the different strands of the gay movement represented by the Gay Liberation Front and the Gay Activists' Alliance, Altman's instincts are with the former. Again, this is a distinction which history has overtaken. The cutting edge of gay radicalism in the early 1970s critically challenged the existing 'gayworld' for its 'ghetto mentality', its emphasis on sexuality to the exclusion of wider cultural issues, its erection of a 'pseudo community' which refused the implications of a wider sexual and social oppression, and hence the meaning of true community. Gay liberation, Altman argues, stands for the realization of such a true community, based on the 'eroticization of everyday life'.

Subsequent writings by gay scholars, including Altman himself, as well as historic experience, have put this argument into a different light. Writers such as John D'Emilio, in *Sexual Politics, Sexual Communities*, and Alan Berube, in *Coming Out Under Fire*, have shown that the emergence of a strong sense of gay community over the previous generation had itself been the necessary precondition for the emergence of gay liberation. Moreover, the main impact of the new gay sense of purpose and militancy over the two decades after 1969 was not the revolutionary transformation of society but a vast expansion of the lesbian and gay world. Altman himself was to anatomize that transformation in his book *The Homosexualization of America, the Americanization of the Homosexual* (1982). In turn, that expansion, with its ease of sexual interaction, was to make possible both the tragically rapid spread of HIV and AIDS in the male gay community after 1980, *and* the extraordinary gay response to it, with its massive mobilization of activism, care, fund raising and creativity, particularly through the invention and widespread adoption of safer sex. Again, Altman was at hand to document the response in his 1986 book *AIDS in the Mind of America* (published outside the USA as *AIDS and the New Puritanism*).

In the past thirty years, then, the relationship between 'movement' and 'community' has shifted. No longer is it possible or desirable to counterpose one to the other. On the contrary, a sense of community is what makes possible a movement or movements, though each is necessarily challenged and changed by the other. But community does more than simply affirm a collective existence, crucial as that is. It also makes possible a greater sense of individuality. It is no longer possible to believe, as Altman suggests in *Homosexual: Oppression and Liberation*, that 'the ultimate extension of gay community is the gay commune'. On the contrary, the past decades have shown that a sense of community and belonging, and the openness about our sexualities that it makes possible, have given rise to a vast variety of possible lifestyles and patterns of relationships. In retrospect, we can see that the emergence of gay liberation was a dramatic, but not isolated, moment in the long-term breakdown of fixed patterns of domestic and sexual life. Gay liberation heralded the public presence and celebration of sexual diversity. The political and ethical implications of that are still being forged in a climate where, as Altman writes elsewhere, sex has become a new front line of politics. But whatever the efforts of moral conservatives and sexual fundamentalists of left and right to the contrary, it seems clear to me that there is no going back to the idea of a single sexual morality or way of life. Diversity and difference are the new watchwords of sexual politics.

This does pose challenging problems for contemporary lesbian and gay politics. On the one hand, developments over the past thirty years have established a strong sense of gay identity and community, giving rise to what has been described as a sort of gay ethnicity, especially in cities such as San Francisco and New York where there is often a strong sense of geographical as well as social rootedness. This has been a vital development in affirming a sense of pride in self and social belonging. But on the other hand, it tends to reaffirm the sense of the separateness and unity of the category of 'the homosexual' which gay liberation sought to challenge, and which the realities of contemporary sexualities make untenable. As Altman recognizes, the new movement of the early 1970s was already straining against the challenge of difference: between men and women, between different racial and ethnic groups, between people with different desires, lifestyles, class positions, or political or religious affiliations. The politics of difference has tended to accentuate these divisions over subsequent years, and the recent development of a 'queer politics' has underlined the dilemmas. For here we have simultaneously the idea of a radical 'queer nation' and a challenge to the patterns of lesbian and gay life as they developed during the 1970s and 1980s.

The spirit of some of the radical queer politics is, in fact, remarkably close to that of early gay liberation, as expressed in Altman's book. For here community and movement are in the end seen not as a confirmation of but as a radical challenge to the idea of a fixed and separate homosexual category. For Altman, the aim of gay politics is ultimately to make the terms 'homosexuality' and 'heterosexuality' meaningless, to bring about the 'end of the homosexual', and of 'the heterosexual'. It is a political movement whose aim is its own demise: 'gay liberation will have achieved its full potential when it is no longer needed'. And it will no longer be needed when the categorical differences between the 'normal' and the 'abnormal' disappear.

This is the third theme I want to look at, and as I have already suggested it is still the most contested. Sexual liberation, for Altman, involved (as the title of his chapter 3 suggests), a move toward 'the polymorphous whole'. Altman's discussion of this concept is, I think, particularly illuminating; note for instance his analysis of the repressed homosexuality underlying the hypermasculinity of a writer like Norman Mailer, where denial of homosexuality is the very definition of what it is to be a true man. In the discussion of the fear and loathing that an anti-homosexual culture generates, Altman is clearly looking forward to the concept of 'homophobia' that George Weinberg was to elaborate in *Society and the Healthy Homosexual* (1972), and which has since become a key analytical term in lesbian and gay studies (for example, in the work of Eve Kosovsky Sedgwick).

Altman owes some intellectual debt here to Marcuse, and to Norman O. Brown, whose writings have gone out of fashion but to whom Altman is clearly indebted. The Freudianism of Altman's work was itself unfashionable at the time the book was written both among gay liberationists (many of whom saw psychoanalysis, at least in the form common in the USA, as repressively normative and anti-homosexual) and feminists. Later feminist psychoanalysis, notably at first the work of Juliet Mitchell, owing much to the recovery of Freud attempted by the French analyst Jacques Lacan, was to open up new perspectives on the Freudian tradition, though little attention was paid in this new critical psycho-analysis to homosexuality. An exception, that again Altman anticipates, though coming from a quite different intellectual tradition, is Guy Hoc-quenghem, whose *Homosexual Desire* puts forward a fuller theory of the impact of anti-homosexual paranoia: 'The problem is not so much homosexual desire as the fear of homosexuality.'

The key lesson of the radical psychoanalytic tradition is that it funda-mentally questions the fixity of sexual identities. For Freud at his most radical, gender and sexual identities are only ever precarious achieve-ments, all the time destabilized and undermined by unconscious desires. The basic bisexual and polymorphously perverse nature of the human animal is constrained and limited by cultural imperatives and norms, but the desires that nature gives rise to are never obliterated; they lurk dangerously in each individual unconscious.

But if identity, and sexual difference, are precarious at the level of the unconscious, they are also in large part a fiction at the level of social and cultural life. This is, I know, a controversial statement, and one that many lesbian and gay activists would bitterly challenge. The search for a gay gene, or special type of homosexual brain, or whatever, which is frequently welcomed by self-appointed gay spokespeople, attests to a constant wish to find an explanation rooted in nature for homosexual difference. As I have already indicated, Altman rejects such fantasies, and anticipating Foucault and other writers argues for the historical shaping of the homo/hetero distinction. This is not to deny the value of construct-ing lesbian and gay identities as an essential way of combating discrimination, and of negotiating the hazards of everyday life. Such identities are, in words I have used elsewhere, necessary fictions. But fictions they are, none the less.

If this is true, if sexual difference is hardened into sexual division because of cultural norms based on a fear of sexual variety, then it follows that in a culture which is more at ease with sexual diversity and plural value systems, and where by implication the dominance of heterosexual and traditional family value systems is questioned, the rationale for rigid distinctions between people begins to disappear; and the end of both the 'homosexual' and the 'heterosexual', in the common usage of those terms, looms.

We seem quite a long way from that situation today. And yet there are signs in contemporary culture of a new willingness and ability to play with identity, to see it as akin to a staged event. Altman's emphasis on the homosexual role becomes in recent writing a stress on identity as a performance, or rather a series of performances (see Judith Butler's book, *Gender Trouble*). In both, however, we can see the dual emphasis: lesbian and gay identities are constructed, but apparently essential; they play with the inherited structures of power, challenging and undermining them; but at the same time they are deadly serious.

Identity, community, challenging the inevitability of the heterosexual/ homosexual distinction: I have suggested that these are the dominating themes of the book. They are not separate themes, because they are intimately connected to the new politics of homosexuality that Altman is simultaneously describing, analysing, and helping to create. Underlying all is the conviction that sexuality should not be easily divided into neat categories in a hierarchical relationship where homosexuality is inevitably marginalized where it is not execrated. On the contrary, 'homosexuals are a minority quite unlike any other, for we are a part of all humans. . . . Everyone is gay, everyone is straight. That is why the homosexual has been so severely oppressed.'

The publication of Altman's book in the early 1970s was a key moment in the popularization and dissemination of the radical sexual agenda that this quotation illustrates. The achievements, disappoint-ments, political setbacks, and personal and community tragedies of the past decades have dimmed some of the utopian hopes, transformed the language of radical politics, and set new and often difficult dilemmas. But Altman's book speaks to us still because its agenda has not yet run its course. Gay liberation, he writes, is a 'process by which we develop a theory and practice out of our experience, living, as it were, our libera-tion'. Few have argued this case with greater *élan* and vivacity.

Note

This essay was originally published as 'Introduction' to a new edition as *Homo-sexual Oppression and Liberation*, New York University Press, 1993.

4

Guy Hocquenghem and Homosexual Desire

Guy Hocquenghem's *Homosexual Desire*, first published in France in 1972, represents a juncture between the politics of homosexuality and a number of significant French leftist theoretical and political currents. These currents have, on the whole, been absent from most English-language debates until very recently, and their appearance now can be seen as the outcome of a certain deadlock in traditional English-language thinking about sexual politics. Hocquenghem's essay itself should not be seen as a definitive theoretical statement or as a clear guide to current practice. Its value lies rather in its summing up of important intellectual tendencies, and their specific application to the question of homosexual oppression.

The focal point of the essay, unifying its theoretical elements and giving it its distinctive *élan* and vitality, is the possibility of social and personal transformation which was opened up by the May events in France in 1968, and which poses, in Hocquenghem's view, the opportunity for a 'revolution of desire'. But the specific argument of the essay is guided by the new possibilities for a radical sexual politics opened up by the emergence of the gay liberation movement in the early 1970s. The movement, which began in the United States in 1969 and rapidly spread to Western Europe in 1970–1, stressed the necessity for a new, open, homosexual politics, a *revolutionary* politics (in rhetoric if not in form) which had as its underlying thrust the goal of personal and sexual self-determination. It is the idea of homosexuals taking control of their own identities, and in doing so rejecting the stigmatizing labels of a hostile society, which poses a real challenge to bourgeois ideologies of familial and reproductive sexuality and male dominance. Hocquenghem sees this transformation of the politics of homosexuality as itself an expression of the new possibilities signalled in 1968.

In outlining this position Hocquenghem identifies with a series of overlapping French intellectual projects, themselves partly transformed by the impact of the theoretical and political stirrings of the late 1960s: the 'recovery of Freud' associated with Jacques Lacan; the linguistic theories derived from Ferdinand de Saussure and others; the debate on ideology and the 'constitution of the subject' stimulated by the work of Louis Althusser; the anti-psychiatry concepts of Gilles Deleuze and Félix Guattari; the historical discussions around the work of Michel Foucault. There is in these a major concern with language, psychoanalysis and marxism which provides the theoretical framework of *Homosexual Desire*. A major interest of the work is its attempt to describe, using this framework, how the 'homosexual' as a social being is constituted in a capitalist society, and the consequences of this for gender and sexual identities. The book itself explores this in three parts: first, it describes and analyses the 'paranoid' hostility to homosexuality that modern society reveals; second, it relates this to the role of Oedipal family and reproductive sexuality in modern capitalism; third, the work states the possibilities of anti-capitalist and anti-Oedipal struggles afforded by the gay movement along with other autonomous movements and 'subject groups'.

Although there has been a longstanding hostility towards male homosexual behaviour in the Christian west, the modern form of this is of relatively recent origin. As Hocquenghem indicates, it was the late nineteenth century which saw the embryonic emergence of notions which have dominated twentieth-century views: in particular the idea of homosexuality as a disease or sickness (the 'medical model') and that homosexuality represents a specific individual 'condition', deriving either from a tainted heredity or a corrupting environment. This represented both a secularization of the old religious sanctions and an individualization of the condition, and was associated with a general increase of social hostility and an 'internalization' of guilt. Even the reformers, such as Magnus Hirschfeld in Germany or Havelock Ellis in Britain, worked within the framework of homosexuality as a specific individual 'variation' or 'anomaly'. This much was common throughout America and Western Europe.[1] But inevitably, there were major national divergences in social and especially legal responses. Unlike Britain and Germany, France saw no tightening of the law in the late nineteenth or early twentieth centuries, and there was a consequent absence of any major legal scandals such as that of Oscar Wilde in England. Under the Napoleonic legal code, homosexuality as such was not subject to specific legal sanctions until 1942. In that year the collaborationist Pétain regime in Nazi-occupied France imposed penalties for homosexual offences with 'minors' under the age of twenty-one. Before this, the 'age of consent' was sixteen, and was applied to heterosexuality and homosexuality alike. The Pétain enactments were confirmed by the post-liberation regime of General de Gaulle in 1945, and it was under the later Gaullist regime of the 1960s that a further tightening of the law took place, when the penalties for public 'indecency' were raised, more sharply for homosexual than for heterosexual offences. Thus while social-democratic regimes in England and Wales, Holland, Germany and Scandinavia were liberalizing the law on male homosexuality in 1960s, the authoritarian Gaullist regime was extending it. (But it is worth nothing, in passing, that even in 'liberal' Britain the reformed law of 1967 was severely limited in its extent, and was followed by an actual increase in police prosecutions relating to 'public decency'.) This partly explains the specific form of homosexual politics in France. There had in fact been a French homosexual organization, known as Arcadie, in existence since the mid-1950s, and it was reputed to have over 50,000 members. But this had been notoriously conservative and closeted. A small, short-lived revolutionary homosexual group did appear in the post-1968 surge of energy, but it was not until 1971 that a gay liberation grouping, the Front Homosexual d'Action Révolutionnaire (FHAR), appeared, explicitly modelled on the American Gay Liberation Front. Although small, it was important in politicizing the question of homosexuality. *Homosexual Desire* reflects these developments, and its aim is clearly to see homosexual oppression as an inevitable part of a wider system of exploitation and oppression. Hence its echoes of Herbert Marcuse's precepts on the moral 'totalitarianism' of modern capitalism and its references to Wilhelm Reich; but more central are the discussions of Freud, the references to the work of Lacan, and the specific criticisms of Lacanian psychoanalysis produced by Gilles Deleuze and Félix Guattari in their joint work *L'Anti-Oedipe: Capitalisme et Schizophrénie*.[2] *Homosexual Desire*, in both its title and its major concepts, demonstrates in particular the author's involvement with the latter work. To understand properly certain formulations used by Hocquenghem, therefore, we must first clarify the terms of the debate.

Desire

The starting point of this debate is the dialogue with psychoanalysis as theory, technique and practice, and its focus is the return to Freud outlined by Jacques Lacan, a 'return' to a Freud purged of the biologism for which he is usually criticized by feminists and focusing on his central discovery, the unconscious. For Lacan and his followers, Freud's work represents the beginnings of a new science of the unconscious whose aim is to uncover the truth of the subject, the 'individual' as a social being. But, as Althusser has put it, 'Freud had to think his discoveries and his practice in imported concepts, concepts borrowed from the thermo-dynamic physics then dominant, from the political economy and biology of his time'.[3] In the hands of Freud's followers (who were encouraged, it has to be said, by tendencies in his own writings) psychoanalysis became a system, heavily encased in the irrelevances of other disciplines, and an orthodoxy in which the major insights were overlaid by a sort of psychic determinism. Lacan, helped by the fact that in France, unlike Britain or the United States, psychoanalysis had never been complicit with medical authority, sought to draw out the kernel of Freud's revolutionary discoveries. In this interpretation, as Juliet Mitchell has said:

> Psychoanalysis is about the material reality of ideas both within, and of, man's history. . . .
> The way we live as 'ideas' the necessary laws of human society is not so much conscious as *unconscious* – the particular task of psychoanalysis is to decipher how we acquire our heritage of the ideas and laws of human society within the unconscious mind.[4]

The unconscious mind, as she goes on to say, is the way in which we acquire the laws of society, for the unconscious is created as the animal child becomes a human child by entering into the social world through the process and resolution of the Oedipus crisis – the acceptance of the 'law of the Father', the fundamental law of society. Through this process, the child enters the symbolic order, an order of signs, meanings, language. Lacan's theorization would itself have been impossible without the emergence of a new science of linguistics, associated especially with the work of Saussure. For Lacan, 'the discourse of the unconscious is structured like a language', and it is through language that the child enters the adult (social) world. Thus Lacan's return to Freud involved a particular emphasis on certain of his works, such as *The Interpretation of Dreams*, where Freud studied the mechanisms and laws of dreams, reducing the variants to two, displacement and condensation. For Lacan, following linguistics, these become metonomy and metaphor. The return, in other words, is to a Freud whose concern is with the unconscious processes of symbolic transformations.[5]

What Lacan set out to do was recover the subversiveness of Freud: the key element which has made Lacan influential both among anti-psychiatrists and on the left is the rejection of the coherence of the 'ego' or 'self', of an essential 'individual'. For a marxist such as Louis Althusser, for example, Lacan's work opened the way to an understanding of the 'structure of misrecognition', or the forms in which the human subject conceives the world; this has been of particular concern therefore to some recent theorists of ideology.[6] The project, here, is the fit between the insights of psychoanalysis as a theoretical tool and marxism. Marx recognized that the individual human subject is not the 'centre' of history, as bourgeois thought believed, and that history has no given centre except in ideological misrepresentation. And this articulates with Freud's discovery, as conceived in Lacanian psychoanalysis, that the individual subject has no given centre or consciousness, but is 'decentred', dominated by a law which he or she does not create but which creates him or her. Lacan undermines those ideas of the 'self' as a coherent whole which are implicit in our language and ideologies.

But as well as suggesting an entrée for marxist theories of ideology, Lacan's interpretation of psychoanalysis is a major link with the anti-psychiatry movement which, in France as in Britain (where it has been represented by the writings of R. D. Laing and David Cooper), has stressed the continuity between madness and reason, so that the decentred self is not qualitatively distant from the fragmentation of the schizophrenic experience. This is a theme developed and transformed by Deleuze and Guattari. It is relevant here because an important part of the radicalism of the late 1960s laid stress precisely on the marginal, the mad, the criminal, as rejectors of bourgeois society, as standing outside the dominant forms of authority and order, the Lacanian 'symbolic order'.

But a third element needs stressing, for Lacan's recovery of Freud has also been suggested as a basis for understanding patriarchy and the structures of male dominance. It is a key to grasping the ways in which the animal child enters the social world as a boy or a girl, the unconscious ways in which psychological 'masculinity' and 'femininity', and male dominance, are accepted as necessary parts of becoming social beings. Such an understanding is essential for a feminist politics. A sketch of Lacan's theory will clarify this process, and also partly explain some of the terms used by Hocquenghem.

The human infant is seen as being concerned at first with the exploration of sensory perceptions, and its main characteristic is its autoerotism. It has no sense of its physical separateness, or of its physical unity. This is the moment which retrospectively is referred to as the phantasy of the 'body in pieces'. The *mirror stage* is the moment when the infant realizes, the distinction between its own body and the outside, the 'other'. It is expressed metaphorically in terms of the child seeing itself in the mirror and identifying with its reflection. But the image is ever external to the child, so that this mirror stage announces the permanent alienation at the heart of identification. The process of identification inaugurates the *imaginary* relation, where the individual misrecognizes himself or herself as the perfect image which appears in the mirror and with which the individual identifies, as being everything he or she imagines himself or herself to be. As interpreted by Althusser this becomes a key term in the understanding of ideology, as an 'imaginary' (but not 'false') misrecognition of the world.

Following the mirror stage, the first form of identification with an object outside the infant is with the mother, a relationship which determines the attitude of the child to the zones of its own body, according to the significance given to them within the relationship. The fact that the genital aspect of the infant's relationship to the mother cannot be developed brings this pre-Oedipal phase to an end. The Oedipus complex is the stage when the intervention of the Father necessitates the child's abandonment of its exclusive relationship with the mother and its entry into the structures of human sexuality. The child is assigned a position in language and the family, in structures of 'masculinity' or 'femininity'. The repression of those elements of the psychic life of the child which do not conform to this positioning constitutes the unconscious.

It is in the unconscious that the child carries the very structures of a patriarchal society. The child's attempt to include genital functions amongst those expressive of the identification of mother and child are unsuccessful because the child has a rival in the Father, against whom it is powerless. This is not necessarily a real male parent but rather the symbolic representation of all Fathers: the Father is the authority which dominates the mother–child relation. Confronted with this authority the child now sees the mother, formerly the repository of all identity, as a testimony only to the authority of the Father. The opening of this fundamental 'absence' in identity inspires the fear of castration, in both boy and girl, though the specific forms vary. This is what forces the resolution of the Oedipal crisis, when the child enters the social world, which Lacan calls the Symbolic, the order of language; the child identifies with certain terms – boy, girl, son, daughter – which receive their significance as ideas through their relation to a central 'signifier' (in Lacan's usage a cluster of words, images, ideas), the *phallus*, the symbolic expression and representative of the authority of the Father. This is intimately connected with the notion of *desire*; indeed, as Juliet Mitchell has put it, the phallus is the very mark of human desire. It is the expression of a fundamental absence which can never be fulfilled, the desire to be the other, the Father, which is both alienated and insatiable: alienated because the child can only express its desire by means of language which itself constitutes its submission to the Father; and insatiable because it is desire for a symbolic position which is itself arbiter of the possibilities for the expression of desire. The phallus and desire are thus key elements, and represent and express the individual's submission to the laws of society. Just as 'desire' cannot be equated with organic or biological need, so the 'phallus' is not coterminous with the physical penis: it is the representation, the signifier of the laws of the social order, the law of the Father, through which obedience to the social (and patriarchal) order is instilled.

What Lacan is attempting to theorize is not a biological development but a social process, and what he is describing are not so much actual events (for example, the threat of castration) as symbolic acts. Thus, as Juliet Mitchell has said, 'In "penis envy" we are not talking about an anatomical organ, but about the ideas of it that people hold and live by within the general culture',[7] and this can be applied to other phases. Hence the analogies, in Lacan as in Freud, with drama, the theatre. As Althusser has put it, 'The Oedipus complex is the dramatic structure, the "theatrical machine" imposed by the Law of Culture on every, involuntary, conscripted candidate to humanity.'[8] What Lacan is describing is the human drama whereby each animal child becomes part of the social world, expressing its structures as a social being.

Against Oedipus

The major problem is that Lacan, like Freud, appears to make these stages, and the Oedipus complex, a transhistorical human experience, though for Lacan it is essentially a cultural not a biological experience. Even Juliet Mitchell, who believes the Law of the Father can be eventually overcome, believes it to be a necessary element in patriarchal societies.

For Deleuze and Guattari, as for Lacan, the forms of desire are not set in nature but are socially created. But they reject psychoanalysis, and in doing so construct a challenge to Oedipus as a *necessary* stage in human development. They attack Lacan for staying *within* the Freudian family framework: as a result, psychoanalysis is trapped within capitalist economic and social demands. Their challenge is expressed in their book *L'Anti-Oedipe: Capitalisme et Schizophrénie*, which was first published in French in 1972. Gilles Deleuze was a philosopher and writer on literature while Félix Guattari was trained as a Lacanian psychoanalyst and has been a marxist activist. Their book, which claimed to re-energize the debate on the relationship between Freud and Marx, created a considerable stir on publication in France and led them to be compared with Laing and Cooper as enemies of psychiatric orthodoxies. Like Lacan, whose writing is complex and unconventional (Freud's readability is often criticized for leading to oversimplification), Deleuze and Guattari attempt to challenge conventional language as well as conventional theory, with the result that in *L'Anti-Oedipe* we are presented with a picture of a world whose complexity and flux defy language. This expresses their basic objection to Freudian theories: any concept of Oedipus implies artificial restrictions on a field, the unconscious, where everything is in fact infinitely open. Deleuze and Guattari see human beings as constituted by 'desiring machines'. Infinite types and varieties of relationship are possible; each person's machine parts can plug into and unplug from machine parts of another. There is, in other words, no given 'self', only the cacophony of desiring machines. Fragmentation is universal, and is not the peculiar fate of what society defines as the schizophrenic. But the crucial point is that capitalist society cannot live with the infinite variety of potential interconnections and relationships, and imposes constraints regulating which ones are to be allowed, that is, essentially those relating to reproduction in the family. Psychoanalysis, by accepting the familial framework, is trapped *within* capitalist concepts of sexuality, concepts which distort the production of desire. Psychoanalytic theory, by concentrating on the Oedipal triangulation of parents and child, reflects the social, political and religious forms of domination in modern society, and is complicit with how capitalism has constructed the family. Deleuze and Guattari argue that the individual's consciousness is determined not by a closed family system, but by a historical situation. So they can analyse and criticize the family, for example, in terms of the desires expressed during May 1968. Desire then becomes an element in the social field, an active participant in social life, not just an element in the individual's psyche. The Oedipus complex, instead of being, as in Lacan, a necessary stage in the development of the human individual, is seen by Deleuze and Guattari as the only effective means of controlling the libido in *capitalist* society. So Freudianism plays a key role under capitalism: it is both the discoverer of the mechanisms of desire, and the organizer, through its acceptance of the Oedipus complex, of its control. For at a time when capitalist individualization is undermining the family by depriving it of essential social functions, the Oedipus complex represents the internalization of the family institutions; it is a policeman of the mind.

Deleuze and Guattari develop their analysis of the relationship between the Oedipalized family and the needs of capitalist society through their theory of entropy (increasing disorder), using concepts borrowed from French anthropological debate. Desiring machines can be coded or decoded: coding puts information about the society and its social language into place, decoding decreases social information. Decoding represents an increase in entropy and it results in society losing control of the machine's interconnections, or 'flux'. Schizophrenia represents the boundary of decoding. Deleuze and Guattari suggest that as society becomes more 'civilized' (capitalist), the level of code in the desiring machines decreases; society struggles against the progressive loss of shared meaning as it would be destroyed by total decoding (schizophrenia). The family is therefore constructed as an artificially 'reterritorialized' unit where social control has been relocated and in which forms of social organization can be reproduced. The father becomes a familial despot, and the mother, for example, an image for earth and country. Thus the privatized 'individual' that psychoanalysis studies within the Oedipal family unit is an artificial construct, whose social function is to trap and control the disorder that haunts social life under capitalism.

Thus psychoanalysis can neither understand desire nor suggest an alternative. As their alternative, Deleuze and Guattari suggest what they term 'schizoanalysis', a process of decoding whose aim is to uncover the unconscious activities of desire in the social field, and the role of the family in responding to the social need to avoid disorder. Where psychoanalysis understands social events in terms of the family, schizoanalysis approaches the family in terms of social needs. And the goal is an emergent understanding of desire. In modern society we can become 'neurotic', that is, accept our Oedipalization (and use psychoanalysis); or we can reject it, by becoming what society describes as 'schizophrenic'; or we can adopt a third alternative, and 'schizophrenize' – that is, we can reject the false coherence of the 'molar' self, and this will lead us to an experience of the self at the 'molecular' level of our desiring machines. We can set out to discover the desiring machine, a process which Deleuze and Guattari, echoing Laing, call a 'voyage' of discovery, and in doing so the 'truth of the subject' will become clearer.

Such a precept has clear political implications, which feed into Hocquenghem's work. For the aim is to find unalienated forms of radical social action, and these cannot be traditional centralized structures (especially of the working class), because these, too, are complicit with capitalism. The model of alternative modes was provided by the spontaneous forms of activity developed in France in 1968, 'fusions of desire' which escape the imprisoning force of the 'normal'. Schizoanalysis provides the alternative: the schizophrenic is not revolutionary, but the schizophrenic process is the potential of revolution, and only in the activity of autonomous, spontaneous groupings, outside the social order, can revolution be achieved. The result, which is central to Hocquenghem's project, is a worship of the excluded and marginal as the real material of social transformation.

The most fierce polemics against these concepts have come from other French marxists. Thus Henri Lefebvre has written:

> It takes a good deal of philosophical arrogance to state, as Deleuze and Guattari do in *L'Anti-Oedipe*, that capitalism only prolongs itself by generating a flux of inanities....It is simply the hypothesis of Bergsonian philosophy revised and corrected by psychoanalysis. By separating time from space, it turns the schizoid into an explanatory principle. It is the belated theorisation of a version of 'leftism' that has run aground on the politicisation of this or that real but peripheral issue (prison, drugs, insanity, etc.) and has then sunk back into a negation of the political. Unfortunately, this also means that they have handed the situation back to the 'pure' politicians.[9]

There is much force in this diatribe, especially in pinpointing the failure to confront the ultimate question of power in society. For instance, can one regard all the 'marginals' as being of equal specific weight? But before discussing some of the problems we must look at the influence of these ideas on Hocquenghem.

The sublimated anus

Hocquenghem employs the theoretical concepts discussed above, first to locate hostile attitudes to homosexuality within a theory of family and reproductive sexuality, and secondly to provide the outline of a politics which can challenge and overthrow these attitudes. His project is explicitly a revolutionary one and in delineating it Hocquenghem skilfully synthesizes a wide range of debates.

Of particular relevance to an understanding of homosexuality is his recognition of the social and culturally specific function of the definition of 'the homosexual'. Very few cultures, in fact, have had a developed concept of the 'homosexual' as a specific type of person different from the 'normal' or 'heterosexual' person, and in the west it was essentially a creation of the nineteenth century. Moreover, in terms of self-identification on the part of those so defined, it is still an emergent and not an achieved identity. We may note here the influence of the work of the historian, Michel Foucault. Hocquenghem makes explicit references to Foucault's essay on *Madness and Civilization*, which traces the growth in the eighteenth century of the social concept of madness as a specific individual quality. Hocquenghem makes the point that what he calls the 'growing imperialism' of society seeks to attribute a social status and definition to everything, even the unclassifiable, and the result has been that homosexuality, traditionally conceived of as a possibility in all sinful creatures (otherwise, why the often severe religious sanctions?), has from the nineteenth century been seen as a specific characteristic (often a 'disease') of a particular ('sick' or 'degenerate') type of individual. Foucault's introductory essay on *The History of Sexuality, La volonté de savoir*, makes this point explicitly (see chapter 5, below).[10] It seems to me an essential starting point for any discussion of homosexuality to recognize this fundamental point, for otherwise we lose ourselves (as most essays into 'homosexual history' do) in a welter of arguments over whether a particular individual was homosexual or not. The core of the problem is (1) what is the effect on individual lives of social definitions of 'the homosexual' (or by analogy the 'mad', 'schizophrenic', etc.), and (2) what are the conditions for the emergence of such definitions and individual meanings.

Hocquenghem confronts these questions by challenging the notion of 'homosexual desire', which he sees as itself misleading. 'Desire', properly speaking, is neither homosexual nor heterosexual. Desire, as Deleuze and Guattari state, is 'emergent', and its components are only discernible *a posteriori*. Homosexual desire, like heterosexual desire, is an arbitrary division of the flux of desire, an 'arbitrarily frozen frame' in an unbroken and polyvocal flux. The notion of exclusive homosexuality is therefore a 'fallacy of the imaginary', a misrecognition and ideological misperception. But despite this, homosexuality has a vivid social presence and Hocquenghem asks – and answers – why. The answer is that homosexuality expresses an aspect of desire which is fundamentally polymorphous and undefined, which appears nowhere else, and that it is more than just sexual activity between members of the same sex. For the direct manifestation of homosexual desire opposes the relations of roles and identities necessarily imposed by the Oedipus complex in order to ensure the reproduction of society. So homosexuality is artificially trapped within the grid of 'civilization' and created as an abstract, separate and excoriated division of desire.

Capitalism, in its necessary employment of Oedipalization, manufactures 'homosexuals' just as it produces proletarians, and what is manufactured is a psychologically repressive category. Homosexuality is artificially cut off from desire, and placed in a separate category. Hocquenghem therefore suggests that the principal ideological means of thinking about homosexuality, which date back to the turn of the century, are intimately, though not mechanically, connected with the advance of western capitalism. They amount to a perverse reterritorialization, a massive effort to regain social control in a world tending towards disorder and decoding. Moreover, the establishment of homosexuality as a separate category goes hand in hand with its repression. The result on the one hand is the creation of a scapegoated minority of 'homosexuals', and on the other the transformation of the repressed homosexual elements of desire into the desire to repress: hence sublimated homosexuality is the basis of the paranoia about homosexuality which pervades social behaviour, and of the panic that the mere mention of the word creates.

It is here that the anti-psychiatry emphasis of Deleuze and Guattari becomes relevant, for Hocquenghem sees that psychiatry has played a vital part in the installation of guilt (expressed, as he notes, even in the works of homosexual writers such as Proust). So the psychiatrization of homosexuality has not superseded penal repression, it has accompanied it. For if repression is to be effective, the culprit must recognize it as necessary, so that modern repression demands an interplay between legal guilt and the psychology of guilt; this is achieved precisely by the Oedipal moment, the victory of the Law of the Father, which is vital for the fulfilment of institutional laws.

Though this is cogently argued, a number of doubts must arise, not so much about the descriptive elements (which empirical work on attitudes to homosexuality tend to validate) as about the theoretical argument. Three specific questions need to be confronted more fully. First, there is the whole question of homosexual 'paranoia'. There can be no doubt that many non-homosexuals display a hysterical hostility towards homosexuality; in recent Anglo-Saxon writings this has been defined as 'homophobia'.[11] But the idea that repression of homosexuals in modern society is a product of repressed homosexuality comes too close to the hydraulic theory of sexuality (the notion that there is a fixed amount of energy which sublimation redistributes) which the Lacanian recovery of Freud sought to undermine. It is not a sufficient explanatory principle simply to reverse the idea peddled by the medical profession that homosexuality is a paranoia into the idea that attitudes to homosexuality are merely paranoid. It does not, for instance, explain the real, if limited, liberalization of attitudes that has taken place in some western countries, or the range of attitudes that are empirically known to exist in different countries and even in different families. Hocquenghem suggests that the relaxation of legal penalties is in effect itself a new form of repression (in Marcusean terms this could be called 'repressive desublimation'), but this does not itself provide a basis for grasping the *shift* in the location of social taboos (for example, in Britain in the 1970s from adult male homosexuality to paedophilia).

Second, there is the problem of why some individuals become 'homosexual' and others (the majority?) do not. Hocquenghem's theories usefully suggest the artificial (and social) nature of the division between 'homosexual' and 'heterosexual', but do not fully explain the processes involved, except in terms of the general Oedipal processes. How, for instance, does the individual enter the symbolic order as a 'homosexual' rather than a 'heterosexual'? What are the specific family pressures, the educational processes, the media images that reinforce the identity? The key reference point is 'reproduction', both of the species and of the Oedipal relationships, as Hocquenghem indicates, but this poses important historical and theoretical problems that demand further exploration.

A third difficulty is closely related to this: Hocquenghem's failure to explore the different modalities of lesbianism. It is important to note that what Hocquenghem is discussing is essentially male homosexuality, for in Hocquenghem's view, although the Law of the Father dominates both the male and the female, it is to the authority of the Father in reproduction (both of the species and of Oedipalization itself) that homosexuality poses the major challenge; as Deleuze and Guattari note, male homosexuality, far from being a product of the Oedipus complex, as some Freudians imply, itself constitutes a totally different mode of social relationships, no longer vertical, but horizontal. Lesbianism, by implication, assumes its significance as a challenge to the secondary position accorded to female sexuality in capitalist society. It is not so much lesbianism as female sexuality which society denies. But Hocquenghem quite fails to pursue this point, which is central if we are to grasp the formation of sexual meanings. It is a criticism which has been cogently levelled at the Lacanian school of psychoanalysis that at the same time as helping us to understand the 'phallocentric' view of sexuality, it actually surrenders to it. In a patriarchal society, female sexuality is defined in relationship to the male. The paradox remains theoretically unexplained (and not only in this work) as to why lesbianism, which ultimately asserts the automony of female sexuality, has historically been ignored, by the absence of legal oppression and even in the work of early liberal sexologists such as Havelock Ellis. Lesbianism has a different history from male homosexuality, and poses specific problems (for example, why did a specific lesbian identity emerge later than a male homosexual identity?), but Hocquenghem's work lacks completeness in failing even to pose the question.

This failure relates to the core of Hocquenghem's theory, which is summed up in the subsection entitled 'The Phallic Signifier and the Sublimated Anus'. Hocquenghem argues that only one organ is allowed in the Oedipal triangle, that which Deleuze and Guattari call the 'despotic signifier', the phallus. And as money is the fetish, the true universal reference point for capitalism, so the phallus is the reference point for heterosexism. Ours is a phallic (or 'phallocratic') society. The phallus determines – whether by absence or presence – the girl's penis envy, the boy's castration anxiety; it draws on libidinal energy in the same way as money draws on labour. And our society is phallic to such a degree that the sexual act without ejaculation is seen as a failure. The result is a denial of all other forms of sexuality, and in particular, the anal. And here is the key to the argument. For while the phallus is essentially social, the anus is essentially private; and for the organization of society around the great phallic signifier to be possible, the anus must be privatized. Hocquenghem quotes Deleuze and Guattari, to the effect that the anus was the first organ to be privatized, and Freud, who sees the anal stage as the stage of the formation of the self. The result is that the 'anus is over-invested individually because its investment is withdrawn socially'.

Homosexuality, Hocquenghem argues, chiefly means anal homosexuality, sodomy. It is always connected with the anus, even though, as all the empirical evidence (such as Kinsey's) suggests, anal intercourse is still the exception even among homosexuals. In our patriarchal society, only the phallus is a dispenser of identity, and any social use of the anus other than a sublimated one creates the risk of a loss of identity, whether the individual is a man or a woman. Hocquenghem quotes Freud's remark that 'the anal becomes the symbol of all that must be dismissed from [the individual's] life'. The conclusion is that homosexual desire is the operation of a desiring machine 'plugged into the anus'.

Clearly, what Hocquenghem is suggesting cannot have a literal meaning (as he says, the empirical evidence does not bear this out); the intention is to suggest the symbolic consequence of the dominance of the phallus. He uses it to argue that since the anus has been privatized by capitalist/phallic domination, we need to 'group' it, which means, in effect, to reject the individualized notion of homosexuality as a problem. Practising homosexuals are those who have failed their sublimation, who therefore can and must conceive their relationships in different ways. So when homosexuals as a group publicly reject their labels, they are in fact rejecting Oedipus, rejecting the artificial entrapment of desire, rejecting sexuality focused on the phallus. And they are rejecting the Symbolic Order. But the major problem here is that the emphasis on the anal has clearly a metaphorical rather than a properly scientific meaning. The historical facts seem to be that the emphasis on sodomy decreased as the conceptualization of 'the homosexual' increased. In Britain, for instance, sodomy carried the death penalty until 1861, but it was *after* the reduction of this penalty (to between ten years and life) that the real process of social definition, and an increase in social hostility, began.

There is an obvious danger in challenging theoretical concepts with historical data, and Hocquenghem is correct to stress the peculiar horror of sodomy that still survives. But without a fuller explanation it is all too easy to believe that the core of Hocquenghem's theory is a flawed attempt to fit his explanatory theses into given Freudian categories. His theory does, however, have the useful function of challenging the centrality of reproductive sexuality: the anal may be seen as a metaphor for this, and it leads to some suggestive insights. He argues that when the anus recovers its desiring function (i.e. when the phallus loses its centrality), when laws and rules disappear, group pleasures will appear without the 'sacred difference' between public and private, social and individual. And Hocquenghem sees signs of this 'sexual communism' in institutions of the gay subculture, where 'scattering' or promiscuity, representing polymorphous sexuality in action, reigns. This point is rarely made and is valuable, challenging as it does the usual condemnation of promiscuity. It can, of course, be overstated. The problem remains for gay people of working out lifestyles and forms of relationship which break away from heterosexist norms; these cannot necessarily be derived from styles that have developed as a reaction to social oppression. For Hocquenghem, however, there is an important political point to be made. He suggests that the 'cruise' (the search for sexual partners) of the homosexual male is reminiscent of what *L'Anti-Oedipe* describes as the 'voyage' of the schizophrenic. Hocquenghem suggests that a promiscuity freed from guilt is the very mode of desire itself. Homosexuals, therefore, breaking free of their guilt, are like the schizophrenics in Deleuze and Guattari's work, the models of revolutionary potential.

Hocquenghem, then, rejects both the traditional homophile movements, with their timidity and acceptance of the artificial divisions of desire, and the traditional leftist organizations. He seeks to show how the struggles of homosexuals have challenged the accepted relationship between desire and politics. Hocquenghem suggests, like Deleuze and Guattari, that there is no real revolutionary centre; the 'centre' lies on the fringes, the marginal. He suggests that we should question the whole basis of 'civilization', understood as the Oedipal succession of generations, and that we should fight, with Fourier (and also, though Hocquenghem does not mention him, with the early English socialist Edward Carpenter), against 'civilization', 'the interpretative grid through which desire becomes cohesive energy', which bolsters the capitalist order. So, like Deleuze and Guattari, Hocquenghem looks to the spontaneous and non-organized workers' movements, ecological movements, community politics and the 'politics of experience', and the gay movement, as the material for radical transformation. Autonomous movements which refuse the law of the signifier, and are brought into being by particular desiring situations, reject traditional political logic and completely upset the political world.

Hocquenghem is here expressing simultaneously the euphoric optimism of post-1968 radicalism and the despair of the traditional politics of the working class, which in the 1960s could be read into the work of Herbert Marcuse and others. Hocquenghem's political outlook rightly stresses the vitality and significance of the new, autonomous movements; more than 'protest' movements, they are attempts at real self-determination. Of course, they are not all of equal social significance, but their very appearance, and their impact on a generation of young radicals, was a significant index of the appalling absences in traditional left attitudes. In rejecting the myth of the 'normal' as natural and given, however, and in emphasizing the need for conscious struggle against it, Hocquenghem, like Deleuze and Guattari, is in danger of creating a new myth: the revolutionary potential of the marginal, a myth which ignores the real problems of power, physical and ideological, in modern societies. Hocquenghem poses here a challenge to traditional concepts of social transformation, without finally responding to it.

The personal and the political

The concerns of French radical debate had their parallels in Britain and North America – in the former largely because of the failures of social democracy, in America largely under the impact of the Vietnam War and the crisis of American imperialism. In fact, the major autonomous movements that Hocquenghem cites – the women's, black and gay movements – all appeared in North America first. But though the concerns have been similar, the intellectual traditions through which they have been expressed have discrete origins.

We have already noted the common anti-psychiatry trends in the work of Deleuze and Guattari on the one hand, and Laing and Cooper on the other, and their specific concern with schizophrenia. Juliet Mitchell has usefully summed up the relevance of this in Britain:

> Laing's early analyses of schizophrenia as a disturbance induced by immediate interaction within the family helped to introduce a new phase of radical humanism to which the women's movement is heir. Both within Laing's own thought and within the theses of those it reflected and inspired, the plight of the scapegoated driven-mad was generalisable. Western society dehumanised persons, categorising them into oppositional stereotypes of mad/sane, black/white and so on. The radical counter-ideology of the restoration of 'whole' (i.e. 'individual') people was thus introduced.[12]

Thus while French anti-psychiatry had clear antecedents in psychoanalysis, the British rejected this tradition from the start and derived many of their concepts from existentialist thought, and had a more clearly individualized outlook. The result was the predominant 'personalism' of the British radicalism of the late 1960s and early 1970s, leading to a pervasive form of radical individualism. This became vitally important in the emergence of the 'new politics' in Britain and America, and led to efforts to sustain a 'radical psychology', as well as influencing the sexual liberation movements. It is worth noting that the first functional group set up in the London Gay Liberation Front was a counter-psychiatry group.

This radical individualism was also clearly reflected in tendencies in sociology in Britain which provided the theoretical basis for the activities of the 'new politics'. An important element of this was summed up in the so-called 'radical deviancy' school of sociology, the chief expression of which was the National Deviancy Conference, set up in 1968 by a number of criminologists who rejected the traditional institutional and Home Office approach to crime.[13] The chief feature of this was the realization that deviance and crime are not inherent qualities of 'actors' but are social definitions that become attached to individuals in a process of social interaction with other people. This had important theoretical implications, which were expressed in Mary McIntosh's 'The Homosexual Role' (see chapter 2, above), exploring how concepts of a specific homosexual 'condition' and a defensive subculture emerged in the eighteenth and nineteenth centuries in England.[14] We should remark here that notions of the social nature of definitions of homosexuality (or any other social 'deviancy') were emerging at roughly the same period in both France and Britain, but through different theoretical routes. In Britain, too, there was a noticeable tendency to glorify the role of the outsider, in radical politics. The theoretical framework here, however, was clearly not marxist at this stage, and there was no engagement as yet with psychoanalysis.

The dominant theoretical framework in Britain derived from 'symbolic interactionism', ultimately an outgrowth of structural functionalism and the sociology of knowledge. Here ideas are not treated in terms of their historical roots or practical effectiveness, but are seen as forming the background to every social process. Social processes are treated essentially in terms of ideas, and it is through ideas that we construct social reality itself. Most of the most valuable work that has informed the theoretical study of homosexuality in Britain has derived from symbolic interactionism (e.g. Kenneth Plummer's *Sexual Stigma*, which was the first major British study of how homosexual meanings are acquired).[15] In this theory sexual meanings are constructed in social interaction: a homosexual identity is not inherent, but is socially created. This has had a vitally important clarifying influence, and has, for instance, broken with lay ideas of sex as a goal-directed instinct. But symbolic interactionism has been unable to theorize the sexual variations that it can so ably describe; nor can it conceptualize the relations between possible sexual patterns and other social variables. It is unable to theorize (and it is here that Hocquenghem's ideas are relevant) why, despite the endless possibilities of sexualization it suggests, the genitals continue to be the focus of sexual imagination, or why there are, at various times, shifts in the location of the sexual taboos. And there is a political consequence too, for if meanings are entirely ascribed in social interaction, an act of collective will can transform them: this leads, as Mary McIntosh has suggested, to a politics of 'collective voluntarism'. Both in theory and in practice it ignores the historical location of sexual taboos. Symbolic interactionism, in other words, stops short at precisely the point where the French debate begins – at the point of social determination and ideological structuring in the creation of subjectivity.

It is precisely for this reason that a number of British feminists began in the early 1970s to explore the work of Lacan and others, with a view to developing a theoretical understanding of patriarchy. The focal point was Juliet Mitchell's *Psychoanalysis and Feminism*, which, as a sympathetic critic stated:

> Opens the way to a re-evaluation of psychoanalysis as a theory which can provide scientific knowledge of the way in which patriarchal ideology is maintained through the foundation of psychological 'masculinity' and 'femininity'. Such knowledge is obviously a precondition of any successful cultural and political struggle against patriarchy – the point being not merely to understand the unconscious but to change it.[16]

This approach points to the need for specific ideological practices in combating patriarchy, although the ways in which this might be done are so far scarcely in outline. It presents, too, the necessity for the struggle of autonomous groupings as an aspect of the struggle against capitalism and for socialism. But there is a twofold problem. First, what form should these specific struggles take? And secondly, what is the relationship between these autonomous groupings and the wider struggle, especially that of the working class, for socialism? It is a pertinent criticism of Mitchell that she completely separates the various struggles in such a way as to reproduce the economism for which marxists are usually criticized by feminists. She seems to see the working class (guided by marxism) as fighting for socialism at the economic and political level, while the women's movement (guided by psychoanalysis) is fighting against patriarchy at the ideological level. In other words, instead of applying historical materialism to the understanding of subjectivity, she effectively sees two separate sciences for two separate objects of study.

Mitchell's book was, however, of great significance in stimulating discussions in the women's movement and the gay movement. And partly as a consequence of its appearance, there was a new interest in the French theoretical debates. In 1977 Lacan's *Ecrits* appeared for the first time in an English translation, while a number of journals explicitly confronted the relevance of the theoretical debates (for example, *Ideology and Consciousness*, which began to appear in London in 1977). The evolution of one Australian journal sums up the theoretical trajectory: founded as the *Gay Liberation Press* in 1972 in Sydney, it later became *GLP: A Journal of Sexual Politics*, and finally in 1976 emerged as *Working Papers in Sex, Science and Culture*, with the aim of critically examining 'the function of language, ideology and scientificity in the construction of sex theories ranging from conventional sciences to liberation movements'. The first two issues made the journal's concerns explicit by particularly examining the work of Lacan, Althusser and Juliet Mitchell.

It is in this developing context that Hocquenghem's book became relevant. His essay was born of a specific conjuncture of theoretical and political concerns, and cannot, of course, attempt to confront all the outstanding issues. But the questions he raises, both implicity and explicitly, have not gone away: the relationship of sexual identity to patriarchal structures; the fit between patriarchy and capitalism; the forms of struggle necessary to combat sexual oppression. A critical reading of Hocquenghem's essay can still help in the continuing debate on these issues.

Note

Hocquenghem continued to be a lively and controversial writer on sexual themes until his premature death from AIDS-related illnesses in 1988. In the early 1990s he was taken up by a new generation of 'queer theorists' as a pioneer of their analysis, which only underlines the truism that ideas do not die but go underground, to re-emerge in slightly rewritten form in new circumstances. The wheel does not need to be reinvented; its spokes keep intruding out of the ground. See the 'New Introduction' by Michael Moon in the edition of *Homosexual Desire* published in 1993 (Durham NC and London: Duke University Press, 1993); and the discussion in Jonathan Dollimore, *Sexual Dissidence: Augustine to Wilde, Freud to Foucault* (Oxford: Oxford University Press, 1991). A very useful overview of Hocquenghem's work can be found in Bill Marshall, *Guy Hocquenghem: Theorising the Gay Nation* (London: Pluto Press, 1996).

References

1   See Jeffrey Weeks, *Coming Out! Homosexual Politics in Britain from the Nineteenth Century to the Present*, London, Quartet, 1977, chs 1–3.
2   Gilles Deleuze and Félix Guattari, *L'Anti-Oedipe: Capitalisme et Schizophrénie*, Paris, Les Editions de Minuit, 1972.
3   'Freud and Lacan', in Louis Althusser, *Lenin and Philosophy*, London, New Left Books, 1971, p. 182.

4 Juliet Mitchell, *Psychoanalysis and Feminism*, London, Allen Lane, 1974, p. xvi.
5 For an interpretation of Freud heavily influenced by Lacan, see Octave Mannoni, *Freud: The Theory of the Unconscious*, London, New Left Books, 1971.
6 See Althusser, *Lenin and Philosophy*; 'On Ideology', in *Working Papers on Cultural Studies*, Birmingham (1977 edition); *Ideology and Consciousness* No. 1, May 1977; *Papers on Patriarchy*, Women's Publishing Collective, Lewes, 1977.
7 Mitchell, *Psychoanalysis and Feminism*, p. xvi.
8 Althusser, *Lenin and Philosophy*, p. 198.
9 Henri Lefebvre, *The Survival of Capitalism*, London, Allison and Busby, 1976, p. 34.
10 Michel Foucault, *Histoire de la sexualité* vol. 1: *La volonté de savoir*, Paris, Gallimard, 1976. An introduction to the ideas contained in this work can be found in Colin Gordon, 'Birth of the Subject', *Radical Philosophy* No. 17, Summer 1977.
11 For a discussion of this concept see George Weinberg, *Society and the Healthy Homosexual*, New York, St Martin's Press 1972. For a critique see Ken Plummer, 'The Homosexual Taboo', *Gay News* No. 106, London, 1976.
12 Mitchell, *Psychoanalysis and Feminism*, p. xviii.
13 For a discussion of this see Mary McIntosh, 'Modern Trends in Sociology', in *Marxism Today*, September 1977.
14 Mary McIntosh, 'The Homosexual Role', *Social Problems* Vol. 16, No. 2, Autumn 1968.
15 Kenneth Plummer, *Sexual Stigma: An Interactionist Account*, London, Routledge and Kegan Paul, 1975.
16 Randall Albury, 'Two Readings of Freud', *Working Papers in Sex, Science and Culture* Vol. 1, No. 1, January 1976, p. 7.

5

Foucault for Historians

Intellectual formation

Foucault was until his death in 1984 professor of the history of systems of thought at the Collège de France in Paris.[1] The point is not the prestige of the title, but the careful delimitation of his areas of interest; not history of thought or of ideas but of 'systems of thought'. The central concern of Foucault was with the rules that govern the emergence and reproduction of such systems, structures of the mind which categorize social life and then present the result to us as truth. There is a rich diversity in his publications: from his early studies of psychology and madness, through the birth of modern medicine and the 'human sciences', to the analysis of modern disciplinary forms and *The History of Sexuality*. Beneath this diversity there were two controlling concerns: exposing the conditions for the emergence of modern forms of rationality, especially the 'human sciences'; and comprehending the complex mutual involvements of power and knowledge. The explicit organization of his investigations around the notion of power was apparent only from the late 1960s, in the wake, as he makes clear, of the dramatic events in France in 1968. It was the academy, supposedly neutral home of knowledge, which provided the spark for the General Strike, and it was in the academy that the effects of 1968 were most visible. There was therefore a new inflection of his work after that, but concern with knowledge and power can be seen as an implicit preoccupation of all his researches from the beginning. It is this double interest – in forms of rationality, and with the analysis of power – which gives his work its distinctive tone.

Given his challenge to the notion of an autonomous, individual 'authorship'[2] he would have been the last person to deny that his thought was formed within the space of contemporary preoccupations. The intellectual trends from which his work emerged have been manifold. Following his philosophy teacher at the Sorbonne, Jean Hyppolite, he grappled with the totalizing philosophical claims of the heritage of Hegel, and in the end rejected them entirely in favour of a deep scepticism about the claims of philosophy, inherited from Nietzsche.[3] At the same time he rejected Sartrean phenomenology and in particular the concentration on individual consciousness and on the constitutive, creative individual. On the other hand, Foucault cannot be easily assimilated into the forms of structuralism which replaced existentialism as the major intellectual vogue in France in the 1960s. He had in common with the loose unity of structuralism a desire to displace individual consciousness, to investigate instead the 'positive unconscious' of knowledge, the hidden imperatives structured like a language, on which social forms are built.[4] But against the claims of structuralism to have produced a theoretical system which could 'scientifically' understand everything from kinship structures to the literary text, Foucault asked: how has this intellectual system become possible, and what have been its effects? These were also the questions he asked of psychoanalysis and marxism; systems which shaped Foucault intellectually but whose scientific pretensions he sought to puncture. A rejection of these claims to truth did not, however, lead Foucault to underestimate their significance. Much of his work, from the early *Madness and Civilisation* to the *Introduction* to *The History of Sexuality*, can be seen as a history (or to use his own term, an 'archaeology') of the emergence of psychoanalysis as a discipline.[5] But it is the conditions of this emergence (in, for example, the religious 'confessional mode', in the categorical separation of madness and reason, in the rise of sexological investigations), and the effects of the resulting psychoanalytic institution, *not* the truth or otherwise of the theory of the unconscious, which preoccupied Foucault.

His attitude to marxism was even more complex. Like many of his generation in the 1940s and early 1950s he was a Communist, but his break came with his recognition of the repercussions of the 'Lysenko affair', where the insights of biological science concerning inheritance were apparently to be subordinated to the party line laid down in Moscow.[6] Here Foucault had an early perception of the intricate involvements of knowledge and power. Here too he had a feeling that marxism was itself an authoritarian discourse which imposed meaning, while claiming to be the truth. Later, in the 1970s, Foucault proved reluctant to distinguish himself from the 'new philosophers' and the 'new right' in France, who saw marxism as inherently poisoned from the days of its 'master-thinkers', and who rejected all socialisms as potentially author-itarian.[7] Evidently Foucault rejected the Althusserian notion that Marx's work can be seen as a scientific breakthrough (or an 'epistemic break'). Simultaneously, however, he recognized the major innovative significance of Marx as the initiator of what he terms a 'discursive practice', a set of social, economic and political activities, governed by a series of rules of exclusion and delimitation, which have had real effects. Moreover, he was unwilling to reject marxism out of hand, either as a political philosophy, or as a tradition of historical exploration. Indeed:

> It is impossible at the present time to write history without using a whole range of concepts directly or indirectly linked to Marx's thought and situating one's self within a horizon of thought which has been defined and described by Marx. One might even wonder what difference there could ultimately be between being a historian and being a Marxist.[8]

It is the totalizing ambition of marxism that he rejected, not necessarily its local claims and commitments and insights. Not surprisingly, his positive points of reference were those writers who have risen up against the norms and certainties of western rationalism, writers such as the erotic, surrealist novelist Georges Bataille, and the poet and philosopher Friedrich Nietzsche. In his appreciation of Bataille we can already see his fascination with the theme of sexuality as transgression, a theme whose emergence he was to begin to trace later in *The History of Sexuality*. He was already aware of the disruptive and decisive power *assigned* to sexuality 'to the degree it is spoken', a significance that derives from the void formed by 'the death of God'. Sexuality, he suggests, is the modern deity.[9] But Nietzsche, as the reference to the 'death of God' suggests, is an even more significant point of departure for he was, as Foucault once put it, the creator of the space of contemporary thought. What Nietzsche and Foucault have in common is a desire to investigate the 'various systems of subjugation', the 'hazardous play of dominations' which are masked by the high-flown generalization of philosophy.[10] For Foucault, as for Nietzsche, the will to power dominates a chaotic and pluralistic world and knowledge is its handmaiden. As Nietzsche put it: 'In so far as the word "knowledge" has any meaning at all, the world is knowable: but it can be *interpreted* differently; behind it lies no meaning but rather countless meanings – "Perspectivism"'.[11] The implication is that there is no single truth to 'reality' but endless perspectives on the truth, each theory constructing its own reality and truths, under the workings of power. Foucault adoped this 'perspectivism' and with it a radical scepticism about the ultimate claims of knowledge.

This preoccupation with the illusory nature of the claims of knowledge partly explains Foucault's interest in a different set of intellectual concerns, represented by the philosophers and historians of science, and especially his teachers, Gaston Bachelard and George Canguilhem. What concerned him here was the status of science and of scientific categories. Foucault noted the correspondence between the concerns of Bechelard and Canguilhem and the Frankfurt School of marxists of the inter-war years:

> In the history of the sciences in France, as in German critical theory, it is a matter at bottom of examining a reason, the autonomy of whose structures carries with it a history of dogmatism and despotism – a reason, consequently, which can only have an effect of emancipation on condition that it manages to liberate itself from itself.[12]

It is this attempt to liberate science from itself that drew Foucault to the work of Bachelard and Canguilhem. Foucault learned from his mentors that the history of sciences is the history of the way in which specific scientific discourses construct their own ways of delimiting truth from falsity. This does not mean that there is no progress in science, or in the discovery of the empirical world; what is at stake though is the belief that science necessarily is based on the progressive uncovering of what is true. That is *not* the guiding light of scientific method, whatever its claims. Knowledge is constituted by ruptures in previous ways of thinking, and on this the influence of Bachelard has been particularly significant. Foucault was concerned, in other words, with discontinuities in thought, and with the impact these ruptures have had on the delimitation of truth. Not surprisingly he has been called a historian of discontinuity, a description which, however, he denied: 'No one is more of a continuist than I am: to recognise a discontinuity is never anything more than to register a problem that needs to be solved.'[13] But it is precisely that problem which guided his work and gives it its historical interest.

Foucault as archaeologist

It should be obvious from what has been said so far that Foucault's history is of a curious sort. He rejects the claims to a 'scientific history' offered by both marxism and Rankean positivism: both make claims to truth which are as dubious as those of other forms of knowledge. But there is, none the less, a vitally important point of reference for Foucault in a great tradition of historiography, the French *Annales* school.

At the beginning of *The Archaeology of Knowledge* he evokes the work of *Annales*, and particularly that of Fernand Braudel. This is an approach to history which has stressed the study of change in material civilization over periods as long as a millennium, as well as the layered and overlapping time scales of historical transformation. The *Annales* influence is evident in Foucault's advocacy of what he calls a 'general history' as opposed to a 'total history'.[14] Total history, he observes, attempts to draw all phenomena round a single causative centre or spirit of a society or civilization. The same form of historical influence is then seen to be operating on all levels, the economic, the social, the political, the religious, with the same types of transformation and influence playing on all these levels. General history, on the other hand, is concerned with 'series, segmentations, limits, differences of level, time lags, anachronistic survivals, possible types of relation'. The aim is not, however, to offer simply a jumble of different histories, or the investigation of analogies or coincidences between them. Nor is it a simple revival of crude positivism, of 'one damn thing after another'. The task proposed by general history is precisely to determine what forms of relation may legitimately be made between the various forms of social categorization, but to do this without recourse to any master schema, any ultimate theory of causation. So the task of historical investigation is not to fish for the 'real' history that glides silently under the surface, or rules behaviour behind people's backs, but to address itself to these surfaces, which *are* the 'real' in the way we live social relations through the grid of meaning and language. This points to the importance of questioning the 'document'. Past histories, Foucault argues, have been concerned to read documents for their hidden meanings, to transform the monuments of the past into documents. In our own time, by contrast, history is that which transforms documents into monuments. Hence history aspires 'to the intrinsic description of the monument', to be, in his terms, an 'archeology'.[15] What he is doing here is distinguishing himself from attempts to understand the emergence of ideas teleologically in terms of their origins in pre-existing ideas, or in terms of their material roots, as simple reflections of something more real behind them. In the first place, what Foucault seeks is 'an archaeology of knowledge', an understanding of the conditions for the emergence of particular forms of knowledge, for the grammar which allows those using the concepts to recognize what they are saying as being true or false. He is interested indeed in the rules of formation of an object of discourse. There are three types of rule: 'surfaces of emergence' (those social/cultural areas, such as the family, social or religious group, work situation, in which a discourse makes its appearance); 'authorities of delimitation' which govern what can be said, such as the medical profession, law, the churches; and 'grids of

specification', systems according to which different types of social categorization, such as madness, could be specified and related to each other.

If his first concern is with an archeology of knowledge, his second is
with the 'genealogy' of particular disciplines, their specific forms of
descent, emergence and transformation. There is no single cause that
can explain what subsequently occurs, but there are moments of 'eruption' in the complex and 'endlessly repeated' play of power. It is precisely
here that he is able to engage in the exploration of the connections
between power and knowledge, for it is through knowledge that power
is operative. And discourse is the point of juncture between knowledge
and power, the form through which power-knowledge operates.

Thirdly, Foucault is concerned not with the analysis of the past for its
own sake, but with the discovery of what he describes as the traces of the
present. History, for Foucault, is a 'curative science'. Archaeology is a
diagnosis of the present, and 'the purpose of history, guided by genealogy, is not to discover the roots of our identity but to commit ourselves
to its dissipation'.[16]

Foucault's work is concerned with the constitution through discourse
of those disciplines which since the eighteenth century have delimited the
boundaries of the economic, the sexual, the medical, the familial, the
disciplinary. He is not saying that more conventional histories are of no
use or are made redundant by his own methods. What he locates is a
specific area of concern which has not hitherto been investigated, a
history of the discursive realm.

But what is discourse? Put at its simplest it is a linguistic unity or group
of statements which constitutes and delimits a specific area of concern,
governed by its own rules of formation with its own modes of distinguishing truth from falsity.[17] Foucault is attempting to reconstruct the
regularities that underscore every discursive formation, the anonymous
historical rules that form its unique emergence. These are what he terms
'discursive practices'. These sets of regularities do not coincide necessarily with individual works even if they are manifested in individual
production. Instead they are more extensive than individual works and
serve to regroup a large number of them. They do not necessarily coincide either with a science or a discipline, but are an assembly of a number
of diverse disciplines or sciences.

Foucault's notion of discursive practices breaks away from the separation of the linguistic from the social. Discursive practices, he argues, are
embodied in technical processes, in institutions, and in patterns of general behaviour. The unity of a discourse, therefore, does not derive from
the fact that it describes a 'real object', but from the social practices that
actually form the object about which discourses speak. The 'social' is
constituted through these practices.

A critique of essentialism

Madness, the ostensible subject of Foucault's first major text, and sex, the apparent theme of his last, seem eminently natural objects to study. There are common-sensical definitions of their nature, and untold texts detailing their abundant manifestations. A history of these phenomena, therefore, it might be supposed, could only be a history of attitudes toward them. But it is Foucault's main task precisely to question the naturalness and inevitability of these historical objects. Their pre-existence as natural unchanging objects is not to be taken for granted. All his work is based on this assumption but it becomes increasingly explicit as his work develops. In *Madness and Civilisation* he does not, of course, claim that phenomena to which the term 'madness' can refer never existed. On the contrary, in this work there is a strong romantic naturalism, which gives the impression that Foucault is posing the truth of madness against the falsity of reason. But even here the main concern is with the way reason was *conceptually* separated from unreason, to provide the conditions for the emergence of modern psychiatric medicine. It is the social categorization which unifies the disparate phenomena known collectively as 'madness'. By the time he comes to write the first volume of *The History of Sexuality* the lingering naturalism has disappeared. In this book, sex, far from being the object to which sexual discourse refers, is a phenomenon constructed within the discourse itself. He does not, of course, deny the existence of the material body, with its desires, aptitudes, potentialities, physical functions and so on, but he argues that the historian's task is to reread the discursive practices which make them meaningful and which change radically from one period to another. So, for example, he writes, 'We have had sexuality since the eighteenth century and sex since the nineteenth. What we had before that was no doubt the flesh.'[18] The notion of 'the flesh' was based on a Christian distinction between the body and the spirit while the modern concepts of sex and sexuality are based on notions of the natural and overpowering force of the instincts which constitute the essence of the individual. Modern sexuality, unlike the Christian idea of the flesh, is constitutive of our individuality: sex has become the truth of our being.

The task of historical investigation is the understanding of the processes of categorization which make phenomena like sex socially significant, and which produce the forms of knowledge which provide the focus for social regulation and control. What is true of madness and sexuality is also true of other objects of discourse. Modern medicine, for instance, produced a new object of observation and treatment, 'the body', which was constituted through a host of social practices – military and economic as well as medical – which displaced concepts relying on the old language of humours and harmonies. The 'medical gaze' as it emerged at the end of the eighteenth century was anchored on a new object which now took on the inevitability of 'naturalness'.[19]

Much of Foucault's work revolves around this crucial period of the late eighteenth century. Here we see the rise of the modern asylum and the emergence of the medical gaze, the birth of the prison and the construction of the apparatus of sexual regulation. But also, and most crucially to Foucault's project, this period saw the birth of the human sciences, with 'man' as its central object. In classical thought, Foucault argues, man as an object of knowledge did not exist. The human sciences therefore were born 'when man constitutes himself in Western culture as both that which must be conceived of and that which is to be known'.[20] The nineteenth century saw the birth of biology, the study of man as an organism, political economy, the study of man as an economic producer, and philology, the study of man as a language maker. Instead of regarding these appearances as no more than the progressive refinement of pre-existing disciplines, Foucault argues that they actually constituted quite different sets of objects, new objects occupying new spaces of knowledge. There occurred in other words what he terms in *The Order of Things* (although the phrase is dropped in subsequent works) the emergence of a new 'episteme'.

A problem with Foucault's argument here is that the changes in forms of knowledge seem to have been willed neither individually nor collectively; they are products, it seems, of knowledge itself. The 'man', in other words, who emerges in late eighteenth-century thought is a creation of discourse, and not a creative being in his own right. He does not speak. Instead he is spoken. This question has invited the criticism of Foucault as an anti-humanist. Man, he writes, 'is probably no more than a kind of rift in the order of things' and *The Order of Things* ends with an almost mystical conception of the 'end of man'.[21] But it has to be said that this displacement of the 'constitutive' individual does not necessarily imply a rejection of humanist values. What it does mean is that humanist values or a political code cannot be straightforwardly built on a supposed real human essence. The very notion of a human essence, the truth of specific individuals, is itself a product of discourse. Our idea of individuality is itself a historical creation. To understand its history, in Foucault's terms, is to understand a dual process of subjection: both in the sense of the creation of 'subjectivity', and in the sense of being imprisoned, 'subjected', within a discourse.

Foucault's account of this subjection leaves unclear the relationship between the discursive process which constitutes subjects and the refractory and resisting consciousness of individuals. He does recognize, however, the possibility of individual resistance to 'subjection': the individual subject is not a product of a single discourse, is not trapped in a prison of dominant meanings, but is in a sense 'inter-discursive', with the potentiality for challenging and reversing the forms of definition, deploying one system of meaning against another. The aim then is not to understand the human individual as an unproblematic biological being, but to grasp that the individual subject acts as a focus of forces: 'It's my hypothesis that the individual is not a pre-given entity which is seized on by the exercise of power. The individual, with his identity and characteristics, is the product of a relation of power exercised over bodies, multiplicities, movements of desires, forces.'[22] All Foucault's work, from the study of madness through the study of the birth of the modern social sciences to the investigation of disciplinary procedures and the organization of sexuality, can be seen as addressing itself to this specific problem: how is the individual constituted in modern thought and in modern social practice?

Foucault's questioning of what are generally seen as pre-eminently natural phenomena, like individuality, sexuality and so on, has been helpful to modern feminism and sexual politics. If gender and sexual categories are historically constructed, and if the mechanisms of their emergence and reproduction can be understood, they are open to transformation. This emphasis on historical construction complements his longstanding critique of the functionalism and determinism inherent in many conventional analyses on the left which seek the hidden cause behind the surface appearance, the master discourse which explains individual discourses. In place of a search for ultimate causes he proposes the genealogical approach. Genealogy, he suggests, demands a vast accumulation of source material, 'relentless erudition', and a patient attention to the discourses which have by and large been ignored, but which in their singularity constitute warnings of the emergence of new ways of conceiving of the world. A discourse is worthy of study *because* it may have been unrealized.[23] The programme of a discourse may have been unsuccessful, but that does not mean it did not have effects. The unintended consequences of social practices may be traced through discourses which have lain forgotten and buried. Thus the aim of the penal reforms of the early nineteenth century may well have been liberal, to produce a rehabilitated person. The unintended effects of the new prison system were, on the contrary, restrictive and oppressive, creating rather than liberating criminals. History does not have a set pattern or ultimate target; it has no inner necessity of response to the functional demands of new modes of production or new class forces.[24]

Foucault helps us to move away from any unthinking reliance on a supposed universalizing capitalist strategy, frees us from an abstract determinism and from an equally deterministic functionalism, and returns us to the probing of the actual relationship between one social form and another, the actual mechanics of power. So the rise of an apparatus of sexuality, a series of practices and institutions defining the domain of the sexual, is located not in any single social necessity but in a host of strategies dealing with relations between parents and pedagogic institutions and children, the relationship of medicine and science to the female body, controversies over birth control and population policies, and the categorization of perverse sexualities. No single approach or necessity is at work in all these practices; they are not pervaded by the same mysterious essence of sex. In fact, sex is defined differently in each practice. It was the work of medical, psychological, educational, hygienic and eugenic practices – articulated in a new sub-discipline of sexology – which defined the unity of these strategies around a new concept of sex as expressive of basic instincts. Each of these strategies and practices had its own conditions of possibility and existence in concrete political, economic, social, ideological practices. But no consistent master plan has been played out, no 'determination in the last instance'. The actual mechanics of power at play have to be studied in their singularity.

In all this, there remains the difficult and over-arching problem of the connections between discourses, and their articulation at any particular moment. Foucault's reluctance to discuss the actual relations between discourses, and between the discursive and the extra-discursive, forces him to rely in many cases on a very crude form of determinism. Thus for example, in his text on Pierre Rivière, the impact of the French Revolution appears as a *deus ex machina*, a hidden hand which is offered as an overall explanation for the specific events which occur.[25] Similarly, in *Discipline and Punish* and in *The History of Sexuality*, the impact of capitalism is invoked as a background factor but only minimally sketched in. Paradoxically, a method designed to free us from determinism in many cases simply offers us a mechanistic determinism by the back door. This is most obvious in his later work. In *Discipline and Punish* and *The History of Sexuality* he interprets the emergence of new forms of disciplinary power as a response to the need to cope with pressure of population from the late eighteenth century onwards. Now this *can* appear as simply a continuation of the long French tradition of demographic determinism, which has at least one source in the Durkheimian emphasis on moral density as being an explanatory factor in the move from mechanical to organic solidarity.[26] In fact Foucault is not arguing that population pressure *caused* changes, but rather that the perception of the population as a problem in specific discourses had important effects. Nevertheless, his comments on the function of the prison from the 1830s in controlling the population can be seen as a latently functionalist and deterministic explanation. Similarly, his suggestion that sex is at the heart of the modern play of power because its control provides access to the regulation of the population implies that sexuality is tied to the imperatives of the social formation as a whole. In *The History of Sexuality* the possibility is left open that there might indeed be a 'need' for the 'repression' of sexuality. But Foucault leaves this suggestion ambiguous precisely because of his reluctance to theorize what the actual relationships are between discourse and social formation.

Power-knowledge

These ambiguities are in large part explained by difficulties with Foucault's notion of power and power-knowledge. As Foucault himself puts it, the whole point of his later work lies in a re-elaboration of the concept of power:

> I believe that power is not built up out of 'wills' (individual or collective), nor is it derivable from interests. Power is constructed and functions on the basis of particular powers, myriad issues, myriad effects of power. It is this complex domain that must be studied. That is not to say that it is independent or could be made sense of outside of economic processes and the relations of production.[27]

The last point is a useful antidote to critics who accuse Foucault of idealism. The message is not that production is unimportant but that the economic or social sources and effects of power cannot be presupposed before the investigation.

So what is power for Foucault? Power is not something that can be held or transmitted, it is not the possession of one class (or of one gender) over another, it is not embodied in the state or any single institution. It is inherent in all social relationships, and plays upon the inevitable imbalance in all those relationships. Foucault is not interested in some fundamental principle of power, but rather in the mechanisms and social practices through which power is actually exercised. His work offers an 'analytics' of power, rather than a theory of power. He argues for the construction of what he calls an 'ascending analysis of power' starting from the specific and infinitesimal micro-mechanisms, which all have their own history and their own development, their own trajectory, their own specific techniques and tactics. He is concerned with the 'technologies' which exercise power over and invest the body. Here power is a positive not a negative force. While his earlier work saw power in terms of exclusion, from the late 1960s he began to analyse it in terms of what it constructs rather than what it denies. His rejection of the 'repressive hypothesis' in *The History of Sexuality* illustrates the point.[28] Far from the nineteenth century witnessing a regime of denial and repression in relation to sexuality, Foucault argues, it witnessed a positive incitement to discourse, a multiple production of sexualities in a host of social practices. The discovery of the significance of sex in a multiplicity of areas, from housing and hygiene to psychiatry and education, amounted to a constitution of new forms of power-knowledge around the body. In *Discipline and Punish* he explores the emergence of new disciplinary forms of surveillance: control not simply of the body but through 'the soul', through producing ever more forms of observation and discipline. In the mid-eighteenth century, a new object of power was defined for the first time: society as a focus of the physical wellbeing, health and life of the population. The exercise of these latter functions, order, enrichment and health, was carried out, he argues, less through a single apparatus of law, negative in its force, than by an ensemble of positive regulatory and institutional forces which in the eighteenth century took on the generic term of 'police'. The concern with policing the population was a product of changes in the constitution of the labour force but more directly a result of the great demographic upswing. Population became a problem to be organized and disciplined, and simultaneously an object of surveillance, analysis, intervention and codification. In this context the body took on a new and crucial importance: as the bearer of those qualities, of health, sickness, strength and weakness, which were crucial to the future of the society as a whole. Hence the emergence of new forms of control, of which the prison, and the Panopticon as its particular ideal form, were representative; and the new importance assigned to the sexual domain. The biological features of the population became relevant factors for economic management and it became necessary to ensure not only their subjection (in the dual sense of subjection discussed above) but the constant increase of their utility. From this emerged the concern with childhood, with the family, with hygiene, and with sexuality.

Much of this is fascinating and convincing, but the stubborn questions recur: what are the points of contact between these social entities; is there a principle of articulation at work between them at any one time; or is there just a chaos of unrelated histories whose actual connections can never be fully elaborated? Where, above all, is the state? Despite the strictures of Foucault's method, his view of the state and its apparatuses is a very conventional and narrow one. As Hussain has noted, Foucault has a command theory of law: he sees the law as a set of commands of the sovereign, which operates by recommending and forbidding certain acts under the threat of punishment.[29] But laws can be as diverse and as disparate as the relations of power which Foucault describes. So in playing down the juridical, negative functions of power, Foucault reduces the law to an instrument of power. In focusing on the forms of power within the walls of institutions, he fails to articulate the relation between these and the juridical framework of social life. This over-emphasis on one aspect of the play of power can be seen as an attempt to compensate for the under-emphasis on the local investments of power in previous studies. But nevertheless it does weaken the overall analytical force of Foucault's studies, and leaves him open to justifiable criticism.

A history of the present

Foucault is ultimately interested not in 'the past' as such but in a 'history of the present'. The present is not a homogeneous whole organized around a single unitary focus. It presents a series of shifting problems each with its specific history. And the chief characteristic of the present is that we live in a society of discipline and surveillance. He stands against all latter-day Whig histories of progress of which 'modernization theories' are embodiments: that the present can be seen as a culmination of inexorable progressive forces, that the liberal present is in some way the product of liberating forces inherent in modern society. In *Discipline and Punish*, for instance, he notes the changes in penal severity over the past two hundred years, and asks 'Is there a diminution of intensity? Perhaps. There is certainly a change of objective.'[30] Power might have changed its form: it might be less 'barbarous' in its investment of the body. But it is no less power. He makes the same point in relation to sexuality. The law might well be less harsh, sex may be more openly discussed. But sex is still regulated and controlled, though now by the more subtle means of medicine and social surveillance rather than by brute interdiction.[31] This argument does break with easy myths of progress, but there are several problems with it. The first concerns the notion, critical to Foucault, of normalization. What is not clear is the degree to which this normalization involves the internalization of the norms. Does the individual become totally disciplined and controlled? Foucault's disciplinary society often seems as all-embracing and inevitable in its effects as the 'iron cage' of bureaucratization and rationalization that Max Weber described. Foucault seems to have realized the difficulties of his position and in interviews he points out the central importance of his notion of resistance. Where there is power, he writes many times, there is resistance; in fact power depends on resistance. The implication of this is that power is a constantly mobile force which can adjust to points of resistance but simultaneously that the resistances inflect the impact of power. This is important because it emphasizes the significance of struggles at the point of the impact of power. But it has to be said that this aspect of Foucault's work is undeveloped and ambiguous.

There is, further, a slippage in Foucault's concept of the workings of contemporary forms of power. In arguing that power is an effect of the operation of social relations, that it is diffuse, omnipresent and polymorphous, Foucault does away with any concept of a hierarchy of power. It is surely evident that some forms of power act as greater 'restraints' and limits, or have greater productive possibilities, than others. The state, for instance, does have a monopoly of legal violence. The media is monopolistic. Capitalists do have more power than workers. Of course Foucault recognizes this, while he rightly refuses to say that one form of oppression is better or worse, more or less severe, than any other. But some powers are more resistant to struggle than others and what is left vague in Foucault's work is any notion of the political strategies, in the conventional sense, needed to transform these powers.

This reluctance to propose any grand, strategic political schema is but an aspect of a wider caution. Like his friend, Gilles Deleuze, he insists on treating theory as a 'box of tools' to be taken up and used, not offered prescriptively. The role of the intellectual in modern society is not to offer prescriptive analysis but to lay bare the mechanisms of power:

> The intellectual no longer has to play the role of an adviser. The project, tactics and goals to be adopted are a matter for those who do the fighting. What the intellectual can do is to provide instruments of analysis and at present this is the historian's essential role ... In other words, a topological and geological survey of the battlefield – that is the intellectual's role.[32]

This in turn derives from a perception of the changed political terrain of the previous twenty years, with the emergence of new struggles around gender and sexuality, the rights of prisoners and mental patients, but also covering a gamut of other social activities. Foucault does not deny that a grand political strategy is possible or necessary (although his own political commitments seem to be in the direction of a mild anarchism). But what he does argue is that any such strategy cannot be the product of the minds of specific intellectuals or leaders but has to be a product of the struggles themselves. Hegemony could only be the end product of a multitude of struggles, not the effect of central planning.

Politically, his recognition of the diversity of current social struggles is healthy. But the relative political weight or potential of the various struggles – of class, sex, prisoners, mental patients and so on – and the nature of the necessary alliances between them are left studiously vague. Similarly, any attempt to construct a Foucauldian social theory is fraught with difficulties. Although there is a guiding series of concerns in his investigations, ultimately what we are left with is a series of separate studies. And the unanswered questions are manifold. Is power ultimately irresistible? Are we all ultimately trapped within a power that is all-seeing yet unseen?

This brings us to another problem: Foucault's main concern is with the construction of subjectivities within discourse. But it is not clear why some individuals recognize themselves within these discourses and others do not. This is a major issue in trying to understand the historical emergence of sexual identities. Much of Foucault's later work was pre-occupied with the construction of sexual categories and their impact on subjectivities, but it is clear that these discourses work differentially on different individuals. What is the relationship between subjectification within discourse and the individual organization of desires and consequent identities?

This is an area that Foucault only began to address in his last works and his attitude towards disciplines which do attempt to address the question – pre-eminently psychoanalysis – remained notably sceptical, as we have seen. At the same time, there is a danger that all general categories – men and women, heterosexual or homosexual, black or white, ruling class and working class – will disappear completely into a welter of specific definitions.

The positive side of this is Foucault's rigorous critique of any simple notion of 'liberation', whether social or sexual. Social relations are inescapably the effect of language and the ceaseless workings of power, and there can be neither any escape from discourse nor any ending of power. What political struggle is inevitably about, therefore, is 'reverse discourses', radically different definitions, different organizations of power relations. How and in what way this is to be done, Foucault leaves vague. This is a radical abstention for a 'political intellectual' and un-likely to endear him to more passionate progressives. But if we can never escape the grid of language, we can at least see its effects, and here Foucault's work is a valuable, if necessarily partial guide.

Note

Foucault's death in 1984 unleashed a torrent of writing, to which I have contributed a little. See my discussion in *Sexuality and its Discontents* (London: Routledge, 1985); *Against Nature* (London: Rivers Oram Press, 1991); and *Invented Moralities* (Cambridge: Polity Press, 1995). Foucault never realized his original six-volume contribution on *The History of Sexuality*. Instead, a further, and apparently final, two volumes appeared posthumously: *The History of Sexuality, Volume 2, The Use of Pleasure* (London: Viking, 1985), and *The History of Sexuality, Volume 3, The Care of the Self* (London: Viking, 1986).

Good discussions of his influence include two books by Lois McNay: *Foucault and Feminism* (Cambridge: Polity Press, 1992) and *Foucault: A Critical Introduction* (Cambridge: Polity Press, 1994), which discuss the shift in his last works, especially the new emphasis on 'practices of freedom'. Contrasting views of the relationship between Foucault's own sexual practices, political commitments and theoretical work can be found in James Miller, *The Passion of Michel Foucault* (London: HarperCollins, 1993), and David Macey, *The Lives of Michel Foucault* (London: Hutchinson, 1993). Foucault is rescued for radical sexual politics in David M. Halperin, *Saint Foucault: Towards a Gay Hagiography* (Oxford: Oxford University Press, 1993).

References

1 Biographical details can be found in A. Sheridan, *Michel Foucault*, London, 1980. A full bibliography of his writings can be found in C. Gordon (ed.) *Power/Knowledge*, London, 1980. Foucault's major works are listed in n. 5.

2 Foucault, 'What Is an Author?' in D. F. Bouchard (ed.), *Language, Counter-Memory, Practice: Selected Essays and Interviews* (hereafter *LCMP*), New York, 1977.

3 See Foucault, 'Orders of Discourse,' *Social Science Information* vol. 10, no. 2, April 1971, where he pays tribute to Hyppolite; and Sheridan, *Michael Foucault*, pp. 4–5.

4 Foucault, *The Order of Things, An Archaeology of the Human Sciences*, London, 1970, p. xi.

5 The main English translations of his work are as follows: *Madness and Civilisation: A History of Insanity in the Age of Reason*, New York, 1965; *The Archaeology of Knowledge*, London, 1972; *The Order of Things*, London, 1973; *The Birth of the Clinic: An Archaeology of Medical Perception*, London, 1973; *Discipline and Punish: Birth of the Prison*, London, 1977; *The History of Sexuality. Volume 1: An Introduction*, London, 1978. For an article which lays particular stress on Foucault's archaeology of psychoanalysis, see Athar Hussain, 'Foucault's History of Sexuality', *m/f* nos. 5 and 6, 1981. See also John Forrester's comments in *Language and the Origins of Psychoanalysis*, London, 1980.

6 On Foucault's reaction to the Lysenko affair see Alex Callinicos, *Is There a Future for Marxism?*, London, 1982, p. 99. More generally see D. Lecourt, *Proletarian Science? The Case of Lysenko*, London, 1977.

7 See Peter Dews, 'The "New Philosophers" and the End of Leftism', *Radical Philosophy* no. 24, Spring 1980, and 'The *Nouvelle Philosophie* and Foucault,' *Economy and Society* vol. 8, no. 2, May 1979.

8 *Power/Knowledge*, p. 53.

9 'Preface to Transgression' in *LCMP*, p. 50.

10 *LCMP*, p. 148. See also *Power/Knowledge*, p. 53, and *The Order of Things*, p. 263. For a discussion of the changing influence of Nietzsche on Foucault see Sheridan, *Michael Foucault*, pp. 115 and ff.

11 Quoted in David Frisby, *Sociological Impressionism: A Reassessment of Georg Simmel's Social Theory*, London, 1981; see *The Archaeology of*

122   *Contested Knowledge*

Knowledge, p. 145; for a discussion of Foucault's 'perspectivism' see Callinicos, p. 106.

12 Foucault, 'Georges Canguilhem: Philosopher of Error', *Ideology and Consciousness* no. 7, Autumn 1980, p. 54. See also 'Orders of Discourse'; C. Gordon, 'Afterword', in *Power/Knowledge*, pp. 233–4.

13 Foucault, 'Questions of Method', p. 5.

14 *The Archaeology of Knowledge*, pp. 3ff.

15 *The Archaeology of Knowledge*, p. 7.

16 *LCMP*, pp. 156, 162.

17 See Foucault, 'Politics and the Study of Discourse', *Ideology and Consciousness* no. 3, Spring 1978.

18 *Power/Knowledge*, p. 211.

19 See *The Birth of the Clinic*.

20 *The Order of Things*, p. 345.

21 *The Order of Things*, p. 387.

22 *Power/Knowledge*, pp. 73–4.

23 On this see Gordon, 'Afterword', p. 248.

24 See *Discipline and Punish*, throughout.

25 Michel Foucault (ed.), *I, Pierre Riviere, having Slaughtered my Mother, my Sister and my Brother...A Case of Patricide in the 19th Century*, London, 1978.

26 See, for example, Emile Durkheim, *The Division of Labour*.

27 *Power/Knowledge*, p. 188.

28 See Part Two, 'The Repressive Hypothesis', in *The History of Sexuality*. See my commentary on this in *Sex, Politics and Society*, London, 1981. See also Hussain, 'Foucault's History of Sexuality'.

29 Hussain, 'Foucault's History of Sexuality', p. 176.

30 *Discipline and Punishment*, p. 16.

31 For a discussion of this see my own *Sex, Politics and Society*, and Stuart Hall, 'Reformism and the Legislation of Consent', in National Deviancy Conference, *Permissiveness and Control*, London, 1980.

32 *Power/Knowledge*, p. 42.

PART II
Histories of Sexuality

6

Sexuality and History Revisited

Writing about sex

Writing about sex can be dangerous. It makes you, as Ken Plummer put it, 'morally suspect' (1975, p. 4). Until recently, in the academic world at least, it marked you also as marginal to the central intellectual preoccupations of the major disciplines.

Nearly forty years ago, the young William Masters felt sufficiently inspired by the example of Alfred Kinsey to want to pursue a career in sex research. He was advised by his obviously more worldly wise supervisor to do three things first: to complete his medical qualifications; to establish his reputation in another field; and to wait until he was 40 before venturing into these treacherous waters.

This little anecdote tells us quite a lot about the moral climate in postwar America, and probably about the present too. Here we find, for example, the hegemony of medicine which has dominated most 'respectable' discussions of sex over the past century. Then there is the emphasis on reputation and credentials, a positive underlining of the importance of a student in this field demonstrating his or her objective, scholarly interest in the subject before venturing into it. And, of course, reputation, credentials, respectability and objectivity are assumed to come with age.

It has always been possible to write about sexuality. But, to do so and be listened to, it has usually been necessary to work within the confines of an acceptable discourse. The authorized voices have been religious, medical, medico-moral, legal, psychological, pedagogical, and certainly 'official'. They have rarely been sensitive to the nuances of history or social variability.

Needless to say, quite a lot of writing about sexuality has gone on outside these parameters. But it is noticeable how, even today, many of us who venture into this field still feel the need to stress our academic credentials for doing so. If you look at any journal whose main concern is sexuality in some form you will find the title page full of the names of impeccably scholarly advisers, complete with a long list of their academic qualifications, from MDs to Ph.D. (Candidate). Academic awards permit us to speak with authority; and to make what we say acceptable.

To get back to my anecdote: the young William Masters followed the advice of his mentor absolutely. And who can say he was wrong? Alongside his partner and future wife Virginia he was to become half of the world-famous sex-research and sex-therapy duo, Masters and Johnson. Their popular success has always been underpinned by their 'scientific' reputation. The very turgidity of their writing style may be seen as a simulacrum of the scientific text.

Some things at least have changed. Since the early 1970s there has been a major expansion in the study of sexuality in general, and of sexual history in particular. We now know a good deal about marriage and the family, illegitimacy and birth control, prostitution and homosexuality, changing patterns of moral, legal and medical regulation, rape and sexual violence, sexual identities and sexual communities, and oppositional cultures. Historians have interrogated old and discovered new documentary evidence; they have deployed extensive oral history sources; and all but exhausted the records of births, marriages and deaths (see Weeks, 1985).

Major scholars, whose reputations were, significantly, made elsewhere, have entered the field. To name just some of the best known: Lawrence Stone has exhaustively chronicled the (largely upper-class) family, sex and marriage in pre-modern England (Stone, 1977). Peter Gay is venturing into the complexities of the 'bourgeois experience' (Gay, 1984; 1986). Most influentially of all, Michel Foucault has essayed a genealogy of the western apparatus of sexuality (Foucault, 1979; 1987; 1988). The subject has achieved an unprecedented range, depth and, dare I say it, respectability.

This signals an important and welcome shift. But it is vital that we understand its real significance, which lies not in who writes but what they write about. The really noteworthy point about the new sexual history lies in the fact that increasingly it is being recognized that far from being a minor adjunct to the mainstream of history, sexuality in its broadest sense has been at the heart of moral, social and political discourse. We cannot properly understand the past, let alone the present, unless we grasp that simple fact.

Two lessons for the historical enterprise flow from this. First, it is imperative to recognize not only the desirability but the absolute necessity of inter-, multi- and cross-disciplinary approaches to the subject. The new sexual history has in fact been fed not only by new sources and new topics, but also by a multitude of approaches, from psychoanalysis to poststructuralism and semiology, and nurtured by a number of disciplines, from the 'new social history' to sociology, philosophy and literature. They go far beyond the conventional intellectual tools of the traditional empirical historian. I would go so far as to say that the study of sexuality as a historical phenomenon fundamentally challenges the existing disciplinary boundaries, illustrating perhaps better than any other topic their contingent natures. Traditional historical methods have proved inadequate to the understanding of sexuality. The history of sexuality should not be studied by historians alone.

The second factor is that sexual history is to a high degree a politicized history, underlined by an energetic grass-roots input into the study of sexuality. To an extraordinary degree, much of the most innovative historical work in this field has come from women and men whose initial concern was as much 'political' as purely 'academic'. Many of the pioneering feminist writers about sexuality in the early 1970s are now in often senior academic positions; their work has grown in empirical richness and theoretical sophistication. But their publications, while achieving the highest scholarly standards, are still clearly within a developing tradition of feminist writing (for example, Walkowitz, 1980; Taylor, 1983; Smith-Rosenberg, 1986). Similarly, within the area of lesbian and gay studies, important historical works have appeared which, though initially stimulated by the moral and political preoccupations of the authors, have begun to transform the wider intellectual debate (for example, Boswell, 1980; Bray, 1982; Freedman et al., 1985). In the study of sexuality, it seems, scholarship and politics, broadly defined, are inextricably intertwined.

I want to devote much of the rest of this chapter to exploring the implications of these factors, concentrating on several interrelated questions. What, for example, is the impact of the new sexual history on our understanding of sexuality? Or, to put it another way, what is it we study when we say we are exploring the history of sexuality? What do our studies tell us about the relationship of the sexual to the social, to power and politics? In what ways do they illuminate our understanding of social and moral regulation, and the role of the state? How, in turn, does this affect our perception of the historic present in which we live? Why, in particular, has sexuality become so important in the contemporary political discourse of both left and right? My aim is not to supply the answers, but to sharpen the questions we must ask if we are to rethink the history of sexuality.

The subject of sexual history

At the heart of the new sexual history is the assumption that sexuality is a social and historical construct. In the famous words of Foucault, 'Sexuality must not be thought of as a kind of natural given which power tries to hold in check, or as an obscure domain which knowledge tries gradually to uncover. It is the name that can be given to a historical construct' (Foucault, 1979, p. 105).

Leaving aside the ambiguities of and problems with this statement, I want to emphasize the revolution in the approach to sexuality that this symbolized. Of all social phenomena, sex has been most resistant to social and historical explanations. It seems the most basic, the most natural thing about us, the truth at the heart of our being. This has been reflected until very recently in even the most sophisticated studies of sexuality. As pioneering sexual theorists sought to chronicle the varieties of sexual experience throughout different periods and different cultures they assumed that beating at the centre of all this was a core of natural sexuality, varying in incidence and power, no doubt, as a result of chance historical factors, the weight of moral and physical repression, the patterns of kinship, and so on, but nevertheless basically unchanging in biological and psychological essence.

Such an assumption governed equally the naturalist approaches of the early sexologists and the metatheoretical approaches of such Freudo-marxists as Reich and Marcuse. It dominated the thoughts of functionalist anthropologists with their commitment to cultural relativism as much as the evolutionists they displaced. It lurked as effortlessly behind the sexual writings of cultural radicals as behind the work of moral conservatives. It was the taken-for-granted of sexual studies (see Weeks, 1985, Part 2).

The new sexual history has changed that. Its origins are disparate, owing, as I have already indicated, something to sociology and anthropology (their emphasis on cultural relativism, social organization and micro-studies: Gagnon and Simon, 1974; Plummer, 1975), something to psychoanalysis (especially the challenge offered by the theory of the unconscious to fixed gender and sexual positions: Coward, 1983), something to the new sexual movements of the early 1970s (their critique of existing social and sexual categories: Weeks, 1977), something to the new social history (in as far as these diverse strands can be disentangled from the new history). Foucault's work made such an impact in the early 1980s because, in part at least, it complemented and helped to systematize work already going on. Unifying the new approach were several common themes.

First, there was a general rejection of sex as an autonomous realm, a natural domain with specific effects, a rebellious energy that the social controls.

Once you begin to see sexuality as a 'construct', as a series of representations, as an 'apparatus' with a history of its own, many of the older certainties dissolve. It is no longer appropriate to state, as Malinowski did, that 'Sex really is dangerous', the source of most human trouble from Adam and Eve on (Malinowski, 1963, p. 127). Instead, we are forced to ask: why is it that sex is regarded as dangerous? We can no longer speculate about the inevitable conflict between the powerful instinct of sex and the demands of culture. Instead, we need to ask why our culture has conceived of sexuality in this way.

Second, it followed that the new sexual history assumed the social variability of sexual forms, beliefs, ideologies and behaviours. Sexuality has not only a history, but many histories, each of which needs to be understood both in its uniqueness and as part of an intricate pattern.

Third, it became necessary to abandon the idea that the history of sexuality can usefully be understood in terms of a dichotomy of pressure and release, repression and liberation. 'Sexuality' as a domain of social interest and concern is produced by society in complex ways. It is a result of diverse social practices that give meaning to human activities, of social definitions and self-definitions, of struggles between those who have the power to define, and those who resist. Sexuality is not a given. It is a product of negotiation, struggle and human agency.

The most important outcome of the resulting historical approach to sexuality is that it opens up the whole field to critical analysis and assessment. It becomes possible to relate sexuality to other social phenomena and to ask new types of question (new at least to the field of sex research). Questions such as the following: how is sexuality shaped, and how is it articulated with economic, social and political structures – in a word, how is it 'socially constructed'? Why and how has the domain of sexuality achieved such a critical organizing and symbolic significance? Why do we think it so important? If sexuality is constructed by human agency, to what extent can it be changed?

Questions such as these have produced an impressive flood of new work – and new questions – across a range of issues from the shaping of reproduction (e.g. Petchesky, 1986) to the social organization of disease (e.g. Mort, 1987), from the pre-Christian origins of the western preoccupation with the association between sex and truth (Foucault, 1987; 1988) to the making of the modern body (Gallagher and Laqueur, 1987).

I'll take a further example from an area which I myself have been particularly interested in – the history of homosexuality. Fifteen years ago there was virtually nothing in the way of serious historical studies of same-sex activity. Such writings as existed assumed an unchanging essence of homosexuality across cultures and over the millennia of human history, as if one could readily identify the experience of the modern gay subcultures with the socially sanctioned male intergenerational sexual patterns of ancient Greece or the institutionalized cross-dressing of certain pre-industrial tribal societies.

I became convinced (following McIntosh; see chapter 2) that this was an inadequate way of seeing this particular past, and my early researches persuaded me that there had been significant shifts in attitudes to, and the organization of, same-sex erotic activities. In particular, it became clear that the idea that there was such a thing as a homosexual person, and an associated homosexual identity, was of comparatively recent origin, no more, in most western cultures at least, than two or three hundred years old (Weeks, 1977). Other work carried on at the same time was reaching similar conclusions (see Smith-Rosenberg, 1975; Katz, 1976; Foucault, 1979).

Since the 1970s this approach has been much debated, and has occasioned a great deal of controversy. There is by no means unanimous agreement about it (Boswell, 1983). It has at the same time become the major hypothesis for the study of homosexual history. For example, a conference at the Free University of Amsterdam in December 1987 brought together over five hundred people from all over the world to debate the relevance of 'essentialist' versus 'constructionist' perspectives in addressing the question 'Homosexuality, Which Homosexuality?'. The history papers covered a wide range of topics, from Aristotelean philosophy to the sexual and emotional proclivities of Eleanor Roosevelt. But central to the majority of them was a sensitivity to historical context that illumined hitherto obscure issues, and largely confirmed the 'constructionist' hypothesis (Altman et al., 1989; Franklin and Stacey, 1988).

But sensitivity to context is one thing; doing away with a unifying concept of sexuality is quite another. One of the problems with the new sexual history is that it is in danger of becoming a history without a proper subject. The history of sexuality is at the same time a history of a category of thought, which, if we follow Foucault, has a delimited history; and a history of changing erotic practices, subjective meanings, social definitions and patterns of regulation whose only unity lies in their common descriptor. 'Sexuality' is an unstable category, in constant flux (Padgug, 1979).

It is, nevertheless, a vital one. All societies find it necessary to organize the erotic possibilities of the body in one way or another. They all need, as Plummer suggests, to impose 'who restrictions' and 'why restrictions' to provide the permissions, prohibitions, limits and possibilities through which erotic life is organized (Plummer, 1984). But they do so in a wide variety of ways. The study of sexuality therefore provides a critical insight into the wider organization of a culture. The important question then becomes not what traditional disciplines such as history or sociology can contribute to our understanding of sexuality, but rather what the study of the sexual can contribute to our grasp of the historical, the social and the political.

Sex, politics and society

This brings me to the second of the major issues I want to explore: what indeed does the new history of sexuality tell us about the relationship of sexuality to other elements of social life, and especially what insights does it give to the nature of power and politics in the modern world?

'To some', the feminist scholar Gayle Rubin has argued, 'sexuality may seem to be an unimportant topic, a frivolous diversion from the more critical problems of poverty, war, disease, racism, famine, or nuclear annihilation. But it is precisely at times such as these, when we live with the possibility of unthinkable destruction, that people are likely to become dangerously crazy about sexuality' (Rubin, 1984, p. 267).

Why is this so? Why is sexuality so thoroughly bound up with the modern play of power, as Foucault suggested (Foucault, 1979)? What is it about sexuality that makes it so susceptible to anxiety, conflict and moralizing zeal?

The first point to make is that this is not always the case. Although our culture attributes a peculiar significance to the sexual, there is plentiful anthropological and historical evidence to suggest that other cultures interpret the possibilities of the body quite differently (Caplan, 1987). While all societies have to make arrangements for the organization of erotic life, not all do so with the obsessive concern we show in the west. Different cultures have varying responses to childhood sexuality, marriage, homosexuality, even reproduction. Some societies display so little interest in erotic activity that they have been labelled more or less 'asexual'. Islamic cultures, by contrast, have developed a lyrical view of sex with sustained attempts to integrate the religious and the sexual – as long, that is, as it was heterosexual (Bouhdiba, 1985; Weeks, 1986, pp. 25–6).

We in the west are heirs of a Christian tradition which has tended to see in sex a focus for moral anguish and conflict, producing an enduring dualism between the spirit and the flesh, the mind and the body. It has produced a culture which simultaneously disavows the body while being obsessively preoccupied with it.

Michel Foucault was centrally concerned with this issue. He abandoned the original scheme for his *History of Sexuality* and went back to the ancient Greeks and Romans in the two volumes published at the very end of his life (Foucault, 1987; 1988) precisely because of his growing conviction that the western preoccupation with the relationship between sex and truth was of very ancient lineage, and crucial to the understanding of power and subjectivity. For the ancients, he argued, concern with the pleasures of the body was only one, and not necessarily the most important, of the preoccupations of life, to be set alongside dietary regulations and the organization of household relations. We, on the other hand, seek the truth of our natures in our sexual desires. In the course of that shift, with pre-Christian as well as Christian origins, sexuality has emerged as a domain of danger as well as pleasure, emotional anxiety as well as moral certainty.

I do not wish here to assess the merits and defects of this argument. I cite it because it illustrates the major point I want to make. The new social history takes for granted that sexuality as an historical phenomenon is in fact a consequence of an obsessive social preoccupation with the body and its possibilities for erotic pleasure. As a result, far from being stubbornly resistant to social moulding, it is a peculiarly sensitive conductor of cultural influences, and hence of social and political divisions.

There are five broad categories of social relations which both are constructed around and in turn shape and reshape sex and gender relations (Weeks, 1986; 1989). First, there are the kinship and family systems that place individuals in relationship to one another, and constitute them as human subjects with varying needs and desires, conscious and unconscious. Second, there are the economic and social organizations that shape social relations, statuses and class divisions, and provide the basic preconditions and ultimate limits for the organization of sexual life. Third, there are the changing patterns of social regulation and organization, formal and informal, legal and moral, populist and professional, religious and secular, unintended consequences as well as organized and planned responses. Fourth, there are the changing forms of political interest and concern, power and policies. Finally, there are the cultures of resistance which give rise to oppositional subcultures, alternative forms of knowledge and social and sexual movements.

These are quite general categories. They have had different weighting at different historical conjunctures. But their intricate and complex interaction in the west has produced a culture which assigns a critical role to sexuality in the definition of subjectivity and self, morality and sin, normality and abnormality.

Modern sexuality has been shaped and defined at the intersection of two absolutely central concerns: with who and what we are as human subjects and social individuals; and with the nature and direction of the society as a whole. And as the state, as the organizing focus of the social sphere, has become more and more concerned with the lives of its members, for the sake of moral uniformity, economic wellbeing, national security or hygiene and health, so it has become more and more involved with the sex lives of individuals, providing the rationale for techniques of moral and legal management, detailed intervention into private lives and scientific exploration of the subject of sex.

As a result, sexuality has become an increasingly important political as well as moral issue, condensing a number of critical issues: with the norms of family life, the relations between men and women, adults and children, and the nature of normality and abnormality. These are central issues in any culture. The debate about them has become increasingly heated and bitter in recent years because debates about sexuality are debates about the type of society we want to live in. As sex goes, so goes society (Weeks, 1986, p. 36).

Power and the state

This is another way of restating that issues of sexuality are at the heart of the whole workings of power in modern society. 'The state', broadly defined, clearly has a crucial role to play here. Through its role in determining legislation and the legal process it constitutes the categories of the permissible and the impermissible, the pure and the obscene. Through its symbiosis with the forces of moral regulation (from the churches to the medical profession) it can shape the climate of sexual opinion. Through its organization of health and welfare it can help to determine the patterns of marriage, child-bearing, child-rearing, and so on.

Of course, the actual practice of the state varies enormously, depending on a variety of historical factors and contingencies. A would-be theocracy like modern Iran can make adultery a criminal offence, with draconian penalties. An ostensibly secular state might formally eschew a direct role in moral regulation (though all the evidence suggests that it is easier to make the declaration of disinterest than to carry it out when faced by the host of pressures to which the modern state is heir). The state can shape through its prohibitions and punishments. It can also organize and regulate through its positive will and injunctions, and influence through its omissions and contradictions.

But however critical the role of the state, both in the abstract and in real historical situations, it would be wrong to see its functions as either predetermined or necessarily decisive. One of the key achievements of the new sexual history is that it has helped us to understand the mechanisms through which sexuality is organized and produced in and through a host of different social practices. And in this complex process a variety of often interlocking power relationships are at play.

Take, for example, the question of gender and sexual difference. Various feminist writers have argued forcibly that the elaboration of sexual difference has been central to the subordination of women, with sexuality not only reflecting but being constitutive in the construction and maintenance of the power relationship between men and women. Sexuality is fundamentally gendered.

On the one hand, this can lead to an argument that all hitherto existing definitions of female sexuality (at least in recorded history) are male definitions, so that the category of sexuality itself is fundamentally corrupted by male power and the actual practices of 'masculinity' (Rich, 1984; Coveney et al., 1984; Dworkin, 1987). On the other, the perception of the symbiosis between definitions of gender and of sexuality can lead to careful analyses of the play of definition and self-definition, power and resistance (e.g. Coward, 1984). In other words, it becomes a sensitizing device which allows us to explore the complexities of practices – theoretical as well as social and political – which have given rise to the relations of domination and subordination that characterize the world of gender.

This has enabled Laqueur, for example, to argue that: 'the political, economic, and cultural transformations of the eighteenth century created the context in which the articulation of radical differences between the sexes became culturally imperative' (Laqueur, 1987, p. 35). The hierarchical model that held sway from ancient times interpreted the female body as an inferior and inverted version of the male, but stressed nevertheless the generative role of female sexual pleasure. The breakdown of this model, in political as well as medical debates, and its replacement by a reproductive model which stressed the radical opposition of male and female sexualities, the woman's automatic reproductive cycle, and her lack of sexual feeling, was a critical moment in the reshaping of gender relations.

It did not arise straightforwardly from scientific advance. Nor was it the product of a singular effort at social control by and through the state. The emergent discourse about sexual difference allowed a range of separate, and often contradictory, social and political responses to emerge. But this new perception of female sexuality and reproductive biology has been absolutely central to modern social and political discourse. Its effects can be discerned in a vast range of political practices, from the legal regulation of prostitution to the social security structures of the welfare state (Weeks, 1989).

If gender is a key variable in the organization of sexuality, class is another. Class differences in sexual regulation are scarcely unique to the modern world. In the slave societies of the ancient world, moral standards varied enormously with social status. But in the modern world class definitions of appropriate sexual behaviour have been sharply demarcated. It has, in fact, been argued by Foucault (1979) that the very idea of sexuality is an essentially bourgeois one, which developed as an aspect of the self-definition of the class against the decadent morals of the aristocracy and the rampant immorality of the lower classes in the course of the eighteenth and nineteenth centuries. It was a colonizing system of beliefs which sought to remould society in its own emerging image.

Undoubtedly, the respectable standards of family and domestic life, with its increased demarcation between male and female roles, a growing ideological distinction between private and public life, and a marked concern with moral and hygienic policing of non-marital, non-heterosexual sexuality, were increasingly the norm by which all behaviour was judged (Davidoff and Hall, 1987).

This does not mean, of course, that all or even most behaviour conformed to these norms, or that the state acted in a uniform way to institutionalize acceptable forms of behaviour. There is a great deal of evidence that the sexual lives of the working class remained highly resistant to middle-class mores (Weeks, 1989). What one can say with confidence is that the complex sexual and moral patterns that exist in the twentieth century are the product of social struggles in which class played an important part.

Not surprisingly, the imagery of class has become a key element in sexual fantasy (Davidoff, 1983; Marcus, 1967). At the same time, the impact of formal regulation of sexual behaviour through the law and social policy is inevitably coloured by class-bound assumptions. In the 1860s and 1870s the Contagious Diseases Acts, ostensibly directed against prostitutes, were perceived to be aimed at working-class womanhood in general. This fuelled the feminist and labour opposition to them, and helped to shape the new sexual regime that followed their repeal in the 1880s (Walkowitz, 1980). More recently, it is impossible to understand the significance of the liberal sexual reforms of the 1960s in Britain without relating them to the re-formation of social boundaries, including, crucially, those of class (Weeks, 1989). Class does not determine sexual behaviour, but it provides one of the major lenses through which sexuality is organized and regulated.

Categorizations by class intersect with those of ethnicity and race. Euro-centric concepts of correct sexual behaviour have helped to shape centuries of response to the non-European world. So in the evolutionary model of sexuality dominant until the early twentieth century, the black person was classed as lower down the evolutionary scale, closer to nature than the European. This view has survived even in the culturally relativist work of twentieth-century anthropologists, who in their eagerness to portray the lyrical delights of other cultures take for granted that this is because the natives are somehow more 'natural' than modern 'civilized' peoples (Coward, 1983).

One of the most abiding myths is that of the insatiability of the sexual needs of non-European peoples, and the threat they pose to the purity of the white races. This has been constitutive of real effects in shaping sexual codes. A fear of black male sexuality was integral to slave society in the American south, and has continued to shape public stereotypes to the present. In South Africa, fear of inter-marriage and miscegenation was at the heart of apartheid legislation. In Britain, immigration policy is shot through with a dense network of assumptions where race, sex and gender are inextricably linked.

As European societies become more ethnically and racially diverse, so dominant racial assumptions shape responses to manifest cultural differences, in family patterns, gender relations and sexual assumptions (Amos and Parmar, 1984). Sexuality here, as elsewhere, becomes a battleground for competing notions of what constitutes proper behaviour.

The boundaries of race, gender and class, as of other social divisions like age or disability I could have discussed, inevitably overlap. They are not clear-cut categories. The essential point is that sexuality is constructed and reconstructed through a complex series of interlocking practices, all of which involve relations of power – and of challenges to that power. In this dialectic of power and resistance, definition and self-definition, the formal bodies of the state inevitably play a crucial part. The state can organize the terrain of sexual struggle through its patterns of legal regulation, its political interventions and social policies. But the state is itself a locale of struggle over the meaning of sexuality: its impact can be highly contradictory as its different organs adopt conflicting policies. There is no functional fit between state intention and sexual regulation. On the contrary, the historian of sexuality must stand amazed at the unintended consequences of state action: laws designed to outlaw homosexuality which encourage it; injunctions to parents to bring forth children for the greater good of the community which are followed by a drop in the birth rate; and attempts to limit childbirth (for the greater good...) which lead to an exponential increase in live births.

The major lesson we can draw from all this is that there is no simple way to understand the social organization of sexuality. Instead of seeing sexuality as a unified whole, we have to recognize that there are various forms of sexuality, that there are in fact many sexualities: class sexualities and gendered sexualities, racially specific sexualities and sexualities of struggle and choice. The historian of sexuality must try to understand these, both in their distinctiveness and in their complex interactions.

History and the present

This brings me to the final theme I want to pursue: the implications of the new sexual history for our understanding of the historic present. As I suggested earlier, a major stimulus to the study of our sexual pasts has come from preoccupations that were clearly located in the present. Feminist history is, for example, by definition a history that has current political concerns at its heart. Thus a book produced by the London Feminist History Group, called *The Sexual Dynamics of History*, observes that 'Our link with contemporary political struggles gives our work as historians a special edge, because our analysis is constantly being reworked and developed' (London Feminist History Group, 1983, p. 1).

At the very least this implies that the questions that are asked of the past are prompted by the concerns of the present. Sometimes these questions can lead to the exploration of new or neglected themes. A good example here is the interest in the history and politics of male violence against women, whose starting point is very much recent experience (for instance, Cameron and Frazer, 1987; Theweleit, 1987, 1990). Sometimes the result is a re-examination of well-worn but controversial subjects in new ways. For example, Boswell's (1980) work on attitudes to homosexuality in the early Christian church is a work of great (traditional) scholarship, but is clearly also part of a fierce debate within both the Roman Catholic Church and the gay community about the real implications of the Christian tradition's attitudes towards homosexuality.

But there is something more at stake than simply finding new or better ways of addressing the past. Sexuality is a highly contentious issue in contemporary society, and at the centre of some highly influential political programmes. I have mentioned feminism and lesbian and gay politics. Perhaps even more important today are the projects of moral regeneration that lie close to the centre of the politics of the New Right in some at least of its manifestations. In the resulting political struggles around sexuality the past is freely raided for its contemporary relevance – as, for example, in the capture by the Thatcher government in Britain of the idea of Victorian values (Walvin, 1987; Weeks, 1989). The new sexual history is important in so far as it contributes to these debates, and to the extent that it illuminates the present.

I do not mean by this that historians should only study the recent past, or concentrate on issues that are of current concern. But at the very least, if the perspectives I have described on the historical construction of sexuality have any merit, the new sexual history should be able to under-mine the certainty with which the past is called in to redress the diffi-culties of the present. As we have seen, sensitive studies of sexual behaviour in other cultures (e.g. Caplan, 1987), or at other times within our own, serve to problematize the whole idea of a single history. Instead they direct our attention to the variety of forces and practices that shape sexual categories.

The historic present is a product of many histories, some of very ancient lineage, some very recent. What we can use the new sexual history for is to question the taken-for-granted, challenge our own cultur-ally specific preoccupations, and to try to see whether what we assume is natural is not in fact social and historical. At the same time, we can explore the continuities and the discontinuities of our sexual histories.

Let's take as an example the ways in which our culture is responding to a crisis that is both personal and social, medical and moral, and also highly political – that relating to AIDS. This is a new problem in that it is a new, or at least newly discovered, disease or group of diseases. It is also a phenomenon that is very closely connected with sexuality, both because it can be sexually transmitted and because, at least in the west, the people most affected so far have been gay men.

What is most striking is the degree to which, in reacting to AIDS, people call on pre-existing discourses and shape them to the current crisis. As Frank Mort (1987) has shown, for example, there is a substan-tial medico-moral tradition, going back at least to the early nineteenth century, linking beliefs about health and disease to notions of moral and immoral sex, 'dangerous sexualities'. The linkage of AIDS with homo-sexual lifestyles evokes a rich tradition that sees homosexuality as itself a disease (Weeks, 1977). Even the question of whether people with AIDS should be segregated and confined refers back to a heated debate in the late nineteenth century about whether the most effective means of con-trolling the spread of syphilis was by compulsorily testing and confining prostitutes (Walkowitz, 1980).

These are political and moral debates where more is at stake than mere historical accuracy. But it so happens that all the issues I have just referred to have been the object of investigation by the new sexual historians, who have effectively demonstrated the social conditions for the emergence of these discourses. It is too much to hope, perhaps, that their work would dispel illusions and prejudices. But at the very least it should force us to pause and ask about the conditions which are shaping our interventions. What their work underlines above all is the living nature of the past – and the historical nature of the present.

Some conclusions

To conclude, I want to offer just three brief observations. First, I want to underline my belief that the new sexual history has fundamentally transformed the way we interpret the sexual past and present. It is no longer possible to see sex as caught in the toils of nature, outside the bounds of history. It is a legitimate subject for historical investigation.

Having said that, it is worth stressing that the particular theoretical position I have adopted on the 'social construction of sexuality', while influential, is by no means dominant. As Carole Vance put it in the late 1980s, 'Social construction theory may be the new orthodoxy in feminist, progressive, and lesbian and gay history circles, but it has made a minimal impact on mainstream authorities and literatures in sexology and biomedicine' (Vance, 1989, p. 29). What this means in practice is that historians have been much more willing to recognize that homosexuality is 'socially constructed' than to examine the historical evolution of heterosexuality. A latent naturalism often survives in even the most advanced history. To my mind the great advantage of the deconstructionist approach outlined here is that it forces us to think beyond the boundaries of existing categories and to explore their historical production.

The second observation I want to make is that deconstruction should also imply reconstruction. There is no point in fragmenting the past into a series of disparate histories unless we deploy them for some purpose. What I have suggested is that an important outcome of the new sexual history is that it contributes to our understanding of the present. Increasingly we can see the present not as the culmination of an unproblematic past but as itself historical: a complex series of interlocking histories whose interactions have to be reconstructed, not assumed.

Finally, I want to suggest that the new sexual history may have a valuable political and ethical outcome. In demonstrating the sexual and moral diversity of the past it may lead us to be a little more accepting of the diversity of the present. Perhaps that is why writing about sex can still be dangerous.

References

Altman, D., Vance, C., Vicinus, M. and Weeks, J., (eds) (1989) *Which Homosexuality?* (London: GMP).

Amos, V. and Parmar P. (1984) 'Challenging Imperial Feminism', *Feminist Review*, No. 17, July 1984.
Boswell, J. (1980) *Christianity, Social Tolerance and Homosexuality* (University of Chicago Press).
Boswell, J. (1983) 'Revolutions, Universals, Categories', *Salmagundi*, No. 58/59.
Bouhdiba, A. (1985) *Sexuality in Islam* (London: Routledge & Kegan Paul).
Bray, A. (1982) *Homosexuality in Renaissance England* (London: GMP).
Cameron, D. and Frazer, E. (1987) *The Lust to Kill* (Cambridge: Polity Press).
Caplan, P. (1987) *The Cultural Construction of Sexuality* (London: Tavistock).
Coveney, L. Jackson, M., Jeffreys, S., Kat, L. and Mahoney, P. (1984) *The Sexuality Papers* (London: Hutchinson).
Coward, R. (1983) *Patriarchal Precedents* (London: Routledge & Kegan Paul).
Coward, R. (1984) *Female Desire* (London: Paladin).
Davidoff, L. (1983) 'Class and Gender in Victorian England', in Newton et al. (1983).
Davidoff, L. and Hall, C. (1987) *Family Fortunes* (London: Hutchinson).
Dworkin, A. (1987) *Intercourse* (London: Arrow).
Foucault, M. (1979) *History of Sexuality: Vol. 1, An Introduction* (London: Allen Lane).
Foucault, M. (1987) *History of Sexuality: Vol. 2, The Use of Pleasure* (London: Viking).
Foucault, M. (1987) *History of Sexuality: Vol. 3, Care of the Self* (London: Viking).
Franklin, S. and Stacey, J. (1988) 'Dyketactics in Difficult Times. A Review of the "Homosexuality, Which Homosexuality?" Conference', *Feminist Review*, No. 29, Summer.
Freedman, E. B. Gelpi, B. C., Johnson, S. L. and Weston, K. M. (eds) (1985) *The Lesbian Issue* (University of Chicago Press).
Gagnon, J. and Simon, W. (1974) *Sexual Conduct* (London: Hutchinson).
Gallagher, C. and Laqueur, T. (eds) (1987) *The Making of the Modern Body* (University of California Press).
Gay, P. (1984) *The Bourgeois Experience: Vol. 1, Education of the Senses* (Oxford University Press).
Gay, P. (1986) *The Bourgeois Experience: Vol. 2, The Tender Passion* (Oxford University Press).
Katz, J. (1976) *Gay American History* (New York: Thomas Crowell).
Laqueur, T. (1987) 'Orgasm, Generation, and the Politics of Reproductive Biology', in Gallagher and Laqueur (1987).
London Feminist History Group (1983) *The Sexual Dynamics of History* (London: Pluto).
McIntosh, M. (1968) 'The Homosexual Role', in Plummer (1981).
Malinowski, B. (1963) *Sex, Culture and Myth* (London: Hart-Davis).
Marcus, S. (1987) *The Other Victorians* (London: Weidenfeld & Nicolson).
Mort, F. (1987) *Dangerous Sexualities* (London: Routledge & Kegan Paul).
Newton, J. L., Walkowitz, J. R. and Ryan, M. P. (eds) (1983) *Sex and Class in Women's History* (London: Routledge & Kegan Paul).
Padgug, R. A. (1979) 'Sexual Matters', *Radical History Review*, No. 20, Spring/ Summer.
Petchesky, R. P. (1986) *Abortion and Women's Choice* (London: Verso).

Plummer, K. (1975) *Sexual Stigma* (London: Routledge & Kegan Paul).

Plummer, K. (ed.) (1981) *The Making of the Modern Homosexual* (London: Hutchinson).

Plummer, K. (1984) 'Sexual Diversity', in K. Howells (ed.) *Sexual Diversity* (Oxford: Basil Blackwell).

Rich, A. (1984) 'Compulsory Heterosexuality and Lesbian Experience', in Snitow et al. (1984).

Rubin, G. (1984) 'Thinking Sex', in Vance (1984).

Smith-Rosenberg, C. (1975) 'The Female World of Love and Ritual', in Smith-Rosenberg (1986).

Smith-Rosenberg, C. (1986) *Disorderly Conduct* (Oxford University Press).

Snitow, A., Stansell, C. and Thompson, S. (eds) (1984) *Desire. The Politics of Sexuality* (London: Virago).

Stone, L. (1977) *The Family, Sex and Marriage* (London: Weidenfeld & Nicolson).

Taylor, B. (1983) *Eve and the New Jerusalem* (London: Virago).

Theweleit, K. (1987, 1990) *Male Fantasies*, vols 1 and 2 (Cambridge: Polity Press).

Vance, C. (ed.) (1984) *Pleasure and Danger* (London: Routledge & Kegan Paul).

Vance, C. 'Social Construction Theory', in Altman, et al. (1989).

Walkowitz, J. (1980) *Prostitution and Victorian Society* (Oxford University Press).

Walvin, J. (1987) *Victorian Values* (London: André Deutsch).

Weeks, J. (1977) *Coming Out* (London: Quartet).

Weeks, J. (1985) *Sexuality and its Discontents* (London: Routledge & Kegan Paul).

Weeks, J. (1986) *Sexuality* (London: Tavistock).

Weeks, J. (1989) *Sex, Politics and Society* (2nd edn) (London: Routledge & Kegan Paul).

7

AIDS and the Regulation of Sexuality

Introduction

The HIV/AIDS epidemic is framed, if not burdened, by many histories. There are histories of past epidemics and diseases, including sexually transmitted diseases; histories of scientific investigation, and of medicine and social hygiene; histories of the various groups affected by HIV and AIDS: of homosexuals, of drug users, of the poor and racially disadvantaged in the urban centres of western nations, and of the poor and exploited in the developing world; and there are histories of social policy and of welfare policies, or of their absence, which can help us to understand the various phases of the political and governmental response to HIV and AIDS. AIDS is already a deeply historicized phenomenon.[1]

But at the centre of any attempt to understand the response to the epidemic in the west must be the history (or rather histories) of sexuality. At the most basic level this is because sexual intercourse is one of the most efficient means of transmission of the virus, and changing patterns of sexual interaction help explain its rapid spread from the late 1970s. There is, however, a more profound reason why we need to situate HIV and AIDS in a history of sexuality. AIDS was identified at a particular moment in that history, when values and behaviour were in a period of unprecedented flux, and when sex-related issues came close to the top of the political agenda.

The syndrome was first identified in a highly sexualized community, the gay community, which was the focus of heated controversy as well as (or perhaps because of) an unparalleled growth and public presence. It was also a period when to an extraordinary degree sexuality had become a major element in political debate and mobilization. Not surprisingly, therefore, AIDS became for many a potent symbol for all that had changed, or threatened to change. Change was not, of course, confined to sexuality, but changes in sexual behaviour seemed to condense all the other changes (in personal behaviour, in the changing demographic make-up of western populations, in forms of social regulation and in the changing relationship between First and Third Worlds) that were transforming western, and world, culture by the early 1980s. The AIDS crisis emerged at a crucial moment of cultural uncertainty, particularly with regard to sexuality, and the initial reaction to the epidemic, as well as the subsequent response at all levels, from popular fear and panic to national and international intervention, has been indelibly shaped by that fact.[2]

This chapter therefore, explores the responses to HIV and AIDS through an exploration of our current sexual preoccupations. I begin with an account of key tendencies in what I shall call the 'new history of sexuality', which can contribute to our understanding of the impact of the epidemic. Then I trace in more detail the changing patterns of the social organization and regulation of sexuality in Britain which helped shape the initial, and continuing, reaction to the crisis. Attitudes towards homosexuality were central to the debates over the appropriate forms of regulation. The gay community in turn bore the brunt of the early 'moral panic' (a contested but to my mind still valuable concept, to which I shall return) and which at the end of the first decade of the crisis still faced the main burden of the epidemic. Responses to homosexuality, then, are necessarily central to the discussion. Finally, I attempt an assessment of the complexity of social responses to HIV and AIDS (both as a syndrome of diseases, and as a symbolic presence) in our deeply historicized present.

AIDS and the new history of sexuality

Since the 1960s there has been a revolution in the historical understanding of sexuality. From being (like gender) scarcely a spectral presence in social history, sexuality has increasingly been seen as a key element for understanding the social dynamics of modern society. At the centre of the new history is a recognition that sexuality is far from being the purely 'natural' phenomenon which earlier historians took for granted, and which largely shaped their avoidance of the subject. If sexuality is a constant, why bother to study it?

We now see, on the contrary, that far from being outside of history, 'sexuality', as the social organization of sexual relations, is a product of many histories, from the *longue durée* of population changes and shifts in the economic and social structure of modern society, to the shorter-term interventions of religious leaders, 'moral entrepreneurs', legislators and sexual activists and minorities. 'Sexuality' in an inadequate but now familiar, if controversial, term is 'socially constructed'.[3]

We can draw from this now substantial body of work three major themes which are central to any attempt to understand the impact of AIDS: the symbolic centrality of sexuality in modern society; the historical nature of sexual, like other social, identities; and the complexity of regimes of sexual regulation. Before deploying these themes for a more detailed analysis, I want to indicate briefly the general ways in which they can illuminate the crisis around HIV and AIDS.

First of all, let us take the symbolic centrality of sexuality. Sexuality has been at the heart of social discourse for a very long time. The regulation of sexual behaviour was central to the institutionalization of Christianity, and hence to the formation of what we know as European civilization. Within the period we now think of as 'modernity', since roughly the eighteenth century, sexual behaviour has been a besetting preoccupation in all the crises and initiatives of industrialization and 'modernization'. This is because sexuality, far from being the most natural thing about us, is in many ways the most socialized, the most susceptible to social organization. To put it another way, the terrain of sexuality is like a conductor of currents, whose origins lie elsewhere, but whose battleground is sexual belief and behaviour. Sexuality, as Michel Foucault put it, has been assigned so great a significance in our culture because it has become the point of entry both to the lives of individuals and to the life, wellbeing and welfare of the population as a whole. But it is also, of course, the focus of fantasy, individual and social, and of judgements about what is right or wrong, moral or immoral.[4]

It is not surprising, then, that the emergence of a sex-related disease, or set of diseases, in the early 1980s became the focus of social anxieties, fears and panics, just as the syphilis epidemic produced significant social, and symbolic, effects in the nineteenth century.[5] The origins of the sense of uncertainty, amounting in many people's minds to a generalized crisis of western culture, may have been complex and diverse, but the emergence of AIDS provided a convenient focus, a symbolic site, for articulating the new social imaginary.

The question of identity was central to what for the sake of convenience I am calling a crisis around sexuality. Here the work of the new history has been perhaps most original and innovatory. What it has sought to demonstrate is that the socio-sexual identities (such as 'heterosexual' or 'homosexual') that we now take for granted as so natural and inevitable are in fact historical constructs, and fairly recent constructs at that.[6] To be more specific, since at least the nineteenth century, and possibly earlier – the debate is still open – western culture has become increasingly concerned with identifying what you do with what you are, with establishing object choice as the key to our sexual natures. In a phrase, heterosexuality and homosexuality may always have existed (if we take those terms to apply to general sexual activity), but 'homosexuals' and 'heterosexuals' have not.

The historicization of sexual identities helps us to understand some of the most important features of the initial reaction to the AIDS epidemic. The existence of the 'homosexual' as a generally execrated category, the description of a particular type of person, the 'other' whose very presence served to define what is normal in the rest of the population, was central to the early definition of AIDS as a homosexual disease, the 'gay plague'. If homosexuality is the exclusive characteristic of the 'deviant', then necessarily the disease must have something to do with the lifestyle of homosexuals. From this stemmed the disastrous reluctance of many early scientists to come to terms with heterosexual transmission, and the dimensions of the heterosexual epidemic, especially in Africa.

This brings us to the third lesson we can draw from the new history, concerning the complex patterns of regulating sexuality. Two key elements stand out: the formal regulation of sexual behaviour through church and state; and the less formal, but frequently closely connected, forms of regulation of sexuality through the discourses of medicine, sexology, 'public health' and social hygiene. The important point here is that these are rarely articulated together in a neat fit: more often than not they are in contradiction with one another, and often are torn by self-contradictions. Different agents of the state (the bureaucracy and the political leadership, central and local bodies) take different views, have different priorities and strategies. Churches have their own moral agenda, and intervene with variable force and effect. The medical establishment might promote a health policy which is sharply at odds with political priorities. All these tensions were manifest in the response to the new health crisis.

At the same time, a deep historical awareness of the shaping roles of the state, religion, science and medicine in sustaining a model of homosexuality as deviant and 'other' helped to determine the early reaction of people with AIDS, and gay activists, to the epidemic. There was a deep-rooted fear that having only recently escaped from the opprobrious definitions of homosexuality (male homosexuals had only recently been partially decriminalized, the 'medical model' of homosexuality was still prevalent) AIDS could easily lead to the remedicalization, and possibly recriminalization, of homosexuality.[7]

All these factors suggest the complex ways in which sexuality is socially organized. Our sense of ourselves, and our place in the world, are shaped at the intersection of a series of often conflicting discourses: religious, legal, medical, educational, psychological, sexological, communal, and so on. Our subjectivities and identities are negotiated through the network of meanings and potentialities these offer. They entangle us, shaping our sense of what we are and can become. But the very complexity of meanings that exist in the contemporary world suggests that we are not trapped within them; on the contrary, they provide the space for constant renegotiations and redefinitions.

The period since the 1960s has seen rapid changes in social and cultural life,[8] and a closely related proliferation of new discourses around sexuality, reshaping and reordering the possibilities for living our sexual lives. AIDS appeared in the midst of a cacophony of debate, experimentation and consequent reaction concerning sexuality. Responses to it were, not surprisingly, complex. In turn, the epidemic has initiated new discourses (for example, concerning 'safer sex', health, and social regulation) which are likely to shape powerfully the ways in which we think and live sexuality for the foreseeable future. The response to AIDS casts a strong searchlight on the sexual preoccupations of our time. It also throws a long shadow on what is to come.

The regulation of sexuality

The key to understanding the impact of the AIDS crisis lies in recognizing that it emerged in the midst of what can best be described as an 'unfinished revolution' in attitudes towards, and in the regulation of, sexuality, and especially homosexuality. On the one hand there has been a striking double-shift in attitudes over the past generation. This has involved both a liberalization of attitudes towards issues such as marriage and divorce, premarital sex, birth control and abortion, and towards homosexuality; and an apparent secularization of belief systems, with the decline of traditional, usually Christian-based, absolutist standards, and the emergence of more pragmatic belief systems. The development from the early 1970s of a vigorously open and diverse lesbian and gay community is one index of the change, though far from being the only one.[9]

But these shifts have been accompanied by a high degree of moral confusion (where attitudes and beliefs have frequently lagged behind behavioural changes). Uncertainty and confusion, in turn, provided the elements for a moral mobilization around sexual issues, which has given sexuality a new political salience. This is most dramatically illustrated by the emergence since the 1970s of a new conservatism, often allied –

though less so in Britain than elsewhere – to fundamentalist religion, which has focused a great deal of energy on key moral issues: abortion, above all, especially in the USA, but also such themes as sex education and, most obviously in relation to AIDS, the claims of lesbian and gay politics. AIDS emerged as a focus of social concern at precisely the moment in the early 1980s when these new political forces were attempting to achieve a new cultural hegemony in North America and Britain especially.[10]

One way into the understanding of the complex forces at work is through the shifting patterns in the regulation of sexuality during this period. The late 1960s had witnessed the most striking changes in the legal framework of sexuality for almost a hundred years. Between 1967 and 1970 there was significant new legislation on abortion, homosexuality, stage censorship and divorce. Together with earlier changes (such as changes to the laws on obscene publications) these constituted what became known as 'permissiveness'.[11]

Behind the legal changes was a collapse of a whole pattern of regulating sexuality, enshrined in the assumption that the law had a right and a duty to state what was right and wrong in both public and private life. In place of a legal absolutism that was widely perceived as being incapable of responding appropriately to a more open and pluralistic culture, a new strategy of regulation emerged, most clearly articulated in one of the key statements of the period, the 'Wolfenden Report' of 1957.[12]

The report, and the raft of legislation that attempted to enact its implications, based its proposals on a clear distinction: between private morality and public decency. The role of the state, it declared, was not to impose a particular pattern of private morals; that was the role of the churches and of individual conscience. The law's role was to uphold acceptable standards of public order and decency.

The legislation of the 1960s was cautious and modest in the actual changes it sought to make. So, for example, the Abortion Act of 1967 did not allow abortion on demand; there was no divorce by consent; and, most significantly, homosexuality was not fully legalized, nor was it in any real sense legitimized. There was no attempt to create new rights, or positively to assert the values of different sexual lifestyles. The declared aim, rather, was to find a more effective way of regulating sexual behaviour than the draconian (and largely ineffective) methods of the old laws had allowed.[13]

So the Wolfenden strategy did not herald any espousal of 'sexual liberation'; its philosophy was well in the tradition of English liberalism, and its policy implications were modest and pragmatic. That was not, however, how it was seen by many, either at the time, or subsequently. For the upholders of legal absolutism and for the morally conservative the approach represented an abandonment of moral standards in favour of moral relativism. During the subsequent decades the legislative revolution of the 1960s became for many the symbol of all that had gone wrong in 'the sixties', the decade of supposed sexual liberation and moral collapse. As the conservative commentator, Ronald Butt, put it, 'In some matters, a charter of individual rights was granted which unleashed an unprecedented attack on old commonly held standards of personal behaviour and responsibility.'[14]

But for some of the radical forces that emerged from the late 1960s, around feminism and gay liberation, the reforms were a symbol also, but this time of a failed liberalism, too little, too late. The British gay movement that emerged in 1970 grew in the space that law reform had helped shape. The new generation of lesbian and gay activists acted *as if* they had been given new rights by law reform. But the spirit of the new radicalism was distinctly different from that of the Wolfenden strategy. By advocating 'coming out', that is declaring one's gayness, it sought to dissolve the privacy of sexual taste, to make sexuality a public issue. Through its militancy and the carnivalesque way in which it demonstrated its new sense of collective consciousness it attempted to break the taboos about public displays of homosexual love and affection.[15]

In other words, the Wolfenden approach, with its rationalistic assumptions about an acceptable distinction between public and private spheres, satisfied neither of the polarized sexual political forces that emerged vocally in the 1970s. For the radicals, it had not gone far enough; for the right, which was becoming politically dominant, especially after the election of the Thatcher government in 1979, it had gone too far. By the end of the 1970s and the beginning of the 1980s, there were clear signs that the Wolfenden strategy itself was losing its purchase on debate, as the political climate shifted.[16]

Behind this was a wider political and cultural crisis, for which the emergence of what Stuart Hall has called the 'authoritarian populism' of the Thatcher governments offered an apparent solution (at least, perhaps, to that section of the British electorate which voted for the Thatcher-led Conservative Party in 1979, 1983 and 1987).[17] Crucially, alongside its commitments to 'a strong state and a free economy' was a moral project, summed up polemically in Mrs Thatcher's potent espousal of a return to 'Victorian values'.[18]

It is important to recognize that this moral project was never during the 1980s pursued with the same enthusiasm as the economic revolution close to Mrs Thatcher's heart, and the impact of Thatcherism on moral attitudes, and even sexual regulation, was in the end limited (see chapter 8 below).[19] Nevertheless, it is relevant to the understanding of the initial impact of, and response to, AIDS that such a forceful exponent of opposition to 'the sexual revolution' was in power in Britain during the early years of the AIDS epidemic. This was a decade when political issues were persistently moralized, and moral issues were ever in danger of becoming political issues, and that profoundly defined the parameters of the response to AIDS. Not least, AIDS raised difficult questions about the relationship between private behaviour and public policy in the most sensitive and controversial area of all, that of sexual behaviour.

The stress on family values, though somewhat erratically pursued, as some of Mrs Thatcher's ideological friends frequently complained, was perhaps the major moral response to 'permissiveness' during the period. Its inevitable accompaniment was a challenge to those who had most fervently sought to undermine the hegemony of the family, and of these homosexuality represented the most potent symbol.

Homosexuality, particularly as represented by the militancy of lesbian and gay politics, represented, in Anna Marie Smith's powerful term, an overflowing of 'radical difference', a challenge to the normality and inevitability of orthodox family life.[20] This not only threatened (at least in New Right discourse, if not elsewhere) the hierarchy of difference between men and women, adults and children represented by the traditional model of the family, but also made public what was best confined to the decency of the private sphere.

It was an historic accident that HIV disease first manifested itself in the gay populations of the east and west coasts of the United States, and subsequently in similar populations throughout the west. But that chance shaped, and has continued to form, the social and cultural response to AIDS. Originally officially designated by their association with the gay community ('gay cancer', GRID or Gay Related Immune Deficiency), and easily encapsulated in tabloid headlines as the 'gay plague', HIV and AIDS were immediately classified as the diseases of the diseased, caused by, and revealing, the problems inherent in a particular way of life: 'promiscuity', 'fast-lane' lifestyles, irresponsibility, and all the other terms deployed against what by the early 1980s was being identified as a clamant, but unpopular, minority.[21]

The lesbian and gay community in Britain never achieved the public presence or sophistication of the American, or therefore the notoriety. It had grown significantly during the 1970s, largely through the stimulus of the radical gay liberation movement which was launched in 1970, in large part under American influence. During the subsequent decade the movement had developed rapidly, absorbing and transforming the older, more reformist, homophile groupings, and in turn stimulating an unprecedented growth of homosexual organizations, social facilities, publications, and a new self-confidence and sense of identity amongst lesbians and gay men.[22]

But by the early 1980s the initial political impetus had exhausted itself. The gay liberation movement itself had fragmented in the early 1970s, and the various militant groupings it had given rise to were themselves in crisis by the early 1980s. Even *Gay News*, which had been central to the identification and articulation of a sense of common experience in the 1970s, entered a terminal crisis in the early 1980s, and had effectively disappeared by 1983.[23] There was a felt mood of vulnerability in the British gay community as policies swung dramatically to the right under Margaret Thatcher. The close ties with the American gay scene, stimulated by a greater ease of transatlantic travel, fed the sense of apprehension. The various anti-gay campaigns of the late 1970s in the USA, most famously the crusade of Anita Bryant to save America from sodomy,[24] had been carefully watched in the UK, and there was a strong belief amongst many activists that the same would follow in Britain.

Yet this sense of vulnerability, and fear of a backlash against the gains of the 1970s, must not lead us to ignore the real strengths of the lesbian and gay communities by the early 1980s. There was a burgeoning commercial subculture, for men at least, which constantly expanded the possibilities for social and sexual interaction. The demise of broad-based campaigning organizations did not mean that a lesbian and gay politics had disappeared. On the contrary, the subsequent decade, in part despite, in part because of, AIDS, saw a new political energy: lesbians active in the women's movement; openly lesbian and gay activists in the major political parties, especially the Labour Party; the emergence of distinctive campaigns for lesbian and gay rights in various local government areas, especially in London, Manchester and other major cities; and a continued development of gay-related information and support services, such as London Gay Switchboard (subsequently Lesbian and Gay Switchboard), with similar organizations throughout the country. Moreover, the example of the gay movement stimulated a proliferation of alternative radical sexual identities, around paedophilia, sado-masochism, transvestism and the like, giving rise to what became known as a radical 'sexual fringe'.[25]

Of course, there was a paradox inherent in this expansion. The ties of community, at least amongst gay men, facilitated the rapid spread of HIV in the gay community. Sex, and a greater freedom in the pursuit of sexual diversity and choice, were bonds that welded the male community together, but that inevitably provided a vector for the rapid spread of disease. On the other hand, the bonds constructed and reaffirmed through a new ease with sexuality also made possible the emergence of a new discourse of 'safer sex', and provided the nexus of friendships and personal ties that was to be a vital factor in the community response to the developing health crisis.[26]

Inevitably, it was the sexuality of the male gay community, and the radical alternative it implied to the traditional values, 'the old virtues of discipline and self-restraint' endorsed by Mrs Thatcher,[27] which became the focus of the early fears aroused by AIDS. But beyond this, as I have already tried to indicate, were a wider set of fears about cultural change that the links between the gay revolution and HIV disease came to symbolize. At the heart of these fears, I would argue, was the challenge posed by diversity.

AIDS, as a syndrome of diseases that pre-eminently during the 1980s affected marginal and marginalized people – male homosexuals, drug users, the poor and black people of American cities, men and women of the Third World – became a symbol of diversity, of the problems posed by cultural and sexual change. AIDS was both global in its impact and implications, and local in its manifestations and effects. It could be represented as the harbinger of that 'sense of an ending' which was at the centre of the new cultural conservatism. It unsettled the enlightenment faith in the triumph of science, and reason. But it also demanded new resources at a time when conservative governments throughout the west were intent on reducing the role of public provision. And it required an empathetic understanding of the implications of cultural pluralism in a climate which was rife with the quest for new absolutes.[28] AIDS, as Nelkin et al. have argued, 'demonstrates how much we as a "culture" struggle and negotiate about appropriate processes to deal with social change, especially in its radical forms'.[29]

The unprecedented nature of the problems posed by the disease as it spread in Britain in the 1980s, combined with the peculiarly uncertain response evoked by the needs of the gay community, helped determine the contours of the immediate response to the crisis. This has been widely characterized as one of 'moral panic', though this description has also been sharply criticized.[30]

The setting of limits, the drawing of boundaries, is precisely one of the functions of the classic elements of 'moral panics', and we can, I believe, still use this concept, with caution, as a helpful heuristic device to explore the deeper currents which shaped the developing HIV/AIDS crisis. The concept was developed to describe the response to the problem of youth in the 1960s, and has been used in a variety of contexts since. Classically, moral panics focus on a condition, person or group of persons who become defined as a threat to accepted social values and assumptions. They tend to develop in situations of confusion and ambiguity, in periods when the boundaries between what are seen as acceptable and unacceptable behaviour become blurred, and need redefinition. Over the past generation there has been an apparently endless series of such panics, many of them around moral and sexual issues: areas, clearly, where boundaries are uncertain, where anxieties about the parameters of legitimate behaviour are most acute. They reveal above all an uncertainty about sexual beliefs, which made it possible to mobilize anxieties and promote symbolic solutions.

In the case of AIDS we can detect several key features. There was, first of all, the characteristic stereotyping of the main actors as peculiar types of monster, leading in turn to an escalating level of fear and perceived threat. The response to the perceived threat from the tabloid press was particularly important here between 1983 and 1986, in shaping the image of the 'gay plague'.[31] This in turn led to the 'manning of the barricades' by the moral entrepreneurs, and the seeking out of largely symbolic solutions: quarantine, compulsory blood testing, immigration controls.[32] More widely there were manifestations of what Susan Sontag has called 'practices of decontamination',[33] against lesbians who at this stage did not seem vulnerable to HIV, as well as gay men who were: restaurants refused to serve gay customers, gay waiters were sacked, dentists refused to examine the teeth of homosexuals, technicians refused to test the blood of people suspected of having AIDS, paramedics fumigated their ambulances, hospitals adopted barrier nursing, rubbish collectors wore masks while collecting garbage, prison officers refused to move prisoners, backstage staff in theatres refused to work with gay actors, distinguished pathologists refused to examine bodies, and undertakers refused to bury them.[34]

These were not universal experiences: there was altruism, self-sacrifice and empathy as well. But all these things happened, to people vulnerable to a devastating and life-threatening disease: and the vast majority of these people were homosexual. It is difficult to avoid seeing such manifestations as anything but panic-driven. The real plague, as the *Guardian* famously put it, was panic.[35]

Of course, AIDS-related illnesses in the early 1980s were mysterious; fear was legitimate. It was not simply dreamt up by the press. There was a general sense of uncertainty, which shaped the early responses of the medical profession as well as politicians. Moreover, to describe these happenings as simply manifestations of a moral panic does not do justice to the complexity of what was happening, or to the prolonged nature of some of the responses. It is perhaps better to see what happened as a series of panics, occasioned by particular events or new information or rumours, unified through a continuing discourse of hostility towards homosexuality (and the pursuit of circulation). Moral panic theory, moreover, does not explain why these social flurries of anxiety occur: they simply draw our attention to certain recurring phenomena, providing a template for description rather than a full analysis. Explanations of the AIDS panic must be found in all the other factors we have discussed.

Nevertheless, with all these qualifications, there is still some merit in using the term 'moral panic' as a way of describing the first major public stage of the response to AIDS, between roughly 1983 and 1986, not least because a perception of how the public was reacting determined the responses both of the community most affected, and of the government.

The complexity of social responses

My argument is that initial reactions to AIDS were structured by a complex history, which in turn produced a complex set of responses. To illustrate this I want, first of all, to look again at the experiences of the gay community. Identities in the contemporary world, it may be argued, are the means by which we negotiate the hazards of everyday life, and assert our sense of belonging.[36] They are rooted in history, or at least 'History' is evoked, but their effectiveness depends on their strategic placing in a complex play of power relations. The response to the new health crisis from the gay community provides a classic example of this. In particular, the early voluntary response to AIDS was able to draw on the sense of a common identity that had developed in the 1970s in order to operate in a situation where national government responses were absent, and where hostility towards the community was increasing. The Terrence Higgins Trust, which emerged in 1983 as the first British voluntary grouping, drew on a wealth of gay organizing and campaigning experience, and this was crucially important. But the emergence of the dozens of other voluntary bodies that followed owed as much to the sense of identity provided by the ties and networks of the community as a whole as to any previous activist experience. Individuals were confirming their sense of common identity through involvement in the fight against HIV and AIDS. At the same time, many who were HIV positive or had been diagnosed with AIDS were affirming new identities, as 'Body Positive' or 'People with AIDS' (see chapter 10, below).[37]

This sense of identity and belonging was crucial to the other major development within the gay community in the early 1980s, the adoption of a regime of what became known as 'safer sex'. It has been suggested that it was precisely the development of a resilient sense of self-esteem that was the 'sine qua non of safer sex education', and this has been confirmed by detailed studies.[38] The idea of safer sex had emerged in the early years of the American epidemic, and became central to the initial work of voluntary bodies and to the coverage of the issue in the gay press. There were clear signs of the success of safer-sex campaigns by the mid-1980s, with a substantial drop in the incidence of sexually transmitted diseases amongst gay men. The detailed reasons for this are unclear, and there were clear variations in the sexual behaviour of gay men. It seemed likely that it was the urban gay man who was most likely to adopt explicit safer-sex guidelines, with self-identification as part of the gay community as a crucial factor, and a sense of equality between partners as perhaps a vital element.[39]

The response of the gay community, and the major voluntary effort it sustained, was an expression of concern and involvement. It was also necessary in the absence of an appropriate official response until 1986. There is now well-documented evidence for the gradual creation of a 'policy community' around the health crisis in the years running up to the adoption of an official government strategy in late 1986, which drew on the expertise of leading figures in genito-urinary medicine, public health officials and activists largely drawn from the gay community. The outlines of what was to become the government response – an emphasis, in the absence of a likely 'cure', on prevention and health education – emerged, building on a much older tradition of public health policy which had its origins in the responses to diseases such as typhoid and cholera in the early days of industrialization and urbanization.[40]

On the other hand, it is difficult not to conclude that the association of AIDS with homosexuality, and to a lesser extent with other forms of social marginality, with all the historical baggage which these factors brought, determined governmental responses throughout the 1980s, particularly in the light of the moral panic in the early years. There was virtually no government response until 1984, when it intervened to secure the blood supply from contamination. It was 1986 before the first major initiative was taken directly by the government, which included the powers to detain people who were highly infectious (though these powers were rarely if ever used). Half of the fifty-nine parliamentary questions on AIDS in 1984–5 dealt with the blood supply, followed by drugs.[41] It is not to minimize the threat of HIV transmission from these sources to note the extraordinary disparity between the actual problem, amongst homosexual men, and the political priorities this suggests. It was to be November 1986 before there was a major House of Commons debate on the subject, four years after the first British deaths.

Two points need to be made. The first is that the government was operating in a situation that was widely perceived to be a gay crisis, at a time when as a result homosexuality was becoming deeply unpopular. The surveys of sexual attitudes during the 1980s are clear on this. The British Social Attitudes Survey for 1987 found that public opinion had become marginally less discriminatory towards homosexuality since 1983, with a greater acceptance also that lesbians and gay men should not be banned from certain professions. But when asked if they approved of 'homosexual relationships', there was evidence of a significant increase in hostility. In 1983, 62 per cent had censured such relations: in 1985, 69 per cent: and in 1987, 74 per cent. There was countervailing evidence also. A 1988 Gallup Poll for the *Sunday Telegraph*, whilst reporting that 60 per cent of those sampled believed that homosexuality was not an acceptable lifestyle, observed that 50 per cent of those under twenty-five were accepting.[42] It is also worth noting that all these surveys of opinion reported increased disapproval of extra-marital sexual relations, suggesting that what was happening was not only a reaction against homosexuality, but a reassertion of more conventional family values amongst significant sections of the population. Nevertheless, it is clear that AIDS was affecting the acceptability of homosexuality, and there was no great public support for more liberal policies towards lesbians and gays.

The second point that needs underlining is that the Thatcher government was highly sensitive to morally conservative currents of opinion. Even as the government was formulating a more considered policy towards the AIDS crisis in late 1986, the Secretary of State for Education was engaged in a complex campaign to prevent schools from providing positive images of homosexuality in response to conservative fears that left-wing local authorities were promoting homosexuality 'on the rates'. And this policy orientation was central to the government's strongest intervention on the subject during the 1980s: the banning by the Thatcher government of 'the promotion of homosexuality' by local authorities through what became known as 'Section 28' of the Local Government Act of 1988.

Behind the specific political context (in particular a government willingness to embarrass the Labour opposition over its ambiguous support for gay rights) was a deeper issue, a concern precisely with the challenge posed to 'traditional family values' by the claim to legitimacy by homosexuals. The famous neologism embodied in Section 28 – rejecting homosexuality as a 'pretended family relationship' – signalled that the claims of the lesbian and gay community in their fullness could not be accepted, because they were outside, antithetical to, the family. Despite the fervent advocacy of the more right-wing supporters of Section 28, this did not represent a challenge to the 1967 settlement, narrowly interpreted. There was no attempt to make homosexuality illegal. It did, however, challenge the claims of the vastly expanded lesbian and gay community as it had developed since 1970. 'Privacy', as far as homosexuality was concerned, was to be narrowly defined according to the interpretation of 1967. Anything beyond that was seen as a threat to the publicly sanctioned private sphere of the family endorsed by the conservative moral discourse of the 1980s.[43]

But even as the government supported what was widely seen as a repressive measure, it had specifically to exclude information about AIDS from its provisions. This highlights the difficulty of policy formation concerning sexuality in a complex society. For the new AIDS policy adopted in 1986 had assumed the need to promote sex education as the only way of halting the threatened epidemic. Implicitly, that meant the co-operation and involvement of the community most at risk, the gay community, a policy that was anathema to the ideologues behind the Thatcherite project.

The new government policy when it came did largely follow the developing policy consensus. The government in practice adopted traditional public health policies aimed at prevention rather than the more punitive policies of detention and segregation advocated by some of its supporters. The simple reason for this was that there appeared to be no practical alternative that would achieve widespread acceptability.[44] The advice that the Health Secretary offered to the nation – to use condoms, and avoid needle sharing – was not only sensible, it was essential. Only a public education campaign to increase awareness of HIV and AIDS, it was believed, would change people's behaviour. This new policy was undoubtedly inspired by the threat of a heterosexual epidemic, which had been dramatized by the publication of the US Surgeon-General's report on AIDS in October 1986. This, combined with mounting evidence that HIV was spreading in the 'heterosexual community' in Britain, propelled the new policy. It made it possible for the proponents of the developing policy and medical consensus to seize the ears of ministers; and it provided ministers, wary of a volatile public opinion and a raucous press, with the opportunity to make a radical departure. Five years into the crisis, AIDS had achieved the 'critical mass' to put it at the top of the policy agenda.

But there were multiple ironies in the policy departure. The policy adopted was basically one of sex education, at a time when the government was elsewhere pursuing a policy of redefining and restricting sex education, by taking it out of the hands of the despised local education authorities and giving responsibility largely to parents, who were thought likely to be more conservative. In part, too, the government was building on the achievements of the voluntary sector, largely led by the gay community which its policies otherwise sought to undermine.

The policy shift in 1986 signalled a new determination on the part of the government to manage the crisis, using by and large the traditional methods of what has been called the 'biomedical elite'. Yet once the period of 'emergency' passed, and crisis management became routinized, there were signs that the government's moral preoccupations had not changed. Hard on the heels of speculation that the heterosexual threat had been exaggerated in 1989, the special AIDS education unit of the Health Education Authority was disbanded, the Cabinet subcommittee overseeing the policy was wound up and Mrs Thatcher personally vetoed government support for a major academic study of sexual behaviour, designed to explore patterns of behaviour likely to facilitate spread of HIV. The media, not only the tabloids, seized the opportunity to state as a fact that AIDS was still a gay disease, and not a real heterosexual threat. It was hard to avoid the conclusion that for many people AIDS only mattered if it was a heterosexual problem.[45]

This certainly was the perception in the community still most at risk. There was a deep sense of frustration amongst lesbian and gay activists, confirmed by the passing into law of Section 28, that gave rise in the late 1980s to a new militancy in the HIV/AIDS and gay communities. A direct action grouping, ACT-UP (AIDS Coalition to Unleash Power), was established in 1989, echoing the American organization set up in New York in 1987, and deliberately recalling the militant gay activism of the early 1970s. A number of individuals who had been heavily involved in the earlier voluntary effort gave their support to the new venture, out of a sense that moderation and discreet behind-the-scenes lobbying had not fundamentally changed government attitudes.[46]

This seemed to be confirmed by an apparent increase in anti-gay prejudice and random violence following the passing of Section 28. By the end of the decade, there was also evidence that prosecutions for consensual homosexual offences had reached a new high (comparable with the previous high total in 1954, before the establishment of the Wolfenden Committee). New government initiatives in 1990/1, threatening to increase penalties for homosexual offences through the Criminal Justice Bill, and attempting to prevent lesbians and gay men from adopting children, sparked widespread opposition and the emergence of new militant lesbian and gay groupings, such as OutRage!.[47]

Yet the paradoxical result of the first decade of AIDS was that homosexuality had achieved a voice as never before. Following extensive gay lobbying and activism, the penalties in the Criminal Justice Bill were modified, and new liaison procedures with the police were established. The new prime minister, John Major, had a much publicized meeting with a leading member of the gay community. In part such successes were the result of that 'legitimisation through disaster' which Altman has seen as a characteristic of the AIDS crisis.[48] As open lesbians and gays were drawn into policy formation and service delivery, as knowledge about gay lifestyles, and sexual practices, spread as a result of discussions of HIV and AIDS, so the homosexual community achieved a new openness and public presence. There was even some evidence that the 'blip' in public acceptability of homosexuality in the mid-1980s caused by the fear of AIDS had been overcome, with a small but important growth of support. Margaret Thatcher, despite AIDS and her conservative moral agenda, had in fact presided over a considerable growth in the self-confidence and social weight of the lesbian and gay community.

Yet the boundaries between acceptable and unacceptable sexual behaviour remained fluid and indeterminate and homosexuality remained ambiguously on the margins of social life, its acceptability still in doubt. Ambiguity was the hallmark also of government policy. During the 1980s there can be no doubt that government was constrained by its moral agenda. That did not stop the development of coherent policies by the policy and medical establishment, or their implementation at national and local level when the crisis seemed acute. But the national policy was implemented in a climate of anxiety which the government's own moral agenda did little to alleviate, and that inevitably had a major impact on how the policy developed.

Meanwhile the health crisis ground on. Though the majority of deaths from AIDS by the beginning of the 1990s were still amongst gay men, the evidence of the underlying HIV epidemic suggested the pattern was beginning to change, with the rate of reported infection rising most rapidly amongst women. It was estimated that by the year 2001, 4,800 men and 1,200 women would die from AIDS annually; by 2011 the annual total would rise to 7,000. HIV, it seemed, would be increasingly a problem for heterosexuals, for women and for black people.[49] By the early 1990s there was evidence that the heterosexual spread was in large part amongst drug users and people from Africa, ominously echoing the development of the epidemic in the USA. But whatever the roots of transmission, the virus was slowly entering the heterosexual population. Once again, the government established a ministerial AIDS action group. Clearly the crisis was not over; in some ways it was still to come, with unpredictable implications for the future regulation of sexuality.

The histories I have outlined demonstrate the unpredictability and complexity of responses when a society is confronted by an unexpected and in many ways unprecedented crisis. In confronting the unpredictability of events 'History' is called upon to offer remedies. These could be drawn from a self-conscious history of resistance (the response of the gay community); from a history of public health (the response of the medical elite); or from a moral history which evoked a value system that probably by this time did not command widespread support, and which underlined a sensitivity to the dangers of rushing too far ahead of public opinion (by and large, the response of the Thatcher government during the 1980s). This suggests the key conclusion: the regulation of sexuality cannot be understood through a monocausal account. On the contrary, it reveals the interplay of diverse forces, burdened (like AIDS) by a multiplicity of often incompatible histories.

References

1 For discussions of the multiple histories of AIDS. see Elizabeth Fee and Daniel M. Fox (eds), *AIDS: The Burdens of History* (Berkeley, 1988), and Elizabeth Fee and Daniel M. Fox (eds), *AIDS: The Making of a Chronic Disease* (Berkeley, 1992).
2 For a fuller contextualization of the points made here, see Jeffrey Weeks, *Sexuality and its Discontents: Meanings, Myths and Modern Sexualities* (London, 1985); and Weeks, *Sexuality* (Chichester and London, 1986).
3 The *locus classicus* of constructionist arguments is Michel Foucault, *The History of Sexuality*, vol. I: *An Introduction* (London, 1979). This little book made a major impact, however, because it fed into theoretical debates already stimulated by the development of what was originally a 'grass-roots history', by feminist and lesbian and gay historians. For a general discussion of these developments, see Jeffrey Weeks, 'Sexuality and history revisited', in Lynn Jamieson and Helen Corr (eds), *State, Private Life and Political Change* (Basingstoke and London, 1990), 31–49. For a sympathetic but appropriately critical overview of the various arguments, see Carole S. Vance, 'Social construction theory: problems in the history of sexuality', in Anja von Kooten Niekerk and Theo van der Meer (eds), *Which Homosexuality?: Essays from the International Scientific Conference on Lesbian and Gay Studies* (Amsterdam and London, 1989).
4 Foucault, *The History*; Jeffrey Weeks, *Sex, Politics and Society: The Regulation of Sexuality since 1800* (Harlow, 1st edn, 1981, 2nd edn, 1989).
5 On the impact of the syphilis epidemic, see Judith R. Walkowitz, *Prostitution and Victorian Society: Women, Class and the State* (Cambridge, 1980).
6 For major contributions on this debate, see the essays in Edward Stein (ed.), *Forms of Desire: Sexual Orientation and the Social Constructionist Controversy* (New York and London, 1990).
7 See, for example, the discussion of this in Weeks, *Sexuality and its Discontents*, chapter 3.
8 On the ever-accelerating rapidity of social change, as the 'juggernaut of modernity' gathers speed, see Anthony Giddens, *The Consequences of Modernity* (Cambridge, 1990).
9 See Weeks, *Sex, Politics and Society* (1989 edn), chapter 15.
10 See the essays in Stuart Hall and Martin Jacques (eds), *The Politics of Thatcherism* (London, 1983) and Ruth Levitas (ed.), *The Ideology of the New Right* (Oxford, 1986).
11 For a conservative view of the period, see Christie Davies, *Permissive Britain* (London, 1975). For a more radical analysis of the period see National Deviancy Conference (ed.), *Permissiveness and Control. The Fate of Sixties Legislation* (London, 1980).
12 Home Office and Scottish Home Department, *Report of the Committee on Homosexual Offences and Prostitution*, Cmnd 247 (London, 1957).

13   Weeks, *Sex, Politics and Society* (1989 edn), chapter 13. On the debates leading to the passing of the Sexual Offences Act 1967, which partially decriminalized male homosexuality, see Stephen Jeffery-Poulter, *Peers, Queers and Commons. The Struggle for Gay Law Reform from 1950 to the Present* (London, 1991). For a comparison with the rights-based developments in the USA during the same period, see Thomas B. Stoddard and Walter Rieman, 'AIDS and the rights of the individual: towards a more sophisticated understanding of discrimination', in Dorothy Nelkin, David P. Willis and Scott V. Parris (eds), *A Disease of Society: Cultural and Institutional Responses to AIDS* (Cambridge, 1991), 241–71.

14   Ronald Butt, 'Lloyd George knew his followers', *Times*, 19 September 1985.

15   Jeffrey Weeks, *Coming Out: Homosexual Politics in Britain from the Nineteenth Century to the Present* (2nd edn, London, 1990), Part 5: 'The Gay Liberation Movement'.

16   The relation of these polarized *political* positions to actual public attitudes and behaviour is a complex one. Broadly, I would argue, there was a long-term 'liberalization' and 'secularization' of attitudes that continued despite AIDS and the dominance of a morally conservative government in the 1980s. See my *Sexuality* and *Sex, Politics and Society* (1989 edn), chapter 15.

17   Stuart Hall, *The Hard Road to Renewal. Thatcherism and the Crisis of the Left* (London, 1989).

18   For a perceptive account of Mrs Thatcher's moral politics, based on her address to the General Assembly of the Church of Scotland in 1988, see Jonathan Raban, *God, Man and Mrs Thatcher* (London, 1988).

19   Martin Durham, *Sex and Politics: The Family and Morality in the Thatcher Years* (Basingstoke, 1991).

20   Anna Marie Smith, 'A symptomology of an authoritarian discourse. The parliamentary debates on the prohibition of the promotion of homosexuality', in *New Formations. A Journal of Culture/Theory/Politics*, 10 (Spring 1990), 41–65.

21   On the early American reaction to the burgeoning epidemic see Dennis Altman, *AIDS and the New Puritanism* (London, 1986), published in the USA as *AIDS in the Mind of America* (New York, 1986).

22   Weeks, *Coming Out*, chapter 17. For international comparisons, see Barry D. Adam, *The Rise of a Gay and Lesbian Movement* (Boston MA. 1987).

23   Gillian E. Hanscombe and Andrew Lumsden, *Title Fight: The Battle for Gay News* (London, 1983).

24   On the situation in the USA in the late 1970s and early 1980s, see Dennis Altman. *The Homosexualization of America, the Americanization of the Homosexual* (New York, 1972).

25   Weeks, *Coming Out*, chapter 15.

26   On the importance of relationships in the gay community, see my essay 'Male homosexuality in the age of AIDS', in Jeffrey Weeks, *Against Nature: Essays on History, Sexuality and Identity* (London, 1991), 100–13.

27   Speech of 27 March 1982.

28   On these themes, see, for example, the essays in Tessa Boffin and Sunil Gupta (eds), *Eestatic Antibodies: Resisting the AIDS Mythology* (London, 1990). On the 'sense of an ending', particularly in relation to AIDS, see Susan Sontag, *AIDS and its Metaphors* (London, 1989); and Elaine Showalter,

Sexual Anarchy: Gender and Culture at the Fin de Siècle (London, 1991). On difference and identity, see the essays in Jonathan Rutherford (ed.), *Identity: Community, Culture, Difference* (London, 1990).

29 Nelkin et al. *A Disease of Society*, p. 3.

30 I first used the concept in relation to AIDS in 1985 in *Sexuality and its Discontents*, p. 45. The concept has been criticized by Simon Watney, 'AIDS, "moral panic" theory and homophobia', in Peter Aggleton and Hilary Homans (eds), *Social Aspects of AIDS* (London, 1988), 52–64; and by Philip Strong and Virginia Berridge, 'No one knew anything: some issues in British AIDS policy', in Peter Aggleton. Peter Davies and Graham Hart (eds), *AIDS: Individual, Cultural and Policy Dimensions* (London, 1990), 245–7.

31 On media response, see Simon Watney, *Policing Desire: Pornography, AIDS and the Media* (London, 1987); and Kaye Wellings, 'Perceptions of risk – media treatments of AIDS', in Aggleton and Homans, *Social Aspects of AIDS*, 83–105.

32 See the discussion in Jeffrey Weeks, 'Love in a cold climate', in Aggleton and Homans, *Social Aspects of AIDS*, 10–19.

33 Susan Sontag, *Illness as Metaphor* (New York, 1978).

34 All these incidents can be documented in the press between 1983 and 1986.

35 'The real plague is panic', leader column, *Guardian*, 19 February 1985.

36 See Albero Melucci, *Nomads of the Present: Social Movements and Individual Needs in Contemporary Society* (London, 1989), and Anthony P. Cohen, *The Symbolic Construction of Community* (Chichester, London and New York, 1985).

37 For some discussion of the voluntary response, see Strong and Berridge, 'No one knew anything: some issues in British AIDS policy', and Zoe Schramm-Evans. 'Responses to AIDS 1986–1987', in Aggleton et al., *AIDS: Individual, Cultural and Policy Dimensions*; and Virginia Berridge, 'The early years of AIDS in the United Kingdom 1981–6: historical perspectives', in T. Ranger and P. Slack (eds), *Epidemics and Ideas* (Cambridge, 1992).

38 Simon Watney, 'Safer sex as community practice', in Aggleton et al., *AIDS: Individual, Cultural and Policy Dimensions*; and Simon Watney, 'AIDS: the second decade: risk, research and modernity', and Mitchell Cohen, 'Changing to safer sex: personality, logic and habit', in Peter Aggleton, Graham Hart and Peter Davies (eds), *AIDS: Responses, Interventions and Care* (London, 1991).

39 Ray Fitzpatrick, Mary Boulton and Graham Hart, 'Gay men's sexual behaviour in response to AIDS', in Peter Aggleton, Graham Hart and Peter Davies (eds), *AIDS: Social Representations, Social Practices* (London, 1989); Ray Fitzpatrick, John McLean, Mary Boulton, Graham Hart and Jill Dawson, 'Variations in sexual behaviour in gay men', in Aggleton et al., *AIDS: Individual, Cultural and Policy Dimensions*; and Cohen, 'Changing to safer sex'. It is worth noting here that by the end of the 1980s there were ominous signs that younger gay men, identifying HIV as a disease of older men, were abandoning safer sex: and the rates of sexually transmitted disease (STD) infection showed signs of increasing once again. One London hospital noted twice the rates of gonorrhea infection in the first six months of 1990 as in the whole of 1989 (*Independent on Sunday*, 14 October 1990). Clearly the adoption of safer sex, though uneven, was much greater in the

gay community than elsewhere, with heterosexual men proving particularly resistant to its messages (see Tamsin Wilton and Peter Aggleton, 'Condoms, coercion and control: heterosexuality and the limits to HIV/AIDS education', in Aggleton et al., *AIDS: Responses, Interventions and Care*). But another history, that making important generational differences within the gay community, was apparently reasserting itself.

40 V. Berridge and P. Strong, 'AIDS policies in the UK: a study in contemporary behaviour', *Twentieth Century British History*, 2, 2 (1991), 150–74: Berridge, 'The early years of AIDS in the United Kingdom'.

41 Berridge, 'The early years of AIDS in the United Kingdom'.

42 Roger Jowell, Sharon Witherspoon and Lindsay Brook, *British Social Attitudes: The 1986 Report* (Aldershot, 1988); *Sunday Telegraph*, 5 June 1988.

43 On the background to Section 28 see Smith, 'A symptomology of an authoritarian discourse'; also my essay 'Pretended family relationships', in Weeks, *Against Nature*.

44 See Berridge and Strong, 'AIDS policies in the UK', and Strong and Berridge, 'No one knew anything: some issues in British AIDS policy'.

45 See 'PM angers doctors by axing AIDS study', *Guardian*, 11 September 1989; 'Thatcher disbands Cabinet AIDS team', *Sunday Correspondent*, 17 September 1989.

46 Tony Whitehead, 'The voluntary sector: five years on', in Erica Carter and Simon Watney (eds), *Taking Liberties: AIDS and Cultural Politics* (London, 1989).

47 See, for example, Labour Campaign for Lesbian and Gay Rights, *Emergency Briefing on Paragraph 16 and Clause 25* (London, 1990); 'Not fit to foster', *Pink Paper*, 5 January 1991; Jayne Egerton, 'Gay parents: nothing natural', *New Statesman and Society*, 16 November 1990; Sean O'Neill, 'Are the police looking the other way', *The Independent*, 18 December 1990; Nick Cohen, 'MPs oppose tough court penalties for homosexuals', *The Independent*, 10 January 1991; GALOP (Gay London Policing Project), *Annual Report* (London, 1990); 'Gay protest sealed with a kiss', *The Independent*, 6 September 1990; and '"Outing group" to name MPs as homosexual', *The Independent*, 29 July 1991.

48 Dennis Altman, 'AIDS and the reconceptualization of homosexuality', in van Kooten Niekerk and van der Meer, *Which Homosexuality?*.

49 *OPCS Monitor*, PP291/1; Chris Mihill, 'AIDS figures prompt race backlash fears', *Guardian*, 9 August 1991.

8

An Unfinished Revolution: Sexuality in the Twentieth Century

What do we mean when we write about 'sexuality'? Sexuality pervades the air we breathe, but we still lack a common language for speaking about it. It is a topic which we can all say something about, and on which we are all in one way or another 'experts', but that, somehow, increases rather than decreases our confusions: sexuality, it seems, has so many 'truths' that we are left with a cacophony of noise, and precious little good sense. There has been an ever expanding explosion of discourse around sexuality in the past century, and the volume seems unlikely to diminish in the near future. Yet it is a subject which arouses the greatest anxieties and controversies, and increasingly has become a front line of divisive political controversy and moral debate.

This is because the sexual touches on so many disparate areas of individual and social existence. When we think of sexuality we think of a number of things. We think of reproduction, which has traditionally been seen as the main justification of sexual activity, and with which western cultures at least have historically been most preoccupied. We think of relationships, of which marriage is the socially sanctioned, but far from being the only, form. We think of erotic activities and of fantasy, of intimacy and warmth, of love and pleasure. We relate it to our sense of self and to our collective belongings, to identity, personal and political. But we also think of sin and danger, violence and disease.

Nothing is straightforward when we try to think or speak of sexuality. It is both the most private and personal of activities, and the most public. We still often speak of it in whispers, while it is all the time shouting at us from bill-boards, newspapers, radio and television, pulpits, the streets. Our own voices compete with, or may even be, those of priests and politicians, medics and militants, and all too many, many more.

So anyone rash enough to try to analyse its social forms, or predict what shape the kaleidoscope will next take, is treading on very dangerous ice. There are so many conflicting elements at play. For sex, despite its immediacy, is very much a cultural and a historical phenomenon. Whatever we like to think, we are not entirely free agents in this matter, any more than we are of anything else. Our choices are real and important, but they are also constrained by a very long and complex history and intricate power relations, which tell us, amongst other things, what is natural or unnatural, good or bad, permissible or impermissible. If there is a 'crisis of sexuality' today, it is because many of the fixed points which we think we need to guide us through the maze have been pulled down or obscured; and because the language of sexuality is muddied by a long and often painful history.

If there is a confusion about values and attitudes, that should not surprise us, nor should we imagine it is anything unique to us. We can find in the history of the past two hundred years or so almost all the themes that preoccupy us now, and similar laments about the decline of morals and a confusion of values.[1] Two hundred years ago, in the wake of the French Revolution, one of the formative moments of modern Europe, we find middle-class evangelists worried about the state of morality in Britain: they saw, or believed they saw, a dissolute, amoral aristocracy, a feckless, overbreeding working class. Surely, these moralists felt, we would end up like the French, drowned in chaos and blood, unless we all learned the importance of 'respectability', what became 'Victorian values'.

Some of the implications of these Victorian values became clearer a generation later as the poverty and disease of the new industrial towns began to confront policy makers. Just as today some conservative commentators seek to blame social ills on the existence of one-parent families, so in the 1840s and 50s individual behaviour was blamed for what were transparently social ills. The result was a renewed effort to moralize the masses into the image of their masters, an effort which by and large failed. The mores of the working classes may have been different from those of the middle class, but, as historians are now discovering, they were no less 'moral'.

Then take sex-related disease. Today our experience of sex is shadowed by the HIV/AIDS epidemic. In the nineteenth century the most feared scourge was syphilis, and we can find in the response to this ominous pre-echoes of our modern reaction. In the 1860s a series of measures, the Contagious Diseases Acts, sought to control the spread of syphilis by enforcing compulsory examinations of those who were suspected of being prostitutes. The model for the acts was allegedly measures to control cattle. The result was inevitable: the intimidation of large numbers of women, growing hostility to state regulation, a radical movement of resistance, and no obvious impact on the incidence of the disease. Many of the more extreme measures proposed in the 1980s to control the spread of HIV – compulsory testing, detention of those suspected of spreading the disease – were prefigured a hundred years before.

As another example, let's take sexual abuse of children. Today we worry rightly about child sex abuse. But sexual abuse of children was raised in the 1830s in the context of debates about the impact of children working in the factories and mines; in the 1870s, in the report, no less, of the Prince of Wales's Royal Commission on Housing, in the context of housing overcrowding and the danger of incest; and in the 1880s, as a result of the panic about the 'white slave trade', when the age of consent for girls was raised eventually from 13 to 16. It takes different forms at different times, but abuse of children is not a new discovery, any more than our confusions and hesitations in confronting it are new.

The history of birth control reveals a similar pattern. Although the roots of the birth-control movement are many and various, and its practice in many forms is probably as old as sexuality, its preoccupations over the past hundred years have been remarkably constant: how to balance the need for social regulation of the population with the rights of parents and of individual women to control their own fertility. When the National Birth Control Council, the immediate predecessor of the Family Planning Association, was set up in 1930 it brought together a number of groups, some of which were deeply shaped by eugenicist ideas, preoccupied with the planned breeding of the best. One of the great fears of the time was that as the population declined, so the balance of the population would shift to those who were least 'fit' to bear the burdens of modern life. Today we are more concerned with the threat of overpopulation in the Third World, or of the implications of artificial insemination or extra-uterine conception, but the same anxieties and fears still intrude: we worry about who should breed, and under what conditions and whose control, as much as why. We do not like apparently the idea of sexuality being uncontrolled and unplanned, a matter of choice rather than social obligation.

Finally, there's the question of sexual identity. It is easy for us today to assume that the sexual categories and identities we work within, pre-eminently those of heterosexual and homosexual, are fixed and eternal, corresponding to essential differences transmitted (who knows how?) from the dawn of time. It is now clear, however, that these distinctions were only formulated in a recognizably modern form in the closing years of the nineteenth century, the result of a complex process whereby the norm of heterosexuality was established and reinforced by the drawing of boundaries between it and its dangerous other, homosexuality. This in turn was intricately related to the reformulation of gender relations, so that sexual and gender identities were locked together: manhood, in particular, was defined by refusing the temptation of homosexuality. The developments of the twentieth century have made possible the emergence of strong and vibrant lesbian and gay identities that have challenged the heterosexual norm, just as social change and the rise of contemporary feminism have undermined the hierarchies of gender, but the point that I want to underline is that the nineteenth century, like the twentieth, was haunted by the spectre of homosexuality. There is a nice historical symmetry in the fact that just over a hundred years after the Criminal Law Amendment Act of 1885 made all forms of male homosexuality illegal, the 'promotion of homosexuality' by local authorities was banned (through what became known as 'Clause 28'). Circumstances change, and so do laws; but a fear of homosexuality apparently remains.[2]

We can, in other words, see in the fairly recent history of sexuality many problems, dilemmas and anxieties remarkably similar to our own. They revolve essentially around boundaries, between men and women, adults and children, 'normal' and 'perverse' sexuality, between orthodox and unorthodox lifestyles and identities, between health and disease. I offer these examples not to suggest that nothing ever changes; on the contrary, I hope to show that there have been profound changes in attitudes towards sexuality. My intention, rather, is to warn against that facile history which looks back to a 'golden age' when somehow everything was better, more fixed and certain, than it is today. It wasn't, and we are not going to be able to deal with the challenges of the close of the twentieth century if we seek a return to the largely mythical, supposedly wholesome values of the last.

Nostalgia for a golden age of order and harmony is one danger when thinking of sexuality. There is another temptation as we approach the end of the millennium, to identify with that sense of an ending which seems to characterize the closing of a century, to reconstruct a *fin de siècle* mood which sees the uncertainty of our own age of anxiety as being the same as that of the most famous *fin* of all, that of the late nineteenth century. Rather than regretting a better past, this mood wallows in the 'sexual anarchy' which some contemporary commentators saw as characterizing the ending of the nineteenth century.[3] This in turn fits into a

postmodern consciousness which in its most deconstructive mood celebrates the impossibility of a master, legitimizing discourse for sexuality,
glories in heterogeneity, the return of the repressed of sexuality, the
bouleversement of all values, and the subversive power of the perverse.

This opens up challenging perspectives for thinking about sexuality
anew. This is especially the case as a new scholarship undermines the
dominant myths and meanings that emerged in the late nineteenth century.[4] As hallowed traditions crumble, we are being forced to raise questions of value: by what criteria, and by whose sanction, can we say that this
activity, desire, style, way of life, is better or worse, more or less ethically
valid, than any other? If the gods are dead, or dying, or the secular myths
of History and Science lie discredited before us, is anything permitted?
Postmodernist writing has been effective in tearing apart for scrutiny and
critique many of our taken-for-granted beliefs. It has been less effective in
elaborating alternative values. I shall return to this issue later.

I want now to look at certain key trends which seem to me to underlie
the changes we have experienced over the past century, and whose
consequences look set to dominate the 1990s. I identify these as, first,
the secularization of sex, an inadequate term which does, none the less,
pinpoint some key changes; second, a liberalization of attitudes, which
has reshaped both the law and social attitudes; and third, the challenge of
diversity, perhaps the key change to which everything else is secondary.
Finally, I want to look at the future of all three in the context of the
current crisis around HIV disease and AIDS. I am not going to offer
predictions, because nothing is predictable in the world of sexuality; nor
do I wish to suggest a blueprint for a new ethics: blueprints are what have
so often led us astray. But I shall try to offer a framework for understanding what too often seems like a meaningless flux.

The secularization of sex

First of all let's look at what I am calling the secularization of sex. By this
I mean the progressive detachment of sexual values from religious values
– even for many of the religious. This has a long history, but perhaps the
key feature was the process, beginning in the mid-nineteenth century,
whereby the initiative for judging sexuality passed from the churches to
the agents of social and mental hygiene, primarily in the medical profession. Science promised to prop up, or replace, religion in explaining or
legitimizing sexual behaviour. Already by the end of the century, some
feminist and other critics were arguing that doctors were the new priesthood, imposing their new (overwhelmingly masculine) imperatives on
the bodies of women. Since then, the arbiters of sexual values have

tended to be increasingly doctors, sexologists, psychologists, social workers, even politicians, rather than priests.

This is, of course, an unfinished revolution, as all those who have
campaigned for birth control, sex education, the rights of sexual minorities or the right of sexual choice know very well. You can still be labelled
as both immoral and sick, sinful and diseased, all at the same time, if you
offend the norms. Nor have the churches of various kinds given up the
struggle. It is only a few years since the British chief rabbi welcomed
the 'swinging of the pendulum' back to traditional values (though as I
have suggested, that tradition was itself pretty confused).[5] Elsewhere in
the world, as well as in Britain, we have seen what W. H. Auden called the
'fashionable madmen' attempting to assert the links between religious
fundamentalism and a particular (restricted) type of sexual behaviour,
and these attitudes have had many local successes to their credit.
The Republican Party convention in the USA in 1992, to quote just one
example, managed to impose on the party an extremely conservative
moral agenda: opposing abortion, campaigning against the recognition
of homosexual rights and affirming the merits of 'family values'.[6]

Yet it seems that despite all the huffing and puffing, the anguished
debates and the like, the process of secularization has gone too far to
reverse fundamentally, as the spectacular electoral failure of the Repub-
licans in 1992 suggests. Even in the most traditional of churches, such as
the Roman Catholic, perhaps the majority of the faithful (and a significant minority of its own priesthood, apparently) ignore the pope's injunctions against birth control, and in the USA we see openly gay Catholic
priests and lesbian nuns. The fevered efforts of religious traditionalists to
turn back the tide testifies, I would argue, as much to the success of
secularization as to the power of religion.

But at the same time as the power of religion is undermined, so the
claims of a scientific morality have been subverted. The early sexologists,
men (usually men) such as Richard von Krafft-Ebing, Havelock Ellis,
Magnus Hirschfeld, even Freud, believed that what they were doing was
to put the laws of sexuality onto a scientific basis, to provide a rational
basis for sex reform: 'through science to justice', proclaimed Hirschfeld
in Germany before his library and legacy were piled on the Nazi book-
burning pyre.[7] Today we are a little more sceptical of the claims of
science to guide us through the moral maze. Many of those labelled
and categorized by the early science of sex (women as the 'dark continent', homosexuals as a biological aberration) have resisted the labels,
and developed their own definitions in a sort of grass-roots sexology
which plays with and subverts inherited descriptions.

The significance of all this is profound, because what it does is to take
responsibility for sexual behaviour away from external sources of

authority and to place it squarely on to the individual. This introduces into the debate on sexuality a contingency that is, for many, troubling and enfeebling. But it is important to recognize that this sense of contingency is not just confined to the domain of sexuality. On the contrary, the existence of a dual consciousness, of the necessity, but difficulty and pain, of individual choice, can be seen as a key element of our late modern sense of self. As the 'juggernaut of modernity', in Anthony Giddens's phrase, gathers momentum, dissolving all certainties and transforming all fixed identities and relationships, so the sense of the contingency of self, its provisional placing in a changing world, a narrative quest for partial unity rather than a fixed attribute of essential being, becomes paramount.[8] In the twentieth century the Enlightenment belief in the constitutive individual, Man (and it was usually male), as the measure of all things has been severely challenged: by Freud's discovery of the dynamic unconscious, by the recognition of cultural and sexual diversity, by the challenges of feminism and lesbian and gay politics, by the historical and deconstructive turns in the social sciences, by the experience of fragmentation which for many characterizes late or post-modernity. In all these contexts sexuality becomes problematized, dethroned from its position of being a determining essence. Yet at the same time, as if by a necessary reflex, sexuality becomes a source of meaning, of social and political placing, and of individual sense of self.

This of course poses many problems, and is probably the main focus of anxiety about sexuality today. The public debates about sexuality since the 1960s, including those around the so-called 'permissive reforms' of the law on abortion, homosexuality, divorce, censorship and birth control, far from being a licence to do what you want, were actually about finding the right balance between private pleasures and public policy, between freedom and regulation. In other ways, the rise of the caring professions, the pressure on organizations like Relate (the National Marriage Guidance Council), and the proliferation of experts and therapies of various sorts indicate the difficulties of relying on ourselves alone. But the conclusion we must draw from this secularization seems to me inescapable: today we see sexual matters as essentially about individual choice. The debate is about the legitimate limits of choice, not about the legitimacy of choice itself.

A liberalization of attitudes

This is closely related to the second trend I have identified, the growing liberalization of attitudes over the past generation. By this I mean the gradual abandonment of authoritarian or absolutist values, and a growing stress on individual decision-taking about sexuality. People are generally more accepting today of birth control, abortion, premarital sex, cohabitation before or instead of marriage, divorce, and homosexuality than ever they were in that supposed haven of the 'sexual revolution', the 1960s. And despite its espousal of Victorian values, and a certain closing of space around a number of key issues, this liberalization continued to grow, perhaps even increase during the Thatcher years, and has continued during the 1990s.[9]

Here are a few examples. About 50 per cent of single women lived with a man before marriage by the end of the 1980s, compared to 7 per cent in 1970, and over triple the figure when Mrs Thatcher took office in 1979. The proportion of children born outside marriage rose from 12 per cent in 1980 to 25 per cent in 1988. For women under 20, the figure is much higher: around 82 per cent in the north-west and north of England. Britain now has one of the highest divorce rates in Europe, over 150,000 a year in the 1980s, and 4 out of 10 marriages will end in divorce in the 1990s.[10]

Then there is the touchstone issue of abortion, a highly contested issue throughout much of the west (it was, for example, one of the issues that threatened to hold up German unification in 1990, because of the conservative fear in west Germany of the liberal laws in the east), and a highly divisive issue in the USA. Despite strenuous efforts since the law was liberalized in Britain in the 1960s to reduce the time during which termination is permitted, all have failed, not only because a majority of MPs were resistant or because of the campaigns of pressure groups, for example, the National Abortion Campaign, but because access to abortion had become the wish of the majority of the population. I am sure that abortion will continue to be a key moral issue, but it is difficult to believe that there will be a consensus in Britain in the near future for restrictive change.

These examples suggest to me that there has been a crucial long-term shift in the way we see sexual activity and relationships. I would be cautious about calling it a revolution. In many ways it is startlingly like a reversion to much earlier, pre-'Victorian values' mores, with a high rate of formal illegitimacy, toleration of certain forms of premarital sex, and a relatively late age of marriage. This is accompanied, however, by a new explicitness in talking about sex which magnifies and dramatizes the impact of the transformations that have taken place.

There is, however, an ambiguity in this continuing liberalization, which underlines the limits of the changes that have taken place, and this is seen most clearly in relation to homosexuality. According to opinion surveys, there was a continuing liberalization in attitudes towards homosexuality from the late 1960s into the early 1980s, then a shuddering setback, which has only recently, according to the survey *British Social Attitudes*, been partially reversed. So while in 1983, 62 per cent censured homosexual relationships, by 1987, in the wake of the AIDS panic, this had risen to 74 per cent of those interviewed. Public hostility was even sharper when asked their attitudes to lesbians and gay men having the right to adopt children. In 1987, 86 per cent would forbid lesbians adopting children, and 93 per cent gay men. A Gallup Poll shortly after the Section 28 controversy in late 1987, early 1988, confirmed a deep-seated hostility: 60 per cent thought that homosexuality should not be considered an accepted lifestyle, compared with 34 per cent who did approve – though perhaps significantly for the coming decade, 50 per cent of those under 35 were accepting.[11] What seems to be happening is a greater acceptance of the fact of homosexuality ('live and let live') whilst there remains an ingrained refusal to see it as of equal validity with heterosexuality.

There is a sharp paradox in attitudes towards homosexuality. While prosecutions for 'homosexual offences' reached a height in the late 1980s only previously attained in 1954, before legalization, suggesting an increased police interest in the issue, while the popular press pursued people suspected of homosexual tendencies fervently, and while the incidence of 'queer-bashing' increased dramatically, there were abundant signs of a more general growth of the homosexual community. Social facilities continued to expand, gay characters appeared in soap operas on television, people spoke more easily about homosexuality than ever before. The prosecutions, 'queer-bashings', and Section 28 can be seen as distorted responses to real changes taking place in attitudes to non-heterosexual behaviour. It is not too much of an exaggeration to say that Mrs Thatcher, despite her rhetoric and actions, presided over the biggest expansion of the lesbian and gay community in its history.

This is in line with the wider point I am making: there seems to be a long-term shift both in beliefs and in behaviours taking place which governments have only a limited power to affect. They can toughen laws, pursue errant fathers, condemn the 'promotion of homosexuality' and the like. They can contribute to the sum total of human misery. But they cannot force people to behave in ways that they don't want to.

This is, in part at least, recognized in the new legal framework that reached its apogee in the liberal reforms of the 1960s, but which still, if inadequately, shapes legal responses. The liberalization of the legal framework that followed the Wolfenden report on homosexuality and prostitution in 1957 signalled an abandonment of legal absolutism, that is a view of the law which saw it as embodying the moral norms of society. Instead, the new approach relied on a clear distinction between the role of the law, to uphold generally acceptable standards of public behaviour, and the domain of morals, increasingly seen as a matter of private choice (the 'Wolfenden strategy').[12] In practice this meant allowing, in the famous phrase, 'consenting adults in private' to pursue their personal ends without interference so long as the public were not unduly frightened. The actual implementation of the new legal framework was less clear cut, however. For example, abortion on demand was tempered by the need for medical authorization of abortions. The rights of homosexuals were restricted by narrow interpretations of 'consent' (which could be given only by those over 21, not at all in Scotland or Northern Ireland until a decade later, and never in the armed forces), and of 'privacy' (which was not recognized if more than two people were present, or potentially present). Regulation was changed, but not abandoned; the locus of control shifted. A form of sexual pluralism was recognized, but it was not fully legitimized. Yet it provided a space which has allowed sexual autonomy to grow. During the 1970s and 1980s there were various challenges to this legal compromise, especially with regard to pornography; but despite a harsher climate and a closing of space for social experimentation, the framework held, even under a political regime committed to moral conservatism. Section 28 is again a test case. Although its intention was restrictive and punitive, it was still clearly within the framework of the Wolfenden strategy. It did not propose making homosexuality illegal, intending instead to prevent 'promotion'. Of course, by doing that, the government's intervention gave unprecedented publicity to homosexuality, and helped to forge a stronger sense of identity and community amongst lesbians and gay men than ever before.[13] But that is one of the paradoxes of legal involvement in sexual lives. The unintended consequences are often more important than the intended. The liberal legal experiment attempted as much to regulate as to free individuals, but its consequences have been to institutionalize a form of tolerance of diversity and choice. That tolerance falls far short of full acceptance of difference, as the case of homosexuality underlines. Nevertheless, it highlights my central point: legal and moral absolutism are fading as the guidelines of policy, but the alternatives have still to be fully worked out.

To close this discussion of what I have called liberalization, I want to pinpoint two further historic shifts that underlie some of the patterns I have mentioned. The first is the changing balance of relations between men and women. This is most obvious in the taken-for-granted assumption today that women have their own sexual needs and desires, with as much claim to satisfying them as men. This has been a long revolution since the nineteenth century, and one that is not clear cut or unproblematic. Some feminist historians have suggested that what has happened is a sexualization of the female body on male terms, and for the servicing of men. Against this it is important to remember the struggles of women themselves for sexual autonomy and freedom of choice.[14]

Beyond this is a more profound questioning of the power relations between women and men, the result both of feminism and of the changing role of women in the economy and society. Despite ups and downs in the path to full equality, there is no doubt that this represents a radical transformation of relationships, whose effects in the next decade are impossible to overestimate. We have already seen its impact in, amongst other things, the changing agenda on rape and sexual violence and a new concern with the sexual abuse of children, in all of which questions of power are to the fore.

The second shift that must be recognized is the growing acknowledgement of the fact of sexual diversity. I have mentioned homosexuality, and the contradictory responses it evokes. But it is clear today that there is a much greater variety of beliefs, identities and relationships than our moral codes allow. The truth is that people's sexual needs and desires do not fit easily into the neat categories and moral systems we build to describe and contain them.

Both these shifts are critical elements in the third major trend I want to outline: the challenge of diversity.

The challenge of diversity

The heart of the challenge is this: we increasingly have to accept the fact of diversity. We know that people have different needs and desires, that they live in different types of household and have various sorts of relationship. But we are reluctant to accept the norm of diversity: that is, we still seek to judge people as if there were a common moral standard by which they should live. One of the key issues of the 1990s has been precisely the attempt to move from recognition to normalization of diversity.

The constant laments about the impact of permissiveness and the evocation of 'Victorian values' during the 1980s suggested that the key changes we have noted – the rise of illegitimacy, the rising divorce figures, the new presence of homosexuality, etc. – indicated a drastic decline of moral standards, a disintegration of old values, leading to a threat to the very existence of the family. Interestingly, more recently, there has been a dawning recognition that something else is afoot: not so much a collapse of morals as a change in their form, not so much a decline of the family as the rise of different sorts of family. Angela Rumbold, when briefly the minister for the family in the late 1980s, suggested that these facts were beginning to filter through into government thinking.[15] The point was made more sharply by the then leader of the Opposition, Neil Kinnock, in a speech in 1990: 'Anyone concerned about the future of the family', he said, 'should understand that in our generation the family is changing, it is not collapsing.'[16] Those who regarded the rise of the non-traditional family as evidence of social delinquency, he went on, showed not only prejudice but impracticality in the face of the problems accompanying change.

Behind such statements is a growing body of social research which has traced the shifts in the domestic patterns which frame sexual behaviour. In many ways, we are still deeply familial in our behaviour patterns. Although the age of marriage has crept up in recent years, most people still get married. Though there has been a recent decline, a high proportion of divorced people remarry. And even though there is a growing percentage of children born outside marriage, they are more often than not born into marriage-like relationships. A majority of 'illegitimate births' are jointly registered by both parents. Although we are more tolerant of premarital sex, we remain very censorious of extra-marital sex. And the majority, as we have seen, still disapprove of homosexual relationships, and the adoption of children by lesbians and gay men. We remain, in the words of the sociologist David Clark, deeply 'wedlocked'.[17]

Yet these overall figures conceal a great deal of variety. A survey by National Opinion Polls for the *Independent* in 1990 showed that the traditional view of the family was held by only a minority, while the under-35s had a 'radically different view of family life to that of their parents' generation'. These different views of the under-35s included a more relaxed attitude to both partners working, joint rearing of children, and a more tolerant attitude (though still only amongst about a third of those polled) to homosexual adoptions.[18] All surveys during the 1990s confirmed these trends.

But beyond such generational shifts is a growing recognition that the word 'family' covers a multitude of forms. In the early 1980s the family sociologists Rhona and Robert Rappoport distinguished five types of family diversity: by internal organization of the family; as a result of cultural factors such as race and ethnicity, religious and other factors; class differences in family life; changes over the life-course; and differing patterns by generation. Others have listed different types of 'family', ranging from non-married cohabitation to single parenthood, from 'commuter marriages' to lesbian and gay relationships.[19] As we know, the latter were labelled 'pretended family relationships' in the Local Government Act of 1988, but once you broaden the definition of the family to include non-traditional forms, it is difficult to know what you can legitimately exclude.

The point I am making is that sexual activity, and committed sexual-emotional relationships, take place today in a number of more or less long-term settings, and have given rise to a range of patterns of domestic organization. We have not yet sorted out, however, the implications of this for policy or ideology. We know, for example, that many women choose single parenthood. We also know that more often than not single parenthood is associated with poverty. The Conservative government in 1990 announced proposals for making errant fathers contribute to the rearing of children, presumably as one sort of response to poverty. But little thought was given to the implications of that response to the question of choice.[20] More often than not we continue to pay lip-service to individual freedom while being punitive to those who exercise it.

These are difficult issues, but ones which have dominated the social agenda in the 1990s. They are likely to shift us away from a moral politics which relies on *a priori* positions towards one which looks at needs and how they can be satisfied. Put another way, we are likely to see less and less emphasis on moral absolutes and an increasing willingness to live with moral diversity.

The impacts of AIDS

Finally, I want to look at an experience which fed into the moral absolutism of the 1980s, threatened to create a sort of backlash against sexual liberalism, and had a tragic effect on the lives of many people – the impact of the health crisis associated with HIV disease and AIDS.

The response to HIV has been coloured by the fact that it has been seen as a disease, in the west at least, of the marginal and the execrated. In America and Britain – but not, it must be said, in all European countries – largely, it has so far affected gay men and intravenous drug users, the so-called 'guilty victims' compared to supposedly 'innocent victims' such as haemophiliacs. It was only when it seemed that HIV was likely to seep through into the heterosexual community that governments in the USA and Britain displayed any urgency on the matter. The British government's launch into urgent action at the end of 1986 was precipitated by the US Surgeon-General's report on the danger of a heterosexual epidemic earlier that year. A tailing off in urgency followed in 1989 after reports circulated that rumours of a heterosexual threat were much exaggerated. It seems that urgency is not required if only unpopular minorities are at risk (see chapter 7, above).[21]

But, and it should not need saying, we are complacent about the risks of HIV and AIDS at our peril. The problem is that the population as a whole seems pretty resistant to warnings about the dangers. The gay community quite early on learnt the need for safer-sex techniques, and the avoidance of high-risk activities. The results were seen in a drop of sexually transmitted disease (STD) infections amongst gay men in the late 1980s, and a slowing down of the expected rate of increase of infection. But there is no similar evidence for a widespread adoption of safer sex amongst heterosexuals.

This suggests that the doom-laden warnings that have characterized much of the public education on AIDS are not effective. Equally in-effective, however, were the calls for a remoralization of behaviour that we heard in the 1980s. There was certainly, as we have seen, a renewed hostility towards homosexuality, and this had very unpleasant effects. A *British Social Attitudes* survey in 1991 indicated that there had been a slight decline in the tendency to see AIDS in moral terms, though there remained strong support for statements that certain sexual practices are morally wrong.[22] Yet there is overwhelming evidence that this does not stop people doing them. What such moralism does do, however, is prevent the full dissemination of knowledge about risk activities and safer-sex techniques.

That moralism is not surprising, however, because the HIV/AIDS crisis dramatizes many of the uncertainties and ambiguities that are shaping sexual mores at the end of this century. It feeds into that sense of an end of an era which I have already noted as an important component of our culture at the present. It dramatizes the existence of sexual and cultural diversity. It underlines the absence of a consensus concerning what is ethnically valid and invalid, acceptable or unacceptable, right and wrong. People with HIV and AIDS have had to endure stigma because our culture has been unable to come to terms with the changes that have transformed sexual life in the twentieth century.

I have suggested in this chapter that sexual behaviour and sexual beliefs are being shaped and reshaped by a number of long-term trends: secularization, liberalization, and the growth of social and moral diversity. During the 1980s, under the impact both of political forces and of AIDS, a number of these trends seemed to be on the point of going into reverse. But it is already looking as if these were blips rather than fundamental shifts. If this is so, then we need to adjust to these trends in our thinking about sexuality. It's time, I suggest, that our moral systems begin to move closer to what we actually do and are, rather than what inherited traditions say we should do and be. If that were to happen we would, I believe, see the development not only of a more humane and tolerant culture, but of one that was also more responsible and healthier in facing the challenges of this particular *fin de siècle*.

References

1 Further details for the examples given can be found in Jeffrey Weeks, *Sex, Politics and Society: The Regulation of Sexuality since 1800*, 2nd edition, Longman, Harlow 1989.

2 On homosexuality see the title essay in David M. Halperin, *One Hundred Years of Homosexuality, and Other Essays on Greek Love*, Routledge, New York and London 1990; Eve Kosovsky Sedgwick, *Epistemology of the Closet*, University of California Press, Berkeley and Los Angeles 1990: and the essays in Jeffrey Weeks, *Against Nature: Essays on History, Sexuality and Identity*, Rivers Oram Press, London 1991.

3 On this theme, see Elaine Showalter, *Sexual Anarchy: Gender and Culture at the Fin de Siècle*, Bloomsbury, London 1991.

4 On the 'sexual tradition', see Jeffrey Weeks, *Sexuality and its Discontents: Meanings, Myths and Modern Sexualities*, Routledge, London and New York 1985.

5 Interview with Sir Immanual Jakobovits, *Independent*, 27 November 1987.

6 See coverage of the 1992 convention in the newspapers of August 1992.

7 See Weeks, *Sexuality and its Discontents*, chapter 4; and Jeffrey Weeks, *Sexuality*, Ellis Horwood/Tavistock, Chichester and London 1986, chapter 6.

8 On this theme see Anthony Giddens, *The Transformation of Intimacy: Sexuality, Love and Eroticism in Modern Societies*, Polity Press, Cambridge 1992.

9 On the Thatcher years see Martin Durham, *Sex and Politics: The Family and Morality in the Thatcher Years*, Macmillan, Basingstoke 1991.

10 See, for example, Roger Jowell, Sharon Witherspoon and Lindsay Brook (eds), *British Social Attitudes – the 7th Report*, Gower, Aldershot 1990; *Regional Trends* 25, HMSO, London 1990; *Family Change and Future Policy*, Family Policy Studies Centre, London 1990; *Key Population and Vital Statistics 1989*, HMSO, London 1990; *Population Trends* 61, HMSO, London 1990; *Single Person Households – Single Living, Diverse Lifestyles 1992*, Mintel International Group, London 1992, quoted in *The Times*, 15 September 1992.

11 Roger Jowell, Sharon Witherspoon and Lindsay Brook. (eds), *British Social Attitudes. The 5th Report*, Gower, Aldershot 1988; Gallop Poll reported in the *Sunday Telegraph*, 5 June 1988.

12 On the Wolfenden strategy and its implications see Jeffrey Weeks, *Coming Out: Homosexual Politics in Britain from the Nineteenth Century to the Present*, 2nd edition. Quarter Books, London 1990, chapter 15; Weeks, *Sex, Politics and Society*, chapter 12.

13 Stephen Jeffery-Poulter, *Peers, Queers and Commons: The Struggle for Gay Law Reform from 1950 to the Present*, Routledge, London and New York 1991, chapter 11; Antony Grey, *Quest for Justice: Towards Homosexual Emancipation*, Sinclair-Stevenson, London 1992, pp. 233–5: Jeffrey Weeks, 'Pretended family relationships', chapter 8 in Jeffrey Weeks, *Against Nature: Essays on History, Sexuality and Identity*, Rivers Oram Press, London 1991.

14 See, for example, Sheila Jeffreys, *Anti-climax*, Pandora, London 1991, for an argument about the limitations of liberalization. For an alternative feminist

argument see the two books by Lynne Segal, *Is the Future Female? Troubled Thoughts on Contemporary Feminism*, Virago, London 1987, and *Slow Motion: Changing Masculinities, Changing Men*, Virago, London 1990.

15 Patrick Wintour, 'Changing attitudes shake family values', *Guardian*, 9 October 1990; Judy Jones, 'Minister urges need to target resources', *Independent*, 22 October 1990.

16 Jack O'Sullivan, 'Labour stakes claim to be party for community care', *Independent*, 21 September 1990; news report of Kinnock's speech, *Guardian*, 21 September 1990.

17 David Clark and Douglas Haldane, *Wedlocked?*, Polity Press, Cambridge 1990.

18 Peter Kellner, 'Traditional view of family "held by minority of people"', *Independent*, 21 September 1990.

19 Robert and Rhona Rapoport, 'British families in transition', in R. N. Rapoport, M. P. Fogarty and R. Rapoport (eds), *Families in Britain*, Routledge and Kegan Paul, London 1982. See the discussion of this theme in Weeks, 'Pretended family relationships'.

20 For the effects of that policy see Sally Malcolm-Smith, 'Single mothers harassed to name absent fathers', *Observer*, 22 September 1991.

21 'AIDS: the intellectual agenda', chapter 7 in Weeks, *Against Nature*; Virginia Berridge and Philip Strong, 'AIDS policies in the UK: a preliminary analysis', in Elizabeth Fee and Daniel Fox (eds), *AIDS: Contemporary History*, University of California Press, Berkeley 1991.

22 Jowell et al., *British Social Attitudes – the 7th Report*.

PART III
Making History

9

The Idea of a Sexual Community

Community, argued James Baldwin, 'simply means our endless connection with, and responsibility for, each other'.[1] And, as Raymond Williams once remarked, the term 'community' is one of the few words which never has negative connotations, and is used pretty promiscuously in a host of political constructions across the political spectrum. It attempts both to express social realities and to offer an aspiration towards something better, more inclusive and tangible. In the form of contemporary communitarianism, the pursuit of community suggests a revulsion against the coldness and impersonality, the instrumentality and narrow self-interest, of abstract individualism with its associated marketization and commodification of human bonds. The idea of community, in contrast to social atomization, suggests that men and women should be members and not strangers, should have ties and belongings that transcend the monad.

As such it has become a key idea in the debate on the postmodern world. Zygmunt Bauman has suggested that it has come to replace reason and universal truth in postmodern philosophy. There are no values or ethics that are not community based, it has been argued; for communities embody certain traditions – many of them, it has to be said, recently invented, but no less potent for that.

Communities are not fixed once and for all. They change as the arguments over time continue, and as other communities exercise their gravitational pull. But at the same time, the social relations of a community are repositories of meaning for its members, not sets of mechanical linkages between isolated individuals. A community offers a 'vocabulary of values' through which individuals construct their understanding of the social world, and their sense of identity and belonging. Communities appear to offer embeddedness in a world which seems constantly on the verge of fragmentation.

A major problem, of course, is that a particular definition of community may undermine a wider sense of community embodied in the best of humanist traditions. The strongest sense of community is in fact likely to come from those groups who find the premises of their collective existence threatened, and who construct out of this a community of identity which provides a strong sense of resistance and empowerment. Seeming unable to control the social relations in which they find themselves, people shrink the world to the size of their communities, and act politically on that basis. The result, too often, is an obsessive particularism as a way of embracing or coping with contingency. And as critics of community have pointed out, social pluralism and the proliferation of associations do not necessarily mean variety for men and women personally: embeddedness means people can get stuck.

The challenge for modern advocates of community, therefore, is to imagine community without either neo-tribalism or self-immolation. The key issue, I would argue, is not whether community, but what sort of community, and what sort of identity, are appropriate at any particular time. Michel Foucault distinguishes between three concepts of community: a *given community, a tacit community* and a *critical community*:

> a given community arises from an identification: 'I am an X'. Tacit community is the materially-rooted system of thought that makes X a possible object of identification; and critical community sees this system of thought as singular or contingent, finds something 'intolerable' about it, and starts to refuse to participate in it.[2]

In the contemporary world, 'given' – or traditional – communities are losing their moral density as old values crumble and uncertainty rules. The latent sense of community that can be detected under the procedural republic of liberalism may provide the necessary support for a wider sense of solidarity, but in it lurks the danger that the communal values that are discernible will be conservative and exclusive – as indeed I believe Amitai Etzioni's communitarian advocacy of a strengthened spirit of neighbourhood and family must be. A critical community, on the other hand, results from a problematization of a given or latent identity. It is open to new experiences and ways of being, which make new subjectivities possible. At its best, I shall argue, the idea of a sexual community as it is evoked in contemporary radical sexual political discourse embraces this notion of a critical community.

In this chapter I want to look at four key elements contained in the idea of a sexual community: community as a focus of identity; community as ethos and repository of values; community as social capital; and community as politics. I shall draw most of my examples from the best-documented sexual community, the lesbian and gay community, with other examples as necessary. There are, of course, many problems with this choice. First of all, it presupposes a unity which is not necessarily there. The differences between gay men and lesbians are well rehearsed; there are many other differences: between rich and poor, white and black, North American and European, urban and rural, right and left, and so on. There is no reason to think that people who share one characteristic necessarily share others but then, that is a feature of all communities. Secondly, it may understandably be argued that there are certain key elements of the lesbian and gay community that make it unique: stigma, prejudice, legal inequality, a history of oppression, and the like. But that, I would suggest, is what makes it a valuable path into understanding the nature of contemporary communities. The idea of a heterosexual community, much used recently in the literature of HIV and AIDS, is pretty much an oxymoron. Precisely because heterosexuality is hegemonic in our general culture, a general heterosexual community does not exist, though of course there are specific heterosexual communities (and as I have suggested, much of contemporary communitarianism assumes as a given that heterosexuality is the very definition of community).

In other words, it is because homosexuality is not the norm, is stigmatized, that a sense of community transcending specific differences has emerged. It exists because participants in it feel it does and should exist. It is not geographically fixed. It is criss-crossed by many divisions. But a sort of diasporic consciousness does exist because people believe it exists. And this belief has material and cultural effects.

To put it another way: a web of narrative, a proliferation of stories, has developed in a particular set of historical circumstances, which gives meaning to the idea of a sexual community for many people. The effectiveness of sexual narratives or stories, as Ken Plummer has argued in his important book, *Telling Sexual Stories* (1995), depends on an ability to tell them, and an audience to listen to them. In recent years we have been witness to the emergence of large groups willing to tell their stories ('coming out'), and the construction of a mass audience for many hitherto implausible narratives, emanating from the private worlds of everyday life. And it is from the conflicts of everyday life that many of the greater conflicts of society are generated; and certainly the new narratives of sexual minorities have both subverted and challenged many of the narrative certainties of contemporary life. But there are other forces that are also shaking the foundations of legitimizing value systems: the emergence of dissident sexual communities is only one index of the jumble of stories now bombarding us. In understanding the idea of community embodied in the new sexual cultures we can also begin to understand the complexities of communities in the postmodern world.

As a way into this question, let me now turn to the four elements of the idea of sexual community that I mentioned earlier.

Community as a focus of identity

It takes two people to make a lesbian, the American feminist Teresa de Lauretis has wittily remarked, and this underlines a profound truth. Sexual identities in the modern world, like other identities, can only ever be relational, shaped in a world of difference. But identities do not exist on an even plane. They are severely marked by a hierarchical ordering, in which lesbian and gay identities are subordinate.

The historical evidence is now massive that, despite the polymorphous nature of sexuality throughout history and across all cultures, the binary division in our culture, between the norm and the perverse, or in practice between hegemonic heterosexuality and dissident homosexuality, has a history, and a recent one at that. Despite the existence of distinct homosexual networks, meeting places, even nascent 'communities', for want of a better word, which are recorded in various European cities since late medieval times, it is only over the past century or so, coincident with the hardening of the binary divide, that distinctive homosexual 'forms of existence', with sexualized identities, communities and sexual political movements, have emerged. A sense of identity, shaped in a sense of community, and articulated through political movements, has been, I would argue, a dominant motif only since the late 1960s.

The social movements concerned with sexuality that have emerged since the 1960s, the feminist and lesbian and gay movements especially, implicitly assume that it is through social involvement and collective action that individuality can be realized and identity affirmed. The new movements can be interpreted as a revolt against the forms of subjectification that the contemporary world has given rise to, a challenge to the technologies of power which define individuals in particular ways and pin them to particular subordinated identities and locations in society. They reveal the complexity of modern social relations, and the intractability of the contradictions and tensions these produce. They simultaneously offer alternative possibilities.

At the heart of the new movements is a rejection of imposed definitions, and a struggle for social space in which new identities can be forged. There is of course a historic irony in this process. The identities are being shaped on the very terrain that gave rise to domination in the first place. Racial and ethnic minorities historically challenged racist structures by affirming their racialized identities ('black is beautiful'). Feminism has historically affirmed the rights of women by asserting the positive qualities of femininity. Lesbians and gays reject the pathologizing of homosexuality by 'reversing the discourse', and affirming pride in being homosexual. In the process, there is a search for a hidden history, a narrative structure which seems to express the truth of repressed or oppressed experience. But a better way of seeing what is happening is to understand it as a social positioning, where difference is asserted as a positive quality rather than an inevitable or naturalized divide.

Movements such as these are not simply expressing a pre-existing essence of social being. Identities and belongings are being constructed in the very process of organization itself. They are effective in so far as they can speak a language which brings people into the activities, alignments and subjectivities being shaped; and the most effective language available is the language of community.

Like a movement, which both grows out of and creates a sense of wider identification, a community must be constantly reimagined, sustained over time by common practices and symbolic re-enactments which reaffirm both identity and difference. A national community may be sustained by allegiance to the flag, national days, the ritual of elections or monarchy, by victories in war, war memorials and military pride, or by the less harmful ephemeral hysteria of athletic competitions or the soccer World Cup. A black community may re-enact its difference through defence of its territory against racist attacks or the symbolic presence of the police. It may also re-enact and celebrate it in carnival, the inversion of the daily humdrum existence where reality is turned upside down, the streets become the property of the oppressed, and the repressed experiences of the community can return, triumphantly, for the day. In the same way, sexual identity and community are expressed through annual events such as Lesbian and Gay Pride; or the losses of the AIDS community can be mourned and the lives of the dead celebrated through candlelit vigils and the sewing of memorial quilts. Without such reimaginings a community will die, as difference is obliterated or becomes meaningless before the onrush of history.

Community stands here for some notion of solidarity, a solidarity which empowers and enables, and makes individual and social action possible. Sexual dissidence is ultimately dependent upon the growth of that sense of common purpose and solidarity represented by the term 'community'. The appeal to the authenticity of one's sexual experience that has been the symblic token of many of the pioneers of radical sexual change becomes culturally meaningful only in so far as it speaks to, and evokes an echo in, the experience of others in a tacit community that is on its way to becoming a critical community. With the development of a sexual movement with a sense of its own history and social role, the idea of community becomes a critical norm through which alternatives are opened up.

Community as ethos and repository of values

Mark Blasius, in his recent book, *Gay and Lesbian Politics*, has argued that the lesbian and gay struggle has produced a sense of community and identity which provides the context for moral agency, and hence for the emergence of a lesbian and gay ethos enacted in everyday life. The lesbian and gay ethos, Blasius suggests, can be understood 'both as coming out and as integrating one's homoerotic relationships within all of one's social relationships'. In practice, though inevitably a prolonged and often anguished practice, that means a challenge to compulsory heterosexuality and the construction of an erotics 'that decenters genital sexuality and de-essentializes gender'. That in turn, Blasius argues, is the grounding for lesbian and gay politics in its various forms. I shall take this text as an example of the arguments being made for the ethical values of sexual community.

Blasius's most important contribution lies in his exploration of the underlying system of values that he sees as existing in the lesbian and gay world. Two significant trends are described: the shift from 'sexuality' to 'the erotic', which in Blasius's argument implies the displacement of traditional hierarchical patterns of the sexual in favour of plural forms; and the emergence of a 'new ethic' which embraces the erotic and is built around not so much an orientation, preference or lifestyle as a sense of self-identified and collectively invented community. They are in a real sense simply two aspects of the same cultural shift: a move towards the evoking, or inventing, of new identities, belongings and forms of intimacy.

Blasius suggests that the gay and lesbian community offers a sense of belonging, an ethos based on erotic friendship 'characterised by reciprocal *independence*'.

> Erotic friendship is an ethico-erotic relationship productive of equality; the participants (whatever they name themselves lovers, exlovers, fuckbuddies, partners, etc) are inventing themselves and become the conditions for such self-invention of each other.[3]

He concludes that, in doing this, lesbians and gays are pioneering an art of living through one's erotic relations, and thereby introducing something new onto the historical landscape.

I agree with that formulation: the dense interconnections, networks, relationships, experiments in living, new forms of loving and caring (above all in response to the HIV and AIDS epidemic), which have been the outstanding achievements of lesbian and gay politics since the 1960s, provide the grounds on which new value systems are developing. But have we said everything when we have said that? The recognition that the basics of a new relational ethos do indeed exist does not in itself answer that fundamental question of 'how should we live'; on the contrary, it poses it in a new way, and this, I feel, is downplayed by Blasius.

We all know how difficult it is to live up to the standards we have communally set for ourselves. Erotic desire can undermine the firmest resolutions. Fear and jealousy and betrayal are not abolished because we disapprove of them. A commitment to safer sex has not stopped unsafe practices. Friendship can turn to hate, and love, like desire, can die. There is a danger that in celebrating the new ethos of lesbian and gay life we may aspire to a utopianism that frail, mere humans can scarcely live up to. So as well as celebrating eros and the possibilities of community, we need to begin to spell out what an art of life, an ethos based on reciprocal independence, means in practice. Are certain forms of behaviour better than others? Are some things right, others wrong, some things true and others false? These are hard questions, because they suggest prescriptive rather than freely chosen answers. The challenge facing us is to avoid prescription and proscription at the same time as we invent forms of conduct which maximize human autonomy and freedom of choice whilst affirming our need for one another, the importance of the human bond. Again, the much used notion of community is an attempt to encompass that objective.

Community as social capital

The sexual movements of recent years have both encouraged and built on a sense of community, a space where hitherto execrated sexual activity and identities have been affirmed and sustained. Such a validation of community has been at the centre of the response to HIV and AIDS by the group most affected in the west, gay men. It has made possible a social and cultural response whose aim is to promote survival, defeat stigma, encourage community and develop self-esteem, the *sine qua non*, in Simon Watney's formulation, of a regime of safer sex. At the same time, the absence of a sense of community around sexual issues amongst other groups affected by the epidemic has been a critical factor in limiting the development of a culture of safer sex and personal responsibility.

For historical reasons, the earliest collective response to the HIV/AIDS epidemic came from the gay community, first of all in the USA and subsequently throughout the west, and even in the developing world. In the absence until the mid-1980s of coherent governmental or international responses, activists schooled in the lesbian and gay community established the first and enduring organizational response to the epidemic – organizations such as Gay Men's Health Crisis in the USA and the Terence Higgins Trust in the UK. These organizations pioneered practices of safer sex, rooted in community experience; developed models of care and mutual support, such as 'buddying'; acted as advocates for people with HIV and AIDS; lobbied, successfully, for a more strategic governmental response; and to some extent became key partners, even agents, of government in responding to the crisis (see chapter 10, below).

These new voluntary organizations embodied a key philosophy developed initially in the sexual communities from which they sprang: that of collective activity and of collective self-help (ironically, though from a different starting point, echoing the philosophical attitude of New Right critics of welfare). As one member of Body Positive, a support group for people living with HIV and AIDS, has commented, 'Self help is about taking control of your own life in your own hands and solving your own problems through helping others in the same situation.'[4] The emphasis on self-help in relation to the new epidemic was at first a matter of *faute de mieux* rather than principle, a community response to the absence of government response in a climate of prejudice and fear. This grass-roots mobilization proved, however, immensely influential in the ideologies of the many other community-based HIV and AIDS organizations that subsequently sprang up (my own research has shown that by the early 1990s well over five hundred HIV and AIDS voluntary agencies existed in the UK, embracing all the major categories at risk). It represents, in the phrase used by Wann, a significant accumulation of social capital by the communities most at risk from the epidemic.[5]

Wann's argument is that a variety of social skills exist in the various communities that now make up an ever more complex and pluralistic culture, and that these are being deployed in a variety of community-based activities. These provide a major resource in the sub-political spheres of social life that are ignored by the last-ditch defenders of traditional statism but are being exploited by the market individualism of the New Right (as can be seen in the ways in which the purchaser/provider split in social welfare provision in part depends on the existence of voluntary activity whilst refusing to accept the radical challenge frequently offered by community action). Community- based activities represent an attempt to gain control of the conditions of one's life, as again can be seen in the activities of the HIV/AIDS organizations.

In the early days of the epidemic, community-based activities were rooted in a growing awareness of personal threat. As a respondent put it, 'We were all in it together... we were desperately in need of support with friends dying... and so we worked together.' Subsequently, the emphasis became more explicitly political, in the notion of self-empowerment; this underlay not only the gay-based AIDS organizations but also those that developed amongst women, black people and other threatened minorities. Hence such comments as: 'I think that is very bad for people's immune system, to be kind of dependent', 'it's more important to help people understand how to go about doing things rather than just taking over and doing things for them'. Of course, in practice, it became very difficult to maintain this commitment: self-help groupings became service-delivery organizations; professionalism replaced voluntary action; statutory funding tied agencies to formal procedures and stricter notions of accountability. Many voluntary agencies have become not-for-profit bodies closely linked to statutory requirements, and ties with the originating communities have often become strained, if they have not been severed. But the essential point remains: the developments occurred in the first place because of the social capital accumulated by hitherto marginalized communities.

Community as politics

For the movements concerned with sexuality what matters more than a single set of goals or a defined programme is the symbolic focus of the activities of the movements themselves, their struggle to gain control over the conditions of life. They cannot therefore be judged solely in terms of their political effectivity in attaining this or that legislative shift, important as this often is. Their ultimate importance lies in their cultural and informal impact on the lives of the individuals who align with them, and are addressed by them as active subjects.

The term 'movement' conveys some of this sense of informality but perhaps carries too strong a suggestion of a cohesiveness in organization which is only spasmodically present. As Alberto Melucci has argued, social movements are normally '"invisible" networks of small groups submerged in everyday life'.[6] They tend to be concerned with individual needs, collective identity, and a part-time 'membership', and constitute laboratories in which new experiences are invented, and tested, in which reality is redescribed, and individuals can develop alternative experiences of time, space and personal relationships. They attempt to shape a new 'grammar' of everyday life rather than political programmes.

One of their key functions is to translate actions into symbolic challenges that upset the dominant cultural codes, and reveal their irrationality, partiality and illegitimacy as products of power and domination. So they have a dual role: to reveal the macro and micro forms of domination that constitute modern life; and to demonstrate the possibilities of alternative forms of life that are not simply prefigurative of some imagined future, but are actually being constructed in the here and now.

So the practical activities of such movements characteristically subvert conventional views of political activities. Consciousness raising, networking, carnival, festivals, candle-lit processions both affirm a sense of collective being and challenge conventional patterns of life, transmitting to the system a picture of its own contradictions. They illustrate both the complexity of power relations, and the possibility of subverting them.

In this way, despite their informality and *ad hoc* nature, these movements can in particular circumstances become active participants in the domain of politics. They regularly make demands on the conventional structure of politics, often couched in uncompromising terms. They also lean towards a politics of direct action, avoiding in most cases the forms of representative democracy. Contemporary social movements are frequently unstable in both their composition and strategic thrust, and there can be no *a priori* guarantee of their progressive nature. During the 1980s, as many feminists have ruefully noted, the women's movement was strongly divided over its attitudes to pornography, with a number of anti-porn feminists making common cause with far right moralists and social authoritarians. Interestingly, and ironically, some of the neofundamentalist movements of recent years are themselves, in the delay in the triumph of their universalist hopes, explicitly redefining themselves as social movements with the same claim to social space, and to difference, as other, overtly progressive groups. The Christian Coalition in the USA, for instance, achieved remarkable success in influencing the right wing of the Republican Party by playing down their Christian fundamentalism and stressing their more acceptable defence of traditional family values.

Politically, radical sexual communities and their associated movements point in two different directions at once – or at least embrace two distinct political moments: what I call the 'moment of transgression', and the 'moment of citizenship'.[7] The 'moment of transgression' is the moment of challenge to the traditional or received order of sexual life: the assertion of different identities, different lifestyles, and the building of oppositional communities. In its recent form it has given rise to 'queer politics', which has sought to break with what has been perceived as the caution of contemporary gay politics with its integrationist approaches. The 'moment of citizenship' is precisely this movement towards inclusion, towards redefining the polity to incorporate fully those who have felt excluded. Its characteristic emphasis has been on the claiming of civil rights, formal equality – and most recently, in continental Europe at least, on the demand for 'partnership rights' for same-sex couples. On the surface at least they seem radically different strategies, and find expression in different organizational forms: for example, in the UK, in the differences between the confrontationalist politics of OutRage! and the lobbying approach of Stonewall.

There are, however, closer similarities than there might appear between the two strategies. As Elizabeth Wilson has written:

> we transgress in order to insist that we are there, that we exist, and to place a distance between ourselves and the dominant culture. But we have to go further – we have to have an idea of how things could be different, otherwise transgression ends in mere posturing.[8]

The claim for citizenship is one possible way in which 'things could be different'. The notion of citizenship has been historically coloured by its familial and exclusively heterosexual connotations: the citizenship models embodied in the post-war welfare state were explicitly built around the nuclear family and a traditional division of labour between men and women. To claim full citizenship for dissident sexual minorities is to argue for the transformation of the concept. This is what I take Ken Plummer to have in mind when he proposes a new notion of citizenship, what he terms intimate citizenship. Intimate citizenship, he suggests, is concerned with those matters that relate to our most intimate desires, pleasures and ways of being in the world. Some of these relate back to more traditional ideas of citizenship. But intimate citizenship is much more concerned with 'new stories': questions relating to control of our bodies, feelings, and relationships; questions of access to representations and spaces; and the problems and possibilities of choice. In other words, issues that have been previously deemed to be outside the concept of social citizenship, because they were part of the private world, are now becoming part of public debate – precisely because it is only through public change that the protection of private space can be guaranteed. The achievement of intimate citizenship, in turn, however, is predicated on the existence of the shared identities, values, social capital and political belongings that we know by the term 'community'.

Conclusion: community as necessary fiction

I have argued elsewhere that the idea of a sexual identity is a fiction (because it is based on the cultural construction of plausible narratives to make sense of individual lives).[9] But it is a necessary fiction because it offers the possibility of social agency in a context where equal access to social goods is denied. In the same way, the idea of a sexual community may be a fiction, but it is necessary fiction: an imagined community, an invented tradition which enables and empowers. It provides the context for the articulation of identity, the vocabulary of values through which ways of life can be developed, the accumulated skills by which new possibilities can be explored and hazards negotiated, and the context for the emergence of social movements and political campaigns which seek to challenge the existing order.

There are, of course, dangers. The new elective communities can be as exclusive and stifling as traditional ones. Social pluralism and a proliferation of communities do not necessarily guarantee variety or autonomy for all members. The co-existence of different communities depends upon a recognition that the condition of toleration of one's own way of life is a recognition of the validity of other ways of life. That, in turn, requires that communities guarantee a freedom of exit and of voice for their members. The communities built around sexuality are no less likely than others to develop their own norms which may exclude as well as include.

But having said that, it should also be acknowledged that in the contemporary world, with its deep sense of uncertainty around values, the idea of a sexual community has developed because of a conviction that it is only through the enhancement of a collective identity that individual autonomy can be realized.

That is not all that could be said about the idea of community in general, or about sexual communities in particular. But it is enough, I hope, to illustrate my main point: in the contemporary world, the idea of a sexual community is both a necessary and an inevitable one. We cannot do without it.

References

1 James Baldwin, *Evidence of Things Not Seen*, Michael Joseph, London 1986.
2 Cited in J. Rajchman, *Truth and Eros: Foucault, Lacan and the Question of Ethics*, Routledge, London and New York 1991.
3 Mark Blasius, *Gay and Lesbian Politics: Sexuality and the Emergence of a New Ethics*, Temple University Press, Philadelphia 1995, pp. 219, 221.

4 P. McCory, 'On Self Help', *Body Positive*, no. 181, 1995. This section on the HIV/AIDS voluntary sector is based on research from an ESRC-funded project. 'The Voluntary Sector Response to HIV/AIDS', which I co-directed with Peter Aggleton. The quotations are from interviews conducted with members of voluntary agencies.

5 M. Wann, *Building Social Capital: Self Help in the 21st Century Welfare State*, Institute of Public Policy Research, London, 1995.

6 Alberto Melucci, *Nomads of the Present: Social Movements and Individual Needs in Contemporary Society*, Radius, London, 1989, p. 6.

7 See Jeffrey Weeks, *Invented Moralities: Sexual Values in an Age of Uncertainty*, Polity Press, Cambridge 1995, pp. 108–23.

8 Elizabeth Wilson, 'Is Transgression Transgressive?', in Joseph Bristow and Angelia Wilson (eds), *Activating Theory: Lesbian, Gay, Bisexual Politics*, Lawrence and Wishart, London, 1993, p. 11.

9 Weeks, *Invented Moralities*.

10

Community Responses to HIV and AIDS: The 'De-Gaying' and 'Re-Gaying' of AIDS

The health authorities haven't really done much for the gay communities. Maybe because they've been scared. Maybe because the funding they get restricts them. Maybe because they don't give a damn. You can't tie it down to one factor. The fact is ... a gay man in the UK is tested positive about once every six hours ... but ... they don't want to address these issues. Other organisations besides the health authorities ... started de-gaying the epidemic for their own particular reasons ... they started to reduce what they were doing for the gay community, till nobody seemed to do anything. And I think it is very important that the gay community, that is the largest community that is affected, should know. ... In the early days when the epidemic first came around it was the gay community that fought back for their own survival. ... Maybe if they hadn't been so quick to mobilise themselves they wouldn't have been left to themselves.

Volunteer, Gay Men Fighting AIDS

The term 'community' has a resonant tone. This resonance is evoked in a variety of ways, suggesting something more than the individual (though it is composed of individuals), less than the state (though the state can embody a sense of community) – a vital intermediary body, or rather series of bodies, between both. Hardly anyone, unless he or she is prepared to deny altogether that society is something more than individuals and their families, is against the notion of community. The difficulty lies in the fact that this evocative term means different things to different people.

When we speak of a community-based response to HIV and AIDS we are actually referring to particular types of community, often those constructed by and for highly marginalized groups of people. The first community responses – indeed in many places, the first responses at all – to the emergence of the HIV/AIDS epidemic came from those most affected by the spread of sickness and death in the gay male and lesbian communities. Later other communities, of black people, of women affected by HIV, of people with haemophilia and so on, developed their own particular responses. But they did so while the wider (that is to say heterosexual) 'community', with notable individual exceptions, displayed a range of unhelpful responses, ranging from panic to indifference, being stirred into managerial action only when contagion seemed in danger of seeping from the marginal communities into what became known as the 'general population'. In the early 1990s, the UK had a government social policy which stressed 'care in the community', a policy whose ideological roots lie in the professed belief that care for the sick and needy is better and more 'cost-effective' when left to individuals and their families, living in diverse communities.

Here we have at least three types of meaning of community: community as a focus of identity and resistance against a backdrop of marginalization and discrimination; community as a euphemism for 'everyone else', that is the 'normal' population; and community as a metaphor for a greater stress on self-help in welfare provision. A term that is so powerful but elastic obviously has its uses in social policy and cultural rhetoric. But in attempting to understand social responses to the HIV and AIDS crisis in Britain, it is vital to grasp that the use of the term can obscure as much as it can clarify, unless it is used with proper attentiveness to an important but often obscured history.

Two central arguments underpin this chapter. The first is a recognition that the vital initial social response to HIV and AIDS came from within the group most affected by, and still most at risk from, the British epidemic – the gay male population. Gay men were not alone in that response. Many women, lesbian and heterosexual, and some heterosexual men, worked alongside them; and the informal alliance between early AIDS activists, physicians and others working in genito-urinary medicine (GUM) clinics, and public health officials was to play a central part in shaping the policy agenda that a reluctant British government was eventually to accept (Weeks, 1993; see chapter 7, above). The point is that gay men, shaped by a strong sense of identification with a political, cultural and sexual community whose achievements of the previous decade now seemed at risk because of a deadly threat of epidemic, took the lead in resistance to it. We can see this both in a community stress on the need to change sexual practices in the direction of safer sex, and in the development of direct services to those who were ill or dying. To say that is not to deny the vital contribution of other individuals or groups, then or since. It is simply to recognize a temporal and moral priority.

The second argument is that community-based activity took the form of a powerful voluntary response, both in terms of volunteering in a range of organizations, statutory as well as voluntary, and in the establishment of a range of specialized HIV and AIDS voluntary organizations, from large service organizations such as the Terence Higgins Trust to local self-help groups, from high-profile care facilities such as the London Lighthouse to a huge variety of national, regional and local help and information lines (Aggleton et al., 1993). A high percentage of the volunteers were, and continue to be, gay men or lesbians. Indeed, the majority of the earliest HIV/AIDS-specific voluntary organizations were founded by, and staffed by, gay people. They were responding to a crisis that particularly affected gay men, and a crisis which, in most of Britain anyway, still largely affects gay men. Yet, as we will see, when the community group Gay Men Fighting AIDS (GMFA) was founded in 1992, it could claim with some justification that it was the first HIV/ AIDS organization in the UK specifically directed at the needs of gay men (King, 1993).

There is a major paradox here which it is the aim of this chapter to explore. The data we use come from the first major national study of the HIV and AIDS voluntary sector. Funded by the Economic and Social Research Council (Grant R 000233669), the project entitled 'Voluntary Sector Responses to HIV and AIDS: Policies, Principles, Practices' began work in 1992 with a survey of some 550 voluntary agencies working on HIV/AIDS issues. These included both HIV/AIDS-specific organizations, founded with the aim of responding to this particular issue, and generalist organizations which had more recently started work in this area. Subsequently, a series of case studies was conducted in a range of individual voluntary organizations; these are the source of the quotations used in this chapter.

From the past to the present

The early voluntary groupings, such as the Terrence Higgins Trust (founded in 1983), were established because of the absence of a co-ordinated national response in the early stages of the crisis. Voluntary services had to develop, because outside the hospitals and GUM clinics caring for people with HIV and AIDS, there was nothing else. The reasons for this have been documented elsewhere (see Berridge, 1993), but lie in the fact that HIV and AIDS first appeared amongst a highly stigmatized group of people, gay men, at a uniquely unfavourable political conjuncture. It was a period when the political impetus of the initial wave of lesbian and gay politics seemed to be weakening, and a New-Right-influenced government had an economic agenda which favoured cutbacks in welfare expenditure and a moral agenda which strongly disapproved of an assertive homosexual politics.

The initial success of this community effort was remarkable, in two senses. First, there was a widespread adoption of safer-sex activities amongst gay men, as they responded to community-based health promotion rooted in a strong awareness of community norms and values (Watney, 1994). Second, embryonic services were established: help lines, self-help groups for people with HIV and AIDS, buddying services, support networks and so on. These were almost entirely supported by voluntary sources of funding (Weeks et al., 1994a).

But there was success of another kind too. A crucial part of the voluntary sector strategy was to campaign for the statutory sector to provide much-needed services. At first, the new sector saw itself as a substitute for absent services, an advocate for better services which it was assumed could and should be provided through the community at large. However, after a change in government policy announced at the end of 1986, there was a more sustained statutory response, directed at limiting the spread of the epidemic. This took the form both of a generalized health education campaign, and of the rapid development of a variety of services funded either directly by central government, or through local and health authorities. In fact between 1985/6 and 1992, central government granted £8.9 million through Section 64 funding to voluntary organizations in the HIV/AIDS field; and over £500 million was made available to statutory bodies for 'prevention, treatment and care', some of which found its way to voluntary bodies (Department of Health, 1992). A consequence of this new government policy was rapid expansion of the voluntary sector.

The origins, and subsequent histories, of the organizations which came into being in this period were diverse. Some developed in response to grass-roots initiatives: of people with AIDS (e.g. Frontliners), of women (e.g. Positively Women), of minority ethnic communities (e.g. Blackliners, Black HIV/AIDS Network), and of injecting drug users (e.g. Mainliners). Others did so as a result, in effect, of partnerships between statutory and voluntary effort (e.g. The Landmark in south-east London). Many started and remained largely informal networks, with few, if any, paid workers. A large number, however, became significant service-delivery agencies.

Though the main stimulus behind the origins of such organizations was a growing recognition of the needs of different populations at risk, in the process of development several tendencies have been widely observed. As the HIV/AIDS sector has developed, so have the expertise and 'professionalization' of the staff. As the size and range of activities of individual organizations have increased, so has the division of labour between management committees, senior managers, paid workers and volunteers. As some of the organizations have acquired formal trust status, and become integrated into a network of inter-agency activities, especially into joint planning with statutory bodies, so have difficult questions emerged about the relation between advocacy, campaigning and service provision. In consequence, and despite their frequent origins in communities of need and at risk, many voluntary agencies have found that their links with their origins are becoming increasingly tenuous.

One sign of this is the clear shift in the populations targeted by the organizations we surveyed. The largest grouping of organizations (44 per cent) stressed that they gave the highest priority to the needs of the 'general HIV constituency'. Some 30 per cent emphasized priority to 'gay/bisexual men', 27 per cent to injecting drug users, 23 per cent to women, 20 per cent to children and young people, 9 per cent to people from minority ethnic communities, and 5 per cent to people with haemophilia. By way of contrast, the reported modes of transmission for diagnosed cases of AIDS between 1982 and 1993 were: 74 per cent through sexual intercourse between men, 7.3 per cent were cases of women through various sources, 4.8 per cent were amongst injecting drug users, and 4.8 per cent among people infected through contaminated blood products.

Such evidence tends to confirm the picture that the early HIV/AIDS voluntary agencies, despite the pattern of the epidemic, were not especially gay-oriented organizations. On the contrary, there is evidence to suggest that those organizations that did have their origins in the lesbian and gay community went out of their way to emphasize that they were generic AIDS service organizations (ASOs). It is this set of circumstances that has given rise to the issue of 'de-gaying'. Briefly, de-gaying has been defined as:

> the denial or downplaying of the involvement of gay men in the HIV epidemic, even when gay men continue to constitute the group most severely affected, and when the lesbian and gay community continues to play a pioneering role in non-governmental (and sometimes) governmental responses, such as the development of policy or the provision of services to people living with HIV.
>
> *(King, 1993, p. 169)*

This raises three types of question: (1) the extent to which it is accurate to talk about 'de-gaying' as having taken place within the HIV/AIDS voluntary sector; (2) the extent to which such an analysis ignores or downplays the needs of other groups at risk of HIV and AIDS; and (3) the extent to which contemporary social policy actually addresses the needs and specific experiences of those people most at risk.

The de-gaying and re-gaying of AIDS

In Britain, the concept of de-gaying has informed the work of a number of gay writers and others long active in the field of HIV and AIDS, for example, Simon Watney (1994), Edward King (1993) and Peter Scott (1993). However, understanding the development of responses to AIDS in terms of de-gaying is not limited to Britain. Cindy Patton, for example, has used the term to account for the links between homophobia and the way in which AIDS has been conceptualized, as well as offering a critique of the way in which voluntary-sector organizations such as Gay Men's Health Crisis (New York) have been transformed from a radical grass-roots origin to professionalized bureaucratic agencies (Patton, 1990; see also Altman, 1993).

As has been amply documented (e.g. Weeks, 1993), AIDS in Britain and most other western countries was originally thought of as a disease which affected gay men only. Since gay men were, in Britain, the first to die of AIDS-related illnesses, there evolved an almost metonymic link between the two 'diseases' – homosexuality and AIDS. At the same time, gay men began to organize to meet the need for information and support of those who were already infected, and to educate others about how to avoid infection. Thus in terms of the epidemiology, and the social responses to that, AIDS rapidly acquired the status of a 'gay disease' – a disease with a corresponding socio-sexuality which served to contain the danger, apparently limiting it to a deviant outsider category of persons.

By the mid-1980s, fears that the epidemic was also likely to affect 'normal' people began to be voiced. In Britain and the United States, government officials predicted that the epidemic could spread into the general population, and parallels were drawn with the African epidemic. An attempt was made to shift the emphasis from categories of person who were (or were not) at risk to types of behaviour which were (or were not) risky.

Organizations formed to assist people with HIV infection were also being transformed both in terms of the dominant discourses they used, and in terms of their relationships with funding agencies. Thus voluntary-sector organizations began to emphasize that they were not gay organizations as such, but offered their services to anyone affected by

HIV. Simultaneously, they began to rely more on funds from state agencies, which led to an increased professionalization of personnel, whereby gay identity became secondary to professional identity, and to an increased conformity to statutory models of organization, including the adoption of equal opportunities policies, a desire for 'respectability', and fear that failure to conform would mean discontinuation of funds.

This 'de-gaying' of voluntary-sector organizations was acutely felt in the area of HIV-prevention work. Gay men who had been involved in initial community-based efforts to educate other gay men about safer-sex practices began to experience difficulty in continuing such work through voluntary-sector organizations keen to reiterate the message that anyone could be affected by AIDS, and concerned that state funders might object to explicit safer-sex education for gay men. At the same time, statutory-sector agencies had begun to undertake generic HIV-prevention work, and work targeting a range of specific constituencies such as women, young people and people from minority ethnic communities.

In the light of these developments, research was conducted in 1992 which sought to confirm the assertion that HIV-prevention work with gay men was not being carried out. King et al. (1992) surveyed 226 agencies – health authorities, local authorities and voluntary organizations – to find out what HIV-prevention initiatives targeting gay and bisexual men were being undertaken. Their study found that there was an 'alarmingly low level' of such work, even though gay and bisexual men continued to be the group most at risk (King et al., 1992, p. 1). Respondents gave various reasons why this might be, such as difficulties associated with contacting gay men (including the belief that there were no gay men in the area); having elected to work with other – or no specific – target groups; believing that work with gay men was too sensitive or illegal; and believing that HIV prevention with gay men was already being carried out by other agencies (cf. King et al., 1992, pp. 12–14).

The establishment in 1992 of GMFA as a new voluntary agency can be linked directly to the frustration of certain gay men long active in the field of HIV and AIDS with the politics and effects of what they would come to describe as de-gaying. The formation of GMFA was, therefore, an attempt to redress the imbalances some saw, and to initiate the process of 're-gaying' AIDS. One of the founding members describes the origins of GMFA thus:

> there'd been an invisible college of a number of gay men working in the
> field who were extremely dissatisfied and distressed at the response to
> the epidemic as it affected them throughout the sectors, and we'd been
> talking for something like two years about the need to set up a specific

organisation which refocused upon gay men's needs because nobody else seemed to be . . . doing it.

(Founding member, Gay Men Fighting AIDS)

A more explicitly gay form of campaigning was seen as essential if GMFA were to begin to influence how resources are allocated. Through articles and advertisements in the gay press, posters, postcards and concerted efforts to recruit gay male volunteers to the organization, the group quickly sought to make itself and its position known. GMFA argued strongly in favour of reallocating resources to meet the need, now well documented through epidemiological data and the demonstrated paucity of HIV-prevention work targeting gay and bisexual men.

At the same time, GMFA volunteers began to devise and implement small, local-level HIV-prevention initiatives. These were part of a training process for volunteers and a demonstration that ordinary gay men were capable of doing such work (as they had done, it was argued, in the early days of the epidemic). Both were seen as necessary as GMFA leaders began to negotiate with statutory bodies for funds to carry out larger-scale work. What was being sought was the power to influence resource allocation, and the power to devise prevention strategies unencumbered by the ethos of statutory agencies, or voluntary-sector agencies perceived to have been de-gayed. Underlying such an approach were two key assumptions: first, that underpinning the de-gaying process was an 'institutionalized homophobia'; and, second, that a strategy of health promotion based on 'community mobilization' had been successful in the early stages of the epidemic, but was in danger of being lost because of de-gaying.

The authors of the 1992 survey of gay men's HIV prevention initiatives remarked that 'underlying all of the reasons given for failing to do work with gay and bisexual men we may detect varieties of homophobia, whether passive or active, frank or implicit, institutional or individual' (King et al., 1992, p. 5). Institutions failed to meet the needs of gay men, to resource health education/promotion specifically for them, because their primary concern was not for the lives of gay men, but to ensure that infection did not 'enter' the heterosexual pool. They also failed to meet the needs of gay men because there have been no real precedents for acknowledging and funding the real needs of gay men.

Against this is counterposed a model of health promotion which prioritizes community mobilization. The existence, it is argued, of a 'moral community' of gay men in the early 1980s provided the basis for a process of health awareness and perception of risk which led to a rapid development of techniques of 'safer sex'. GMFA, for example, claims that the early days of the epidemic saw a reduction in HIV

infection because gay men themselves 'passed on the word' about how to
have safer sex, on how to avoid infection. The methodology employed by
GMFA – community mobilization – seeks to create the conditions
whereby that 'naturally occurring' safer-sex movement will be repeated.
This strategy requires that there be a 'community' to mobilize, and so it is
argued HIV-prevention work should begin in the nucleus of gay communities that already exist, most obviously among men with a confident gay
identity who use gay structures, venues and community groups. When
questioned about the role of GMFA, one volunteer replied:

> to be very basic it's there for the survival of the gay community. Without
> organisations like GMFA, the gay community will die or be driven under-
> ground.... The amount of gay men that are coming out and amount of gay
> men that are dying will soon overtake each other because HIV and AIDS is
> not limited to age barriers ... so unless there are organisations such as GMFA
> to educate people ... not just about sex but about gay sex, gay way of life, the
> age of consent, issues regarding couples and council houses and not being
> able to leave it to your partner, unless people know about discrimination
> such as that it won't change.
>
> *(Volunteer, Gay Men Fighting AIDS)*

Such an analysis marks a striking change of emphasis from the early days
of the epidemic when AIDS activists emphasized the importance of
making the distinction between 'risk groups' and 'risk activities'. It was
the latter, it was argued, that should be targeted, because everyone was
potentially at risk unless they modified behaviour which could transmit
the virus. To target the former would be to remain complicit with a
discourse which blamed gay men for the epidemic.

There are, however, some problems with the above analysis. First, it
assumes that 'de-gaying' had taken place across the board, whereas it
may be more appropriate to suggest that most HIV and AIDS voluntary
organizations were not in a position to be de-gayed because they were
never explicitly gay to start with. As part of our study of voluntary-sector
responses, we have looked closely at two non-London organizations in
areas of relatively low HIV prevalence. The first, a local volunteer-led
community group, has one part-time paid worker and between 30 and 40
volunteers. Although the group was originally formed by a core of
individuals, predominantly gay men, who were dissatisfied with the
then existing Body Positive local group, members are keen to stress
they have never been a gay-oriented organization. The group's constitution, for example, states that one of their primary aims is 'To promote the
benefit of the inhabitants [of the local community] living with HIV and
AIDS without distinction of sex, sexual orientation, race or of political,
religious or other opinions'. However, the vast majority of support for

the group, particularly with regard to fund raising, comes from the local gay community. As one member put it:

> This group isn't just for gay people, it's for heterosexual people, men, women, children, haemophiliacs, drug addicts...It's for everyone....I could never stand any group anywhere and being part of it and saying it's only for gay people.... Talking about the gay community, the group is very much on the gay scene, very, very well known and in every gay pub and club we have our leaflets, our posters.

The other agency, a significant regional one founded in the mid-1980s, again had a strong lesbian and gay membership and staffing, and most people in the area affected by HIV were gay men, but it has always seen itself as a generic agency. Indeed, it is only in the past few years, with statutory funding, that it has been able to support explicitly gay outreach work. This in turn has led to tensions within the organization over the priority that should be given to this sort of activity, and its weakening effect on other, broader-based activities. It is an ironic fact that statutory funding for gay health promotion has been seen as undermining the generic ambitions of a gay-founded and -run service agency.

Both of these examples illustrate the point that while staff and volunteers might be lesbian and gay, and specific work (fund raising, outreach) may be targeted at the gay community, beyond large centres like London there may be no alternative but for voluntary agencies to be generalist in their work. This contrast does not in itself invalidate the arguments of GMFA, but it highlights the difficulties of developing a community-based model of HIV/AIDS health promotion that would be straightforwardly applicable throughout the UK.

The broadening constituency of AIDS

The recognition of different populations at risk, and of their diverse needs, has posed difficult questions about the sensitivity and appropriateness of existing services. The articulation of new needs, or existing needs that are unmet within current service provision, coupled with the release of public funds, stimulated the emergence of a whole range of HIV/AIDS groups during the 1980s. To exemplify the diversity of the response, such groups included Positively Women, founded in 1987 by a small group of women in response to the lack of appropriate support services available at that time to women living with HIV; Positively Irish Action on AIDS, founded in 1989 by a group of Irish HIV and drug workers and Irish gay men who were increasingly concerned about the number of Irish people with drug and HIV problems; the NAZ project, formed in 1991 by a group of concerned and affected people who felt that the needs of South Asian, Turkish, Irani and Arab communities were not being adequately addressed by the statutory and voluntary sectors; Blackliners, which came into being as a telephone help line in 1989 out of concern that people of African, Asian and Caribbean descent living with or affected by HIV/AIDS did not have the much-needed sources of information and advice; and the Black HIV/AIDS Network (BHAN), formed in 1988 to offer self-help and provide services to Asian and African–Caribbean people living with and affected by HIV and AIDS.

The emergence of these new community-based groups was made easier because of a conscious policy reaction by some local authorities. Influenced by the notion of general risk, these authorities applied an equal opportunities framework to their resource distribution, targeting their funding at specific communities in response to a new recognition of identity. Some, within minority communities, have been highly critical of the resulting 'category policies':

> While great progressive social changes have resulted from self organised communities that are based in a collective identification, this is not the same as the identity politics that is dominant in parts of the voluntary sector and in some local authorities and which informs a great deal of work around race, gender, sexuality, disability and HIV disease.
>
> *(BHAN, 1991, p. 9)*

The danger of such a critical response, however, is that it suggests that the flourishing of these new community-based groups was the result of a top-down decision. Our own research suggests that organizations such as Blackliners did not simply arise because there was money available, but were born out of the sense of exclusion and the identification of real need by the people themselves. However, this development coincided with efforts to decouple AIDS from homosexual identity. As noted above, the need to stress that 'AIDS is everyone's problem' led to a shift in the nature of much HIV/AIDS health-promotion activity. The coupled effects of the shift in understanding from high-risk groups to high-risk activity, and the homophobic responses to AIDS as the gay plague, led to attempts to unravel the 'natural' association of AIDS with a gay identity/lifestyle. It is precisely this juncture in the late 1980s – the identification of unmet need; the resulting, and sometimes inflexible, application of an equal opportunities response; a lack of adequate understanding of the epidemiology of the disease; and a movement within gay/AIDS activists to delink practices and identity – that led to the development of 'diverse' needs-led community-based organizations.

In America, Cindy Patton (1990) has documented the rise of the new HIV/AIDS groups which addressed the needs of African American, Latino, Haitian and Asian communities. She argues that these newly emergent groups developed for two reasons, out of existing multi-service agencies and cultural affirmation projects, and as projects with a more liberationist ethos. Pointing to the fact that 'government planners, the media and funders often failed to recognise how communities of colour organise around AIDS by extending church or community programmes' (Patton, 1990, p. 11), she argues that the planning of service provision had not taken into account the diversity of social formations and the different philosophies of particular communities that would impact on appropriate HIV/AIDS provision. In some respects, the British experience has closely followed the American situation:

> We know of many Black people who have been made clearly unwelcome in some voluntary sector organisations, particularly if they are heterosexual or women, or go with their family, even though the services are clearly intended for all people living with HIV and AIDS. The low use of support services established by well known voluntary organisations extends even to many Black gay men living with HIV. There have also been some serious incidents of racial harassment and abuse of black people with AIDS attending voluntary organisations.
>
> *(BHAN, 1991, p. 40)*

The argument suggests that within a few years of their inception many of the existing organizations were not meeting the needs of the black communities. While Black people facing HIV/AIDS will have some of the same needs as white people, others will be specific to their race and ethnic experience (e.g. poorer housing conditions, a greater likelihood of unemployment, racial discrimination in health care and in housing allocation, racial violence and harassment). Their medical condition is thus only one of many problems they may face.

This justification for specialist services is in part a critique of existing services, but also a demand for greater choice in health care – people are more comfortable with services which address their particular needs. This has led to changes in some organizations targeting the black population. Blackliners, for example, in its short history has shifted many of its priorities. As already stated, it began as a help line managed by volunteers from diverse backgrounds. In the early days, many of the calls received were from black gay men. Five years after its foundation it continued to provide services for gay men and other men who have sex with men, but also offered services for single women, women with children and other groups in need. Blackliners believe that it is important they acknowledge the diversity within their own client groups, as well as the more subtle workings of culture:

> There's your Afro-Caribbeans, Africans, Asians, even within different Asian communities, the people operate differently and culture is to do with lots of things, it's not just to do with your colour. . . . It's not about all this lumping of people together, it doesn't work.
>
> *(Management Committee Member, Blackliners)*

The existence of organizations such as Blackliners and BHAN is not only a response to existing service provision, or lack of services, it is also bound up with the history of the epidemic, and media representations of HIV and AIDS. For many black people, AIDS has been presented not only as a gay disease, but also as an African disease. Such media sensationalism stigmatized people living with HIV and AIDS, and acted as a pressure to hide HIV/AIDS in black communities.

The situation becomes even more complex when looking at individual social and sexual experiences. Many black men who have sex with men do not identify as gay, and many black lesbians' and gay men's activities are separate from the 'white' scene. In daily life, therefore, there are important practical questions about where to go for services, be they from the gay community, the black community or the wider social relations of the family.

In other words, different minority communities can and do make the same claims for specialist directed services as gay activists around AIDS. As King (1993, p. 271) states, 'it would be unthinkable to attack an organisation such as Positively Women . . . because it does not provide services for men; or to criticise the Black HIV/AIDS Network . . . for not working with white people. These organisations are properly recognised as being not separatist, but specialist.' In fact, it is precisely the need for specialist groups that offers support to recent demands for a re-gaying of AIDS. If specialization is the best way to get an appropriate model of provision, then gay men need their own specialist groups.

However, this attempt to reprioritize gay men's needs has not gone without comment. In a polemical article in Mainliners' newsletter, Nicola Field has argued strongly against the existence of organizations such as GMFA: 'Fighting solely on one issue and from one corner, GMFA does nothing to challenge the system and undermines the gradual moves towards unity that have been growing since the mid-1980s' (Field, 1993, p. 20). She sees AIDS as a 'crisis of poverty, homophobia, racism and misogyny' (Field, 1993, p. 20), and accuses GMFA of 'ducking issues' which link struggles. Although it is easy to write off her views as 'queer bashing', her thoughts probably echo wider reservations voiced elsewhere within the voluntary sector about specialist gay organizations.

Our own research suggests, however, that such a view is misguided. It would be absurd to argue that all groups regarded as at risk need specialist and targeted services, except for gay men. Gay men are still the group most affected by HIV, and it is clear that the gay community requires culturally sensitive services and targeted health promotion as much as any other group. On the other hand, in most parts of Britain, there is no scope or opportunity for specialist agencies addressing the needs of a specific community. The best that can be expected is targeted services within more generalist organizations. Within such organizations, a community mobilization model might well be an appropriate one by which to address the needs of the gay population. It is not, however, the only available health promotion model. What our analysis suggests is that services, statutory as well as voluntary, need to be acutely sensitive to the differences of particular communities at risk – their histories, their communal norms and traditions, and their assessed needs.

Targeting

The evolution of the HIV/AIDS voluntary sector illustrates the need for services and wider social policies to be targeted to the needs of specific communities. The difficulty, however, lies in the fact that this has to happen in a cultural climate influenced by several contradictory factors. First, as we have seen, a number of early AIDS service organizations which were rooted in the gay community have achieved a certain legitimacy by stressing that they are not specifically gay organizations, but meet the needs of all at risk. This hard-won credibility is unlikely to be readily abandoned. Second, the emergence of organizations to articulate the needs of other groups at risk has diversified the HIV/AIDS voluntary sector, and created potentially competitive interests and diverging emphasis in relation to targeting. Third, all of this is occuring in a climate where there is a developing funding crisis (Hopper, 1992), and where government emphasis on targeting may have different implications from those of the community-based agencies themselves (Weeks et al., 1994a).

Shifts in government policy, in fact, provide the crucial context for understanding developments in the HIV/AIDS voluntary sector. The National Health Service and Community Care Act 1990 resulted in a 'shifting climate' for both the voluntary and statutory sectors, characterized by a sharp demarcation between the statutory sector as the 'purchasers' of services, and the voluntary sector as 'providers'. While there might be some potential benefits in such a system, in providing 'quality' and 'choice' of services to clients, while ensuring the targeting of resources to areas of greatest need, commentators have also focused on the complex contracting arrangements and increased bureaucratic procedures that have ensued.

The extent to which AIDS community-based groups have entered into the arena of service contracts depends largely on their own relationship with the statutory sector, and their ability to attract purchasers. This, in turn, is influenced by a range of factors including the group's own organizational culture, their style and structure of management, and the extent to which funders see them as a 'professional' organization (Weeks et al., 1994a). These important criteria are viewed by funders as a means of gauging how able a group is in coping with more explicit criteria for funding. However, funders may also rely on their own political sensibilities and discretion when entering into funding negotiations with potential voluntary-sector providers.

Although government rhetoric in the early 1990s advocated the targeting of resources to those populations most affected, cuts in Section 64 funding and the ending of ring-fenced money in this period directly affected HIV voluntary organizations who may be 'better placed than statutory bodies to reach those populations most at risk' (Rudd, 1993, p. 8). This led to HIV/AIDS voluntary organizations having to compete with other voluntary organizations who cater for more 'popular' constituencies; the loss of HIV-specific posts; a breakdown in collaboration between the voluntary sector and statutory sector particularly in the area of HIV prevention for marginalized groups such as gay men; the loss of intersectoral developmental strategies; and a reduction in the range and quality of specialist HIV/AIDS services in favour of more mainstream activities.

The implications of such far-reaching cuts in community-based initiatives are many. In some parts of the country, for example, HIV-related prevention and care are provided solely by voluntary organizations via the deployment of statutory funding. This has raised fears that, with the amount of money available to statutory agencies shrinking, contracts may not be offered to voluntary agencies that are too 'political' or deemed to represent 'unpopular' or 'marginalized' groups such as gay men.

In a workshop attended by a range of national and local HIV voluntary organisations (Weeks et al., 1994b), Trisha Plummer of Blackliners suggested that the advent of a contracting culture and increasing restraints on resources would necessitate painful choices being made over prioritization, equal opportunities, and specialization versus generic services. The integration of HIV/AIDS services into more generalist provision, she suggested was proceeding alongside the targeting of resources and services, and had obvious advantages both in addressing HIV/AIDS and in combating the continued stigmatization and marginalization of those particular populations most affected and most at risk.

For many agencies, however, the ending of ring-fencing and the gathering pace of 'mainstreaming' mean not only that purchasers are now at liberty to 'select' the types of voluntary-sector provider they fund, regardless of the local epidemiology, but also that purchasers are at liberty to determine the level of local HIV-specific services they provide. The move towards generalized HIV education and funding seems only to marginalize further the needs of those most at risk.

Targeting, therefore, has a dual implication. If intended as the necessary channelling of inevitably limited resources to those most at risk, it opens opportunities for meeting the criticisms of groups like GMFA. If, on the other hand, it means targeting resources to those organizations which are least challenging or controversial, least 'political', it can have the effect of magnifying the impact of the epidemic within the communities most at risk, among those who tend still to be the most marginal and least 'popular' parts of the population.

This returns us to the discussion of the concept of community with which we opened this chapter. It is clear that without the mobilizing energy provided by communities at risk, the response to HIV/AIDS would have been severely retarded. Yet at the same time, voluntary action on its own has neither the scope nor resources to combat the growing magnitude of the challenge posed by the epidemic. Diverse communities are a reality. They are also a model ideal, offering a stance from what could be achieved through which we can see the limitations of what has been achieved. The communities struggling to articulate need are offering an image of what is both necessary and desirable. Governments, on the other hand, have a responsibility to choose between often conflicting priorities in a context of limited resources. Not all needs can be met. But if government ignores the voices of those at risk, then the dimensions of the crisis are likely to grow as scarce resources are misdirected.

Particular communities can articulate need, campaign, provide support and care for those falling ill or dying, but without the properly targeted support of the community as a whole, as represented in statutory agencies, they cannot hope to cope with all the dimensions of the epidemic. This is why community-based organizations have been essential and necessary elements in combating HIV and AIDS, but on their own their actions can never be sufficient. A successful voluntary sector still requires an activist and compassionate state.

Note

The AIDS epidemic has been a protean experience for all drawn into its wake. Its history has been complex, and rapidly changing. This essay was originally written in 1994, and published in 1996. Since then several things have changed significantly. First, the community-based response advocated by GMFA did indeed become the embedded practice of many health authorities with substantial populations of gay men at risk. Second, it has been more widely recognized that several ethnic minority populations are at risk also, and new resources have been targeted towards HIV health education in these communities. Third, with profound implications for the future, the advent of new combination therapies has brought new optimism about the likelihood of HIV becoming a manageable, chronic disease; and has certainly lengthened the lives and improved the quality of life of people with HIV and AIDS in the richer North. But fourth, on a global scale, where poverty, ignorance, and often government incompetence hold sway, the epidemic still threatens catastrophic loss. AIDS continues to be a core feature of our sexual history.

I am grateful to Peter Aggleton, Chris McKevitt, Kay Parkinson and Austin Taylor-Laybourne, with whom this essay was researched and originally written.

References

Aggleton, P., Weeks, J. and Taylor-Laybourn, A. (1993) 'Voluntary Sector Responses to HIV and AIDS: A Framework for Analysis', in P. Aggleton, P. Davies and G. Hart (eds), *AIDS: Facing the Second Decade* (London: Falmer Press).

Altman, D. (1993) 'Expertise, Legitimacy and the Centrality of Community', in P. Aggleton, P. Davies and G. Hart (eds), *AIDS: Facing the Second Decade* (London: Falmer Press).

Berridge, V. (1993) 'Introduction', in V. Berridge and P. Strong (eds), *AIDS and Contemporary History* (Cambridge: Cambridge University Press).

BHAN (Black HIV and AIDS Network) (1991) *AIDS and the Black Communities* (London: Grosvenor).

Department of Health (1992) *HIV Infection: The Working Interface Between Voluntary Organisations and Social Services Departments* (London: Social Services Inspectorate/The AIDS Unit).

Field, N. (1993) *Mainliners Newsletter*, reprinted in *Rouge*, 12: pp. 20–1.

Hopper, C. (1992) 'The Role of the Voluntary Sector', in *HIV and AIDS in the Community*, Occasional Paper no. 2 (London: All Party Parliamentary Group on AIDS).

King, E. (1993) *Safety in Numbers* (London: Cassell).

King, E., Rooney, M. and Scott, P. (1992) *HIV Prevention for Gay Men: A Summary of Initiatives in the UK* (London: North West Thames Regional Health Authority).

Patton, C. (1990) *Inventing AIDS* (New York: Routledge).

Rudd, L. (1993) 'Analysis', *AIDS Matters*, 13: p. 18.

Scott, P. (1993) 'Appendix 1: Gay and Bisexual Men or Men who have Sex with Men?', in B. Evans, S. Sandberg and S. Watson (eds), *Healthy Alliances in HIV Prevention* (London: Health Education Authority).

Watney, S. (1994) *Practices of Freedom: Selected Writings on HIV/AIDS* (London: Rivers Oram Press).

Weeks, J. (1993) 'AIDS and the Regulation of Sexuality', in V. Berridge and P. Strong (eds), *AIDS and Contemporary History* (Cambridge: Cambridge University Press). See Chapter 7 above.

Weeks, J., Taylor-Laybourn, A. and Aggleton, P. (1994a) 'An Anatomy of the HIV Voluntary Sector in Britain', in P. Aggleton, P. Davies and G. Hart (eds), *AIDS, Foundations for the Future* (London: Taylor & Francis).

Weeks, J., Aggleton, P., McKevitt, C., Parkison, K., Taylor-Laybourn, A. and Whitty, G. (1994b) *Maintaining Momentum: Voluntary Sector Responses to HIV and AIDS* (London: HERU, Institute of Education, University of London).

11

Everyday Experiments: Narratives of Non-Heterosexual Relationships

---

Unlike the 1960s, when the questioning of traditional forms produced a search for alternatives to the family, increasingly today there is a pronounced tendency to speak of 'alternative families', differentiated by class, 'race' and ethnicity, life-cycle, single parenthood, chosen lifestyles and the like (Weeks, 1991). Yet while many of these forms have become increasingly acceptable (though not without frequent political controversy, as in the case of one-parent families), there is a continuing stigma attached to non-heterosexual (lesbian, gay, same-sex or 'queer') forms. As the pejorative term 'pretended family relation-ships', legally enshrined in the Local Government Act of 1988, suggests, non-heterosexual patterns are somehow not real. Perhaps it is hardly surprising, then, that the legitimacy of non-heterosexual relationships has recently become a major topic of political controversy, in debates over adoption and surrogacy (in the UK), partnership rights (in many parts of Europe), and same-sex marriage (in The Netherlands and the USA). When the queen of The Netherlands threatens to resign rather than sign into law an act legalizing 'gay marriage', and when a notoriously tardy US Congress rushes into law a bill refusing recognition of the same, something is clearly afoot in the moral undergrowth. At the same time, however, there is growing evidence that lesbians and gay men are establishing sophisticated social forms, which we describe as 'families of choice', with that sense of involvement, security and continuity over time traditionally associated with the orthodox family, and yet which are deeply rooted in a specific historic experience.

During the past generation the possibilities of living an openly lesbian and gay life have been transformed, with the construction of new spaces for everyday life (Bell and Valentine, 1995; Weeks, 1995), and the development of complex cultural patterns. The unprecedented public presence and volubility of lesbians and gays since the late 1960s are in themselves an index of profound changes in the private existence of the non-heterosexual population (Plummer, 1992). In part this amounts to the construction of difference, and certainly the public presentation of homosexuality can be seen as the shaping of new narratives which affirm the distinctiveness of the homosexual experience. Not surprisingly, this has been reflected in a literature, and social and cultural stance, which asserted the importance of sexual identity, allied to a growing assertion of difference. This was supported by the emergence of a social movement which affirmed positive lesbian and gay identities, and which in turn grew out of and strengthened a concept of a distinctive lesbian and gay community (see chapter 9).

Since the early 1980s, however, two marked shifts are discernible. The first is the emergence of a new discourse concerned with wider aspects of homosexual existence than simply sexuality and identity: with relationships, friendships, experiences of intimacy, homosexual parenting, as well as partnership rights and marriage, which could be described as the development of a 'relationship paradigm' (see Weeks et al., 1996, for an overview). Increasingly, political campaigns around homosexuality have extended beyond traditional preoccupations with equal rights and legal protection to embrace questions about relationships: the legal recognition of partnership rights, same-sex marriage, equal rights to adoption and the like (Sullivan, 1995).

On one level, this can be seen as an inevitable consequence of the developing cultural acceptance, and social embeddedness, of the lesbian and gay community as part of a growing pluralization of society. On another level, however, these changing preoccupations are an aspect of the second shift: a recognition of the opening up of all social identities, and what Giddens (1992) has called the 'transformation of intimacy'. On a theoretical level, the poststructuralist and postmodernist challenges to social theory have stressed the fluid, historical, negotiable, contingent nature of all social identities, including sexual identities (Weeks, 1995). Increasingly, it can be argued, identities are not pregiven; they have to be articulated in increasingly complex social circumstances. The lesbian and gay assertion of identities is only one aspect of a wider construction of identities. And if, indeed, identities are contingent, and changeable, it becomes important to understand both how and why identities emerge, how they are stabilized, and how they can be transformed. The relational possibilities – whether in the distinctive social worlds where identities are shaped and affirmed, or in the intensely personal world where intimate involvements are cemented – are keys to the understanding of personal identity. Identity is shaped in and through intimate relationships.

Modernity, Giddens (1992) has argued, is a post-traditional order in which the question 'how shall I live?' has to be answered in day-to-day decisions about who to be, how to behave and, crucially for this discussion, whom and how we should love and relate to. Intimacy, in its modern form, implies a radical democratization of the interpersonal domain, because it assumes not only that the individual is the ultimate maker of his or her own life, but also equality between partners, and their freedom to choose lifestyles and forms of partnerships. Despite the particularism of the homosexual experience, one of the most remarkable features of domestic change over recent years is, we would argue, the emergence of common patterns in both homosexual and heterosexual ways of life as a result of these long-term shifts in relationship patterns (see Bech, 1996). In both, it can be argued, the central drive is the search for a satisfactory relationship as a key element in personal affirmation. The relationship, whether marital or non-marital, heterosexual or homosexual, becomes the defining element within the sphere of the intimate, which provides the framework for everyday life. It is also the focus of personal identity, in which the personal narrative is constructed and reconstructed to provide that provisional sense of unity of the self which is all that is possible in the conditions of late modernity. What Giddens (1992) calls the 'pure relationship', dependent on mutual trust between partners, is both a product of the reflexive self, and a focus for its realization. It offers a focal point for personal meaning in the contemporary world, with love and sex as the prime site for its attainment.

This can be put in another way: the transformations of intimacy, themselves the product of the breakdown of traditional narratives and legitimizing discourses under the impact of long-term cultural, social and economic forces, are making possible diverse ways of life which cut across the heterosexual/homosexual dichotomy. So alongside the discourse of difference which marks the non-heterosexual experience, we can also see the emergence of a certain logic of congruence. Non-heterosexual relationships are shaped in and through these apparently divergent tendencies.

A key aspect of these changes is that as we culturally prioritize individual choice and the acceptance of diversity, commitment becomes
increasingly a matter of negotiation rather than ascription. Recent studies of family and kin obligations (Finch, 1989; Finch and Mason, 1993)
suggest that although ties to family of origin remain highly significant,
they cannot be assumed, and are as much a product of 'working out' as of
blood. The authors prefer to use the concepts of 'developing commitments' and of a sense of responsibility that is worked out over time, so
that while kin relationships remain distinctive, the extent to which they
differ from other relationships, particularly friendships, is blurred. This is
clearly of great significance in relationship to non-familial commitments.
Nardi (1992), for example, notes that friends can provide that sense of
commitment and shared responsibility which kin relationships traditionally do offer, in a 'friends as family' model. In both examples, commitments are seen as products of negotiation.

What we are witnessing, we would argue, is the emergence of
new ways of conceiving family and intimate life, which emphasize
individual needs and meanings, the prioritization of intimacy as the
focus of domestic arrangments, and the negotiated nature of commitment
and responsibility. Plummer (1995), among others, has conceptualized
these in terms of new narrative forms, or stories, that are significantly
reshaping the ways in which we conceive intimate life. As Plummer puts
it:

> The ceaseless nature of story telling in all its forms in all societies has come
> to be increasingly recognised . . . . Society itself may be seen as a textured
> but seamless web of stories emerging everywhere through interaction:
> holding people together, pulling people apart, making societies work . . . the
> metaphor of the story . . . has become recognised as one of the central roots
> we have into the continuing quest for understanding human meaning.
> Indeed culture itself has been defined as 'an ensemble of stories we tell
> about ourselves'. *(Plummer, 1995: 5)*

If this is the case, then the emergence of new ways of expressing basic
needs and desires ('new stories') may be seen as highly important. They
are indicative both of changing perceptions and of changing possibilities.
New stories about sexual and intimate life emerge, it has been argued,
when there is a new audience ready to hear them in communities of
meaning and understanding, and when newly vocal groups can have their
experiences validated in and through them. This in turn gives rise to new
demands for recognition and validation as the new narratives circulate.
These demands may be the expressions of a minority, but they resonate
with broader changes in intimate life. It is in this context that we can

begin to understand the significance of the new stories about non-hetero-sexual families of choice.

The family of choice

'Family' is a resonant word, embracing a variety of social, cultural, economic and symbolic meanings. In social policy discussions, however, it is conventionally used to denote relationships which involve the care of children. It is striking, therefore, that the term is in common use among self-identified non-heterosexuals to denote something broader: an affin-ity circle which may or may not involve children which has cultural and symbolic meaning for the subjects that participate or feel a sense of belonging in and through it. These two quotations illustrate this broad-ening, almost metaphoric, use of term. The first is from a black les-bian:

> I think the friendships I have are family. I'm sure lots of people will say this, but, it's very important to me because my family are not – apart from my mother, who's *kind* of important – on the whole my family's all I've got. And my family are my friends. And I think you make your family – because I've never felt like I belonged anywhere. And it's taken me a long time to realise that it comes from me. . . . It doesn't matter where I go or who I am with, I'm not going to just suddenly be given a family, or a history, or an identity, or whatever. You don't just get it on a plate. You have to create your own. So far as I am concerned, that's how important friends are.
>
> *(FO2)*

The second is from a white gay man:

> we call each other family – you know, they're family. I'm not sure whether that's family in the sense of being gay. . . . I have a blood family, but I have an extended family . . . my friends.   *(MO4)*

There are several points that can be made about such statements. In the first place, the use of the term suggests a strong perceived need for the sorts of value and comfort that the traditional idea of the family suggests (though the reality of the family of origin may be starkly different). Although some lesbians particularly disliked using the term 'family' because of its oppressive heterosexual connotations, for many others friendship circles are like the idealized family (and infinitely preferable to the real one), offering 'a feeling of belonging to a group of people who like me' (MO5); 'affection, love if you like – you share the good things, and you share the bad things too' (M44); 'they support me . . . I socialize with them, talk about things that are important to me' (FO1). Friendships provide the 'lifeline' that the biological family, it is believed, should provide, but often cannot or will not for its non-heterosexual offspring. For a young lesbian, the family of origin is 'homophobic', and cannot offer what friends do provide. Friends are:

> supportive, and understand in a way that your family should and often doesn't. And because of people's situations, they often end up spending more time with their [friends].... I think they become like family.   (F43)

This brings us to the second point: the most commonly used terms applied to such relationships are 'chosen' and 'created'. For one gay man, friends are:

> more important than family.... I take my family [of origin] for granted, whereas my friendships are, to a degree, chosen, and therefore they're created. And I feel a greater responsibility to nourish them, whereas my family will always be there.   *(M21)*

The narrative of self-invention is a very powerful one, particularly in relation to self-identity and lifestyle. As a gay man in his late thirties put it:

> speaking from my generation ... discovering that I was homosexual meant having to invent myself because there was nothing there ... there weren't any role models. It may well be different for gay men coming out now.... But there's still that element of self-invention.   *(M17/18)*

This story of creating your own life is widely echoed in the theoretical literature (e.g. Foucault, 1979; Giddens, 1992; Weeks, 1995) and reflects (as well, no doubt, as reflexively contributing to) the perceived reality in a postmodern world of fluid identities. It peculiarly relates, however, to the common discourse of many lesbians and gay men who see themselves as breaking away from the constraints of traditional institutional patterns, which denied their sexuality and identity. Heterosexuals, a gay man suggests, 'slip into roles that are preordained and it goes along that route. Whereas we don't have any preordained roles so we can actually invent things as we want them' (M17/18). Or as a lesbian sees it: 'With my family of choice it's somewhere that, you know, it's an environment where I can be myself' (F15).

In practice, of course, there are clear overlaps between homosexual choices and the choices of many self-identified heterosexuals. But for non-heterosexuals the idea of a *chosen* family is a powerful signifier of a fresh start, of affirming a new sense of belonging, that becomes an essential part of asserting the validity of homosexual ways of life. When a gay man was asked whether gay and heterosexual relations differed, the reply was significant: 'Essentially, no. Strategically, yes' (M21). In other words, by affirming the values of choice, new possibilities were opened up for non-heterosexuals: the new type of family stands for something different.

Identity, and thereby difference, built around sexual preferences and choices, are confirmed through a sense of community that friendships can provide:

For me [family] means the gay community. (F03)

> I suppose I don't feel part of a big community, but I think there are lots of smaller communities... because I can't think of myself as being anything other than a gay man, having those friendships and support networks, I suppose, is extremely important. I think I'd be a very sad and pathetic person without them.   *(M05)*

'Community', with all its historic baggage and ambiguity, nevertheless provides the context for asserting personal values, and is also the precondition for putting homosexuality on the public agenda.

Identity, community, choice: these are key terms in the lives of many non-heterosexuals. They are seen as the necessary context for the shaping (or 'invention') of what a gay man called the 'queer construct family'. But if choice is the ruling discourse, it is also important to recognize the limits on choice. This is the third important factor to note. It is easier for someone now coming out into the lesbian and gay social world to enter a network of friends than it would have been for someone from an earlier generation (although, of course, homosexual networks are historically well established – see, for example, Porter and Weeks, 1990). Similarly, it is easier to construct elective families in metropolitan centres than in rural areas. Political factors can also be important. One black lesbian was battling with her perception of institutionalized racism, and had made a conscious decision to shape her life choices around a community of black women. Choices are contingent on many factors, constrained by the socio-economic, cultural and historical contexts in which we live (see Allen, 1989; Weston, 1991). Moreover, these forms of interaction lack the social recognition of more traditional family patterns. The important factors, however, are not the limits, real as these are, but the ethos and values that many non-heterosexual women and men are expressing: that a sense of self-worth and cultural confidence is realized in and through the friendship networks that we describe as families of choice.

There can be no doubt of the potent meanings attached to these friendship networks by many lesbians and gay men. Do they really, however, represent something new? One way of looking at this is to compare families of choice to other recognized social forms. The most obvious is the phenomenon of friendship itself. A recent study (Roberts and McGlone, 1997) has suggested that most people still make a basic distinction between friends and kin in terms of obligation and commitment, and this is also apparent among many non-heterosexuals. However, for many lesbians and gays, their circles meant more than the term 'friendship' usually denotes: 'For my part I don't have friendships on the level that I think heterosexuals have friendships. I think my friendships are more intense' (F43). Friendships flourish, it has been argued (Heinz Kohut, quoted in Little, 1989: 149), when overarching identities are fragmented in periods of rapid social change, or at crucial moments in individual lives, especially for lives lived at odds with social norms. This would certainly describe the context of lesbian and gay lives over the past generation. On the surface, at least, this lends credence to the idea that for many people friendships offer surrogate or 'pretend' families: substitutes for the real thing. This is not, however, how non-heterosexuals see the significance of their relationships, or how these relationships are characterized in the recent literature. Bozett (1987), for example, sees lesbian and gay relationships as having all the significant defining features of biological families, and Nardi (1992) has described friends *as* family. Weston (1991) has concluded that in creating 'families we choose' lesbians and gays are involved neither in imitating heterosexual families, nor in necessarily replacing or substituting a family of choice for a family of origin. Like Weston's research, our own suggests strongly that for many non-heterosexuals the term 'family' embraces a variety of selected relationships that includes lovers, possibly ex-lovers, intimate friends, as well as blood relatives, and is as real as the family of origin.

A useful approach may be to conceive of elective families as something new sociologically, as an index of changing social possibilities and demands. Clearly they build on historical experience. They are in many ways like changing patterns of friendship, with much in common with the extended networks of support created by other marginalized groups. But they are also examples of what Giddens (1992) sees as the 'everyday experiments in living' that people are required to undertake in an ever more complex world. This is certainly how it is seen and expressed by a number of respondents. In this quotation a respondent is speaking about the ways in which he and his partner test the limits of what is possible:

> we're constantly experimenting with just how far we want to go, and sometimes feel that we have some degree of mobility in a given situation.... It's

not so much political flag waving, it's just doing what we want to do and trying to push the boundaries a bit, to see how people cope with it.   *(M21)*

These everyday experiments are best characterized as fluid and adaptable networks, which, as we have seen, can include blood relatives, but whose core is made up of selected friends. These relationships are sometimes created across class and ethnic barriers, and may be intergenerational. They are also strikingly non-hierarchical, in the sense (in the absence of children) that there is no perceived ordering of significance along lines of age, precedence or role division – which is not to say there are not disparities of income or personal or social power, or any absence of potential conflict. Such divisions are not, however, intrinsic to the relationships. But like many friendship networks, there appears to be a tendency towards social homogeneity. Often they are single-sex: a number of male respondents claim not to know many lesbians, and vice versa. In the nature of things, friendships often stretch across the homosexual/ heterosexual binarism, but the inner core tend to be both homosocial and homosexual. Frequently, the inner core includes former sexual partners as well, of course, as current lovers. However, partners may have overlapping but different circles of friends. There has been a tendency in the literature to concentrate on lesbian and gay couple relationships as the exclusive focus of intimacy, and as we shall see couples are indeed important. But for many individuals who are not in long-term couple relationships, families of choice are the prime focus of emotional support. Friends may change; new people may enter the circle. But friendship networks seem permanent – certainly, individuals act on the assumption that they are.

Couples

Until fairly recently it was conventional to play down or ignore the dyadic relationships of homosexual men: a stereotype of predatory promiscuity was prevalent in the literature and in popular perceptions. By contrast, lesbians were seen as more likely to form couple relationships, and this difference was strongly related to assumptions about different male and female sexual and emotional needs (see Gagnon and Simon, 1974, for a discussion of this).

But the dominant belief in the non-heterosexual world is that lesbian and gay relationships offer unique possibilities for the construction of egalitarian relationships. This echoes wider historical studies which have indicated that the twentieth century has seen a significant shift in the traditional pattern of homosexual interactions for men and women

(Abelove et al., 1993; Dunne, 1997). There are also significant historical accounts, of course, which indicate that this is true for relations between men and women, largely as a result of the changing role of women and the 'transformation of intimacy' (Giddens, 1992; Beck and Beck-Gernsheim, 1995). The interesting feature, however, is that many lesbians and gay men have consciously shaped their relationships in opposition to assumed heterosexual models. A number of women, particularly, see their lesbianism as a conscious alternative to subordination to men. As a lesbian in her early fifties puts it:

> Much more sort of helpless, weak, I think that's one of the things heterosexuality does to women. And I feel I've got stronger and stronger [since coming out as a lesbian]. And of course, some of that could be just getting older and more experienced. But I think some of it is being a lesbian.
>
> *(F30)*

Another woman makes a complementary, and frequently repeated, point:

> [in heterosexual relationships] there is an essential power imbalance that there are certain roles, which are backed up by economics and backed up by sanctions. And also...men and women are socialized differently in terms of what...heterosexual relationships are. Yeah, I think they're very different – very. *(F34)*

The assumption, among men as well as women, is that 'it's much easier to have equal relations if you're the same sex' (M31) because this equalizes the terms of the intimate involvement. Or as a lesbian says: 'The understanding between two women is bound to be on a completely different wavelength' (F33). Equal standing means that issues around, for example, the division of labour in the household are seen to be a matter for discussion and agreement, not *a priori* assumption, because of 'being able to negotiate, being on an equal level to be able to negotiate in the first place' (M04); 'Everything has to be discussed, everything is negotiable' (F29).

Equality is also seen as integral to intimacy:

> I think there is...less a kind of sense of possession, or property, in same-sex relationships, and more emphasis on...emotional bonding...that's not quite what I mean, but they're less ritualized really. *(M39)*

There is plentiful evidence as well, inevitably, that egalitarian relations do not automatically develop. They have to be constantly struggled for against inequalities of income, day-to-day commitment, emotional labour, ethnic difference and the like. Inequality of income is perhaps the most frequently divisive factor, especially as for some couples sharing income or even ownership of a home was not only practically but politically difficult, as this little exchange illustrates:

> Q: Did you ever have joint bank accounts?
> A: No. No. That was too heterosexual.   *(M05)*

Whatever the practical difficulties, however, there is a strong emphasis among lesbians and gays on the importance of building intimate couple involvement: 'being in a relationship helps to affirm one as a person and we all need that' (M44); 'I love the continuity. . . . I like the sex. I like doing some things jointly. . . . A sense that you are loveable' (F06). Affirmation through involvement in the democratic, egalitarian relationship appears to be the dominant homosexual norm, conforming closely to Giddens's definition of the 'pure relationship':

> a situation where a social relation is entered into for its own sake, for what can be derived by each person from a sustained association with another; and which is continued only in so far as it is thought by both parties to deliver enough satisfaction for each individual to stay within it.
> *(Giddens, 1992: 58)*

This clearly suggests a contingency in couple relationships, which is echoed in the interviews: couples act as if a relationship might last for ever, work at making it work, but also realistically recognize that it might not:

> we said at the beginning that we'd work at it and see what happened, or something along those lines. . . . But we weren't going to make plans or a life-long commitment because . . .   *(M17/18)*

> We've never ever said, that, you know, 'till death us do part'. But we do plan long term – while the relationship is going well, we will be planning long term. Because you can't keep planning short-term and expect long-term things to sort themselves out.   *(F06)*

Sexual attraction is the most obvious factor that draws individuals together in the first place, and provides the basic dynamic. But sex is not in the end the decisive factor. When asked if his relationship was primarily sexual, one gay man replied:

> No. I would say it's very much more a friendship . . . we don't have a tempestuous relationship at all. I think we have a very stable relationship. Sex is obviously part of it, but . . . I wouldn't say our relationship was based on sex.   *(M12)*

A lesbian similarly put sex in its place:

> [Intimacy] is about closeness really. And there's different degrees of it. It's about trust ... friendship, right through to sexuality. It's about being close and trusting. *(F40/41)*

It is in this context that the question of sexual fidelity must be considered. For many couples, male as well as female, sexual and emotional fidelity were inextricably linked. For some, however, the most important factor was emotional faithfulness:

> Tim could sleep with somebody, and have sex with them, and I wouldn't feel that was being unfaithful. I would feel he would be unfaithful if he never told me about it. *(M04)*

Monogamy itself was frequently seen by men and women as something that needed both negotiation and redefinition in the changing circumstances of relationships. As a lesbian commented: 'I had to decide what was real for me, and what wasn't. So, I don't believe in monogamy. I may be monogamous, but I don't do it for its own sake' (F14).

Bauman (1993: 98) has argued that there are two characteristic strategies for dealing with the perceived flux of modern relationships, what he calls 'fixing' and 'floating'. Fixing takes place when the potential openness of what Giddens (1992) calls 'confluent love' is set firmly in place by the demands of duty. Floating occurs when the labour of constant negotiation on the terms of a relationship leads to people cutting their losses, and starting all over again. This is often the case in non-heterosexual relationships:

> a lot of lesbians and gay men split up more often than heterosexuals because they're not necessarily conventionally married, and they don't have to go through all the hassle, so it is easier to split up, I think, in some cases. *(F44)*

This is not, however, the only pathway. Many work through the vicissitudes of their relationship, constantly remaking it, trying to 'make a go of it' by affirming their long-term commitment. Part of this may be through the creation of special rituals, celebrating together and with friends: 'anything we can think of, we celebrate' (F33). Some seek religious blessings or have 'gay weddings' to confirm their partnerships. Others just remake their relationships on a day-by-day basis: 'just the sort of very fact of carrying on living together is a sort of ... daily renewal of commitment' (M15). In other words, neither floating, nor fixing, but continuously confronting the challenge of relationships, 'working through' the ups and downs.

So far we have discussed same-sex couples as if they were undifferentiated. In fact, on both male and female sides there are strong perceptions of difference between lesbians and gay men. Here are comments from a lesbian woman:

> I see women's level of commitment, or emotions, more intense in their friendships....I know lots of gay men would probably disagree with me...gay men, they talk about sex a lot...whereas lesbians don't.... Oh, this is all very varied, but I think women talk a lot more about emotional things than men do. And I don't think that's just a fallacy. I don't think that's just a myth. I think it's true.   *(F36)*

Alongside these well-established perceptions, there is a degree of ignorance about each other's lifestyles, with both lesbians and gay men claiming not to know many non-heterosexuals of the opposite sex. Although there are differences, however, which are both political and personal, these are minor compared to the similarities in terms of life plans. Among both non-heterosexual women and men there is a similar engagement with the shaping of egalitarian, caring and enduring relationships. The role of sexual desire within these relationships varies widely, but equally important for many are wider concepts of commitment.

Care, responsibility and commitment

As same-sex relationships are constructed and maintained outside conventional institutional and legal support systems and structures, they are less likely to be characterized by predetermined obligations, duties and commitments. There is no lack of evidence that such issues matter to non-heterosexuals, but as part (though a critical part) of the negotiation of relationships among equals, a matter of free and conscious choice:

> I would like to think that people in gay relationships stay together because they actually want to stay together to a greater extent than people in heterosexual relationships do.   *(M15)*

Within this sort of ethos, terms such as 'duty' or 'obligation' tended to be avoided by our subjects, having, as one gay man said, 'a negative connotation' (M39). Duty is 'like some kind of moral code that people use to put on you. . . . I don't think I need that kind of external thing put on me' (F04/F05). These terms were compared unfavourably with the concepts of responsibility and mutual care and commitment:

> Responsibility is something I decide to do and I keep to; obligation is when I feel I have to. *(F01)*

> Duty is something that is imposed on you . . . if you feel responsible for someone. I mean, being a parent, you're responsible for your children, then you do that because you feel you want to, not because somebody else feels you ought to. *(M44)*

Ideals of care and responsibility appear to be situational, dependent on the needs of parent and blood relatives, as well as of friends, but the ideas themselves are potent, organized around notions of 'the right thing to do' (M11), especially with regard to parents (see Finch and Mason, 1993). Freely chosen relationships, however, have the potentiality to be both free of imposed obligations, and therefore more intense. For many gay men particularly the experience of the AIDS crisis has confirmed the importance of a commitment to care and mutual responsibility (see Adam, 1992): 'It makes some relationships more intense because they are inevitably going to be foreshortened' (M03).

Parenting raises questions of obligation, commitment and responsibility most sharply. Many non-heterosexuals, men and women, are involved in parenting in one way or another, as biological or adoptive parents, or as non-biological co-parents. There is evidence, moreover, that a significant generational shift is taking place in attitudes to parenting. For most gay men over forty without previous heterosexual relationships, fathering or caring for children had appeared virtually inconceivable. Many lesbians, however, had considered having children, and for younger men as well as women the question of children is now a live issue. This is partly the result of changing attitudes more generally, and a wider public discussion of questions surrounding non-heterosexual parenting, custody and adoption. It is partly, however, the result of an increasing interest in non-traditional ways of conceiving, especially through donor insemination (Saffron, 1994; Griffin and Mulholland, 1997; Harne and Rights of Women, 1997). A number of lesbians have been involved in discussions with gay male friends about artificial insemination, and some have conceived in this way. This raises often delicate questions about the role of the male donor in co-parenting, and is sometimes the subject of considerable anguished discussion. More traditionally, lesbian couples particularly frequently want children, to complete their relationship.

The resulting parenting arrangements can be quite complex, involving biological parents, lovers, even ex-lovers in an extended family-type arrangement. Those involved in such arrangements tend to be highly conscious of the wider cultural anxieties around such arrangements, and acutely alive, especially, to the sensitivities of the child. Take this example. Two men (M. aged 23 and G., 38) are in a couple relationship and co-parent a 12-year-old daughter with her two lesbian mothers who live nearby. The older man is the biological father through a previous heterosexual relationship and marriage with one of the lesbians:

> *Do you feel that you get recognition from other people as an important person in B.'s life?*
> M:...well, not in a broader sense, because at school, if I...go swimming, and B.'s and the school have gone, and I know not to say hello because that would cause problems, and I have to respect that, and I do. You know, I don't want to make her life difficult for her...
> G: It's like the difference between being out personally and the fact that you're out as a family. I think we're out as individuals, but the family isn't.
> (M17/18)

Similarly, two lesbian parents, when asked what they most feared about being openly homosexual, replied it was 'the crap' their daughter would get:

> S: I think with adolescence she's going to have a lot of problems of her own without.... It's more a concern, you know, for her than for ourselves really, isn't it?
> J: Mm. We're already aware that she has to be secretive.   *(F04/05)*

Yet, whatever the means of giving birth or being involved in parenting, whatever the social and personal hazards, the care and wellbeing of the child remains the first and ultimate responsibility of same-sex parents, over and above the relationship itself. This seems to be the common thread across the diversity of parenting practices.

The power of new stories

Care and legal responsibility for children raise in an acute form the legal status, and social policy implications, of the emergence of elective families and the public affirmation of lesbian and gay relationships. The evidence from European countries which have legally recognized the registration of same-sex partnerships suggests that parenting, and especially access to adoption rights, is a last taboo: characteristically, as in Denmark, when partnership rights are recognized, they exclude adoption (see Waaldijk, 1994; Bech, 1996). Attempts to give lesbian and gays full rights to marriage, as currently in The Netherlands and Hawaii, are highly controversial precisely because they involve parenting rights also. The rights of lesbian parents, especially to custody of their children when marriages break up, have been challenged for some twenty years, often on the grounds that children need fathers for healthy development (Hanscombe and Forster, 1982; Martin, 1993; Saffron, 1994), despite evidence of the success of lesbian parenting (see Tasker and Golombok, 1991, 1995, 1997; Saffron, 1996). Recent cases in Britain suggest some flexibility in legal decisions over lesbian custody (Williams, 1994), but the statutory situation remains unfavourable to lesbian and gay custody and adoption rights.

This is only one aspect of a wider lack of legal recognition of the implications of non-heterosexual domestic patterns (on the general issues, see VanEvery, 1991/92; Carabine, 1995). On a range of issues, from access of lesbians to donor insemination through parenting to immigration, health insurance, pension rights, mortgages and joint home ownership and inheritance rights, the legal status of same-sex relationships is at best ambiguous and at worst discriminatory. It is in this context that we need to consider the implications of the new narratives of non-heterosexuals about relationships and rights.

Many, if not most, self-identified lesbians and gays have a strong sense that the cultural privileging of heterosexuality inevitably denies full humanity to non-heterosexuals, and therefore fails to legitimize their most significant commitments. This is expressed by the frequent use of the terms 'homophobia' and 'heterosexism' to describe prevailing cultural norms. While there is a recognition that social attitudes had changed, often dramatically, in the past generation, making a new openness possible, there is also a strong sense that change had not gone far or fast enough. Many non-heterosexuals have experienced some form of informal discrimination, ranging from enforced self-censorship to physical attack. Above all, there is a strong sense that their most valued relationships are not given full recognition, sometimes even within families of origin, let alone the wider society.

A sense of injustice leads inevitably to a claim to rights. Essentially, non-heterosexuals wish for the same rights as heterosexuals to choose their ways of life, without being discriminated against. Many, lesbians in particular, favour full individualization of social and economic rights, which would remove the legal consequences that flow from married status, so that rights and responsibilities would belong to individuals (see Waaldijk, 1994). As a lesbian observed:

[marriage is] not going to give equal rights to everyone – it's only going to give equal rights to people who are in long-term relationships. And that doesn't seem fair to me. *(F02)*

Others want full access to the same couple rights as heterosexuals, including pension rights, inheritance, immigration and so on, without necessarily having formally to register a partnership. The most controversial issue, however, relates to the formal recognition of partnerships, and the question of same-sex 'marriage'. It sometimes divided couples, as this exchange indicates:

J: T. doesn't feel the need to do something like that, and I'd like to do something like that.
T: That's just your insecurity.
J: It's my insecurity, or you could reframe it the other way round. I think we've been together now for over seven years. I think that it's appropriate that we do something that celebrates and acknowledges our relationship.
T: We don't argue on it! We just agree to disagree...I suppose it's conforming to the way that heterosexuals live. We're not heterosexuals.
(M01/02)

On the one hand, there is the desire for the same rights as heterosexuals:

I'm totally in favour [of same-sex marriage]...because if I met someone who I cared for that much and we couldn't make it legal in some respects, I would be so angry....I mean, you don't have to have the commitment, but it's nice to have the opportunity, to actually go through the ceremony of being legally married....I don't want partnership rights, I want marriage. *(M10)*

On the other hand, there is the discourse of difference:

I just think it's a piece of nonsense, really – not a piece of nonsense, but, I don't like saying 'aping heterosexuality' because....I believe we should all be treated equally in the eyes of the law, but...I believe now we are not the same as straight people, that we do have differences, and that we are diverse and that we are creative, and that we take a lot more risks around a lot of things. *(F36)*

This leads, finally, to the question of the meaning of full citizenship in the contemporary discourse of non-heterosexuals. Plummer (1995) has suggested that historically there have been three key concepts of citizenship which have successively commanded the political agenda: political (access to equal rights in the state), social (equal access to social rights), and economic (equal access to economic opportunities). He argues that these are now being joined by a fourth claim, to intimate citizenship, which:

> speaks to an array of concerns too often neglected in past debates over citizenship, and which extends notions of rights and responsibilities.... [I]t is concerned with all those matters linked to our most intimate desires, pleasures, and ways of being in the world.   *(Plummer, 1995: 151)*

There are no blueprints in terms of policy or practice about how such claims to intimate citizenship should be worked through, because there is inherent in them both a sense of the contingency of all rights claims, and of the diversity of social and personal practices which they entail. Claims to intimate citizenship involve difficult questions about the relationship between private and public, about responsibilities as well as rights, about the social and political implications of any notion of complex, and different, 'equalities', about balancing a sense (and affirmation) of difference with a sense of common belonging and common values (see Weeks, 1995). The general point that can be made, however, is that these issues are, in part, on the agenda because they are being raised in the diverse interpretative communities that make up a complex society, and are being clearly articulated by lesbians and gay men. They are, in Plummer's (1995) formulation, part of 'a field of stories, an array of tellings, out of which new lives, new communities and new politics may emerge' (Plummer, 1995: 151–2).

As we have already suggested, many of the new stories of lesbian and gay lives are very close to those that might be told about rapidly changing patterns of heterosexual lives. That does not lessen the importance of the new narratives about non-heterosexual relationships. On the contrary, they underscore the significance of what is happening to our notions of 'family'. These non-heterosexual narratives of family and of choice, of care and responsibility, of love and loss, of old needs and new possibilities, of difference and convergence, are prime examples of those everyday experiments which are contributing to the creation of the 'new family'.

Note

This chapter is based on research conducted for a project funded by the Economic and Social Research Council, entitled 'Families of choice: the structure and meanings of non-heterosexual relationships' (reference no.: L315253030). The research took place between 1995 and 1996, as part of the ESRC's research programme on Population and Household Change, and was based in the School of Education, Politics and Social Science, South Bank University, London. I was the director of the project, with Catherine Donovan and Brian Heaphy as the research fellows. The core of the research involved in-depth interviews with forty-eight men and forty-eight women who broadly identified as non-heterosexual. All the first-person quotations in this chapter come from these interviews. All female interviews are denoted by 'F', the male interviews by an 'M', each followed by a number. The numbers reflect the order in which the interviews took place. Because our respondents used a range of self-identifications – lesbian, gay, bisexual, queer, homosexual – we have preferred to use the terms non-heterosexual or same-sex throughout when referring generically to key findings.

The chapter was written with Catherine Donovan and Brian Heaphy, and I am grateful for their collaboration throughout our joint work.

References

Abelove, H., Barale, M. A. and Halperin, D. M. (eds) (1993) *Lesbian and Gay Studies Reader* (London: Routledge).

Adam, Barry D. (1992) 'Sex and Caring Among Men', in Ken Plummer (ed.), *Modern Homosexualities: Fragments of Lesbian and Gay Experience* (London: Routledge).

Allen, Graham (1989) *Friendship: Developing a Sociological Perspective* (Boulder CO: Westview).

Bauman, Zygmunt (1993) *Postmodern Ethics* (Oxford: Blackwell).

Bech, Henning (1996) *When Men Meet: Homosexuality and Modernity* (Cambridge: Polity Press).

Beck, Ulrich and Beck-Gernsheim, Elisabeth (1995) *The Normal Chaos of Love* (Cambridge: Polity Press).

Bell, David and Valentine, Gill (1995) *Mapping Desire: Geographies of Sexualities* (London: Routledge).

Bozett, F. W. (1987) Preface, in F. W. Bozett (ed.), *Gay and Lesbian Parents* (New York: Praeger).

Carabine, Jean (1995) 'Sexuality and Social Policy', paper given at Social Policy Association, Women's Interest Group.

Duncombe, Jean and Marsden, Dennis (1996) 'Can We Research the Private Sphere?: Methodological and Ethical Problems in the Study of the Role of Intimate Emotions and Personal Relationships', in L. Morris and E. S. Lyon (eds), *Gender Relations in Public and Private: Changing Personal Perspectives* (Basingstoke and London: Macmillan).

Dunne, Gillian A. (1997) *Lesbian Lifestyles: Women's Work and the Politics of Sexuality* (Basingstoke and London: Macmillan).

Finch, Janet (1989) *Family Obligation and Social Change* (Cambridge: Polity Press).

Finch, Janet and Mason, Jennifer (1993) *Negotiating Family Responsibilities* (London: Routledge).

Foucault, Michel (1979) *The History of Sexuality, Vol. 1, An Introduction* (London: Allen Lane).

Gagnon, John and Simon, William (1974) *Sexual Conduct* (London: Hutchinson).

Giddens, Anthony (1992) *The Transformation of Intimacy* (Cambridge: Polity Press).

Griffin, K. and Mulholland, L. A. (eds) (1997) *Lesbian Motherhood in Europe* (London: Cassell).

Hanscombe, G. and Forster, J. (1982) *Rocking the Cradle: Lesbian Mothers – A Challenge in Family Living* (London: Sheba).

Harne, L. and Rights of Women (1997) *Valued Families: The Lesbian Mothers' Legal Handbook* (London: Women's Press).

Little, G. (1989) 'Freud, Friendship and Politics', in R. Porter and S. Tomaselli (eds), *The Dialectics of Friendship* (London: Routledge).

Martin, A. (1993) *The Guide to Lesbian and Gay Parenting* (London: Pandora).

Nardi, Peter (1992) 'Sex, Friendship and Gender Roles Among Gay Men', in Peter Nardi (ed.), *Men's Friendship* (London: Sage).

Plummer, Ken (ed.) (1992) *Modern Homosexualities. Fragments of Lesbian and Gay Experience* (London: Routledge).

Plummer, Ken (1995) *Telling Sexual Stories: Power, Change, and Social Worlds* (London: Routledge).

Porter, Kevin and Weeks, Jeffrey (1990) *Between the Acts: Lives of Homosexual Men 1895–1967* (London: Routledge).

Roberts, C. and McGlone, F. (1997) *Kinship Networks and Friendships: Attitudes and Behaviour in Britain 1986–1995*, Population and Household Change Research Programme, Research Results No. 3, Swindon: ESRC.

Saffron, Lisa (1994) *Alternative Beginnings* (London: Cassell).

Saffron, Lisa (1996) *What about the Children? Sons and Daughters of Lesbian and Gay Parents Talk about their Lives* (London: Cassell).

Sullivan, Andrew (1995) *Virtually Normal: An Argument about Homosexuality* (London: Picador).

Tasker, F. L. and Golombok, S. (1991) 'Children Raised by Lesbian Mothers', *Family Law*, May: 184–7.

Tasker, F. L. and Golombok, S. (1995) 'Adults Raised as Children in Lesbian Families', *American Journal of Orthopsychiatry*, 65 (2), 203–15.

Tasker, F. and Golombok, S. (1997) *Growing up in a Lesbian Family: Effects on Child Development* (New York and London: Guilford Press).

VanEvery, J. (1991/92) 'Who Is "The Family"? The Assumptions of British Social Policy', *Critical Social Policy*, 11(3), 62–75.

Waaldijk, K. (1994) 'Homosexuality: European Community Issues', in G. Zijlstra, M. Odijk and G. Ketelaar (eds), *Family? Partners? Individuals?* (Amsterdam: RoseLinks).

Weeks, Jeffrey (1991) 'Pretended Family Relationships', in *Against 'Nature: Essays on History, Sexuality and Identity* (London: Rivers Oram Press).

Weeks, Jeffrey (1995) *Invented Moralities: Sexual Values in an Age of Uncertainty* (Cambridge: Polity Press).

Weeks, Jeffrey, Donovan, Catherine and Heaphy, Brian (1996) *Families of Choice: Patterns of Non-Heterosexual Relationships. A Literature Review*, Social Science Research Papers No. 2 (London: South Bank University).

Weston, Kath (1991) *Families We Choose: Lesbians, Gays and Kinship* (New York: Columbia University Press).

Williams, F. (1994) 'Lesbian Couple Granted Parental Rights', *Gay Times*, 191, August: 29.

12

Millennium Blues and Beyond: Sexuality at the Fin de Millennium

---

Marking the passing of time

Elaine Showalter (1991), in her comparison of the last *fin de siècle* and the one now impending as I write, has a striking image of a digital clock on the Pompidou Centre in Paris ticking down the seconds, minutes and hours to the end of the millennium, and the beginning of the new – evoking a sense of the inexorable passage of time, to a fixed point, a final destination, a date with a decisive but impenetrable future.

We know of course that the date is an arbitrary one, not even an end of a century, which pedants say should be a year later, marking a thousand years after nothing particularly significant, and not even precisely two thousand years after its founding, and possibly mythical, 'real event'. The millennium's exact symbolism derives from a particular religious tradition which, however influential, is only one among several world faiths, and which in any case has been largely sidelined in most of the preparations for it outside Rome. The date itself is a fiction of the human mind, and, as Steven Jay Gould (1997) has pointed out, even the meaning of a millennium has itself changed. Originally it meant a period of a thousand years that would follow the great battle between good and evil. Now rather more tamely we see it as celebrating the passing of a thousand years, with all the apprehension for an unknown future that might generate. Even that digital countdown now reminds us of something else: the power but fragility of the massive technological revolutions of the late twentieth century which gave us the digital computer, currently threatened by the millennium bug. And indeed, the last time I was in Paris the clock had disappeared from the Pompidou Centre, victim of repairs to the building.

Yet the countdown has become fraught with meanings, even if those meanings are absolutely unfathomable to most people. The apparently meaningful but fundamentally contingent nature of the millennium may, in fact, be its most significant feature, a signal of the increasing arbitrariness of the ways in which we conceive of the world and our existence. Which is why I want to begin with an arbitrary but, at least to me, meaningful linkage, between the Pompidou Centre, the most popular architectural product of high modernity, co-designed by the architect Richard Rogers, and another of his designs currently inexorably rising by the river Thames in London, the Millennium Dome, which at one stage could claim to be the most derided building of postmodernity.

I am, I should confess, a great admirer of the new Dome, and although I write before it is completed, and its success is unknown, I wish it well. When I hear the complaints of my friends in the chattering classes about it I am reminded that 'intellectuals' first emerged as a coherent caste in a mass protest from the French clerisy over the rise of the monstrous Eiffel Tower in Paris in the late nineteenth century. I hope current sceptics are as magnificently wrong now as they were then. But there is something wonderfully symbolic about the dome project. It has been constructed on the prime meridian, in sight of the glorious buildings of historic naval Greenwich, evocative of past world-historic greatness, but on a windswept, desolate, deindustrialized peninsula whose very ground has been poisoned by industrial waste, a space history has let go. No one, even the best disposed towards it, is entirely sure what it is for, how long it will be there, what its long-term future could be. It is a beautiful, mysterious structure, half circus tent, half UFO, pegged to the ancient, meandering river, yet apparently about to take flight to unknown destinations. It is an empty vessel built on a wasteland, with a controversial past, a confused present, an undetermined future, a vehicle for a multitude of contradictory meanings, fears, hopes and dreams, a metaphor for the age of uncertainty in which we live. And at the heart of that uncertainty is one of the most controversial and derided features of the project, an image of everyhuman.

Originally proposed as an androgynous, sexless figure, holding a baby, which visitors would be able to enter to explore the workings of the human body, following media scorn the designers wavered over whether it was a man or a woman, whether its external organs should be shown, indeed what they were, how and where we should enter, what pleasures we should expect to experience when we are in there, and finally compromised on having two figures, a male and a female. Here we have another metaphor: at the centre of contemporary uncertainty is an uncertainty over the representation and meaning of gender and sexuality. The uncertainty is, however, for lack of anything better, recuperated in traditional terms of masculinity and feminity, a man and a woman linked in a gentle embrace. The ostensibly infinite possibilities of late modernity are finally inescapably locked into conventional hallowed dichotomies, because that is the easiest way out. After all that has happened over recent decades, is that all we can look forward to? I shall try to answer that in what follows.

Endings

Let me first of all look again at why we have been preoccupied with the end of a millennium and the beginning of a new one. However arbitrary, however fictional, the idea of the millennium may be, the fuss it has generated has chimed for many people with a generalized sense of an ending which has haunted many of our cultural assumptions (Weeks 1995). We have, of course, been here before. In many ways the last *fin de siècle* foreshadowed many of our own preoccupations, with much the same degree of hope and anxiety. As Showalter argues (1991: 2), the crises of the *fin de siècles* are 'more intensely experienced, more emotionally fraught, more weighted with symbolic and historic meaning, because we invest them with the metaphors of death and rebirth that we project onto the final decades and years of a century'. And perhaps it is not surprising that many of these anxieties are focused on the crucial triplex, for individuals and societies, of family, gender and sexuality. Here we intimately experience the rhythms of life, the challenges of love and loss, filtering the great moves of history in the grind, hopes, despairs and delights of everyday life. Despite their apparent stability, rooted in nature and tradition, the pleasures and pains of the body and our closest relationships are sensitive conductors of every ripple from the waves of change.

It is easy to see significant parallels between the ends of the nineteenth and twentieth centuries., as this simple listing demonstrates (see Weeks 1995):

Late nineteenth century	*Late twentieth century*
The threat to the family	The decline of family life
First wave feminism	Second wave feminism
The rise of the 'new woman'	'Liberated women'

Late nineteenth century	Late twentieth century
The moral challenge to male privilege	'De-manning'
The Victorian patriarch	The 'new man'
The sexual exploitation of young girls	Paedophilia
The invention of the homosexual	The lesbian and gay
'Decadence'	Sexual transgression
The syphilis epidemic	AIDS
The 'fallen women'	'Girl power'

I could go on. The point is that in each period fundamental questions around the body, desire, masculinity and femininity were raised and became the subject of heated controversy, which in turn both reflected and shaped profound changes in the relationships between men and women, women and women, men and men, adults and children, and their combination in the intimate sphere. At the heart of each of these relations is deep anxiety about the renegotiation of boundaries, and the unsettling of the assumed 'natural order' of things. 'Sexual anarchy', in the novelist George Gissing's phrase, used by Showalter as the title of her book, seemed loosed on the world in the late nineteenth century, just as many fear it is today. As Durkheim noted at the beginning of the twentieth century, in terms which many could have echoed at its end:

> Today traditional morality is shaken and no other has been brought forward to replace it. The older duties have lost their power without our being able to see clearly and with assurance where our new duties lie. Different minds hold opposed ideas and we are passing through a period of crisis. It is not then surprising that we do not feel the pressure of moral rules as they were felt in the past. They cannot appear to us in their old majesty, since they are practically non-existent.
>
> *(Durkheim 1974: 68–9)*

But of course we are not simply reliving the *fin de siècle* blues. Just as changes in the late nineteenth century were responses to the unsettling of all relationships in the wake of unprecedented change, so today we observe features which are products of a distinctive conjuncture as the juggernaut of modernity grinds on. Many things are the same; much is different. We can signal that difference in one example, the role of sexology, the *soi disant* scientific study of sexuality (Weeks 1985). The nascent science in the late nineteenth century was centrally implicated in all the debates about gender and sexuality, weaving a web of meaning around the body and its desires through its descriptions, categorizations, definitions, neologisms and theoretical speculations. Its project was no less than to discover the 'laws of nature' to aid rational understanding and reform. It was the Enlightenment project applied to the body, a new master narrative to explain the mysteries of desire. But as we now recognize, as well as trying to describe reality in all its confusing forms, it also helped to constitute it in ways which not only reproduced existing relations of sex but also invented new classifications which helped to produce new norms and truths. Sexology sexualized the female body, but in ways which many argue locked women ever more tightly into subordinate relations to men, eroticizing unequal power relations. It defined the existence of 'the homosexual' as a member of a separate species, thus constructing a new binarism which has dominated thinking about heterosexuality and homosexuality in the twentieth century. Sexology constructed itself as an expert discourse, the codification of new knowledge, the purveyor of the truth of our bodies.

By the late twentieth century, however, the locus of sexual expertise has radically shifted. Scientific knowledge has been challenged by the eruption of many subjugated knowledges. Expert discourse is constantly battling against counter-discourses emerging from the feminism and sexual movements of the past generation. Scientific truth is being challenged by the multiplication of truths. Sexual knowledge is contested as never before.

Let me offer an example, that of the AIDS epidemic. It has often been commented on (see chapter 7) that one of the remarkable features of the AIDS crisis has been the extraordinary degree to which those most affected by the syndrome took the lead in responding to it: in helping to define the nature of the crisis, in advocacy, in developing community-based models of care, in the search for palliation and cure, in terms of involvement in the processes of scientific investigation and medical intervention, and in the elaboration of new, safer forms of pleasure. The immediate context for this was the existence in the USA and to varying degrees in other western societies of a powerful and sophisticated constituency – the gay and lesbian community – whose very survival was seen to be at stake, and which had the acquired skills and social and cultural capital which enabled it to mobilize for a more adequate response than was at first offered in a society increasingly dominated by conservative social objectives. But over and beyond that were longer-term changes where issues about risk, trust and expertise, the delegitimization of traditional forms of authority, and the insurgence of grass-roots knowledges were contributing to a new climate, at the heart of which was a profound question of representation: who has the right to speak for whom in a diverse society.

A community that had defined itself against the medical codification of its pathology was hardly likely to bend a knee to a profession that blindly proclaimed its scientific objectivity and purity. But at the same time that profession was integral to finding solutions to the devastating health emergency. The communities at risk needed 'good science' and dispassionate (and accessible) medicine (Epstein 1996). But all too often the grass roots and the professionals, despite assumed common goals, had different priorities, conflicting definitions of correct procedures, disparate world views, and spoke different languages. The result was what Epstein (1996) describes as a series of 'credibility struggles' over who had the right to speak about and control the defintion of HIV and AIDS, and to determine the appropriate responses to the epidemic. 'The AIDS crisis is a case in which the normal flow of trust and credibility between experts and lay persons has been disrupted. The autonomy of science has therefore been challenged; outsiders have rushed into the breach' (Epstein 1996: 17). Epstein shows in meticulous and sometimes devastating detail the agonizing process which led to a new balance (never stable or fixed, but on a new level of interaction): a multiplication of the successful pathways to credibility in the fight against AIDS, and a diversification of the personnel who claimed the right to be heard way beyond the authorities traditionally accredited by our culture.

This is the real mark of what is different about the late twentieth century: those who used to be spoken of are now struggling, in various ways, using different, often hesitant or incoherent languages, to speak for themselves. The result is inevitably confusing, but enormously significant. We are here in a world where the imperatives of history, nature and science are being displaced by the norm of sexual choice, and where a master narrative is being displaced by a multiplication of new narratives, each claiming its own truth.

This is, I want to argue, the result of two closely interrelated tendencies, which I will call for convenience globalization and the transformation of intimacy – though each term is contested (compare Giddens 1992; Weeks 1998)

Globalization

I am using 'globalization' as a metaphor for the complex process of capitalist reconstruction, the creation of a world market, technological innovation, the creation of the 'informational society', cultural integration, even on hegemonic terms, and all the other forces which are dramatically changing the size, integration, opportunities and tragedies of our global village. Three parallel processes within this broad tendency are vital for understanding what is, I am suggesting, a real revolution in sexual possibilities. I will call these 'detraditionalization', 'individualization' and 'identity creation'.

Detraditionalization is one of the most dramatic results of the new world we are entering. The new economic, social and cultural forces sweeping the world are fundamentally undermining many of the traditional focuses of legitimacy and belonging, from long-established religious institutions and political forms to old class, regional and geographical loyalties. As I shall discuss in a moment, many of these are being replaced by new belongings, which in some cases are no less forceful, intimidating even, than the ones they replace. New traditions are being invented as fast, it seems, as old ones are fading. But these can only be understood properly if we do indeed see them as reflexes to the dissolution of old verities, a signal that we are living through a new age, where the old is dying, and the new is struggling to be born: a world of manufactured risk, breakdown of trust, ontological insecurity, but also new meanings and possibilities, where negotiation replaces imposed interpretations. The most important results of this for our discussion are the breakdown of the traditional family as we have known it in myth, ideology and often painful practice (see Silva and Smart 1999), the undermining of gender hierarchies through the rise of women on a world scale, and the diversification of sexual practice, the proliferation of polymorphous desires, as old bonds are weakened and Eros floats free from the imperatives of reproduction.

This is related to a second impact of globalization: a process of individualization. As old belongings weaken there is an inevitable emphasis on the centrality of individual autonomy, the person seizing control of his or her own life. This was already a potent element of the cultural revolts of the late 1960s and early 1970s: 'my body is my own', 'not the church, not the state, but women must control their fate' ... Oddly, on the surface at least, this explicitly counter-cultural tendency proved complicit with the renewed emphasis on economic individualism that fuelled the revival of market economics from the mid-1970s and that had swept the world by the late 1990s, until challenged by the threat of global recession. The New Right political leaderships of the 1980s sought to combine neo-liberal economics with social authoritarianism on moral issues, propelled by the energy of the culture wars that attempted to sweep back the sexual revolution (see chapter 8 above). But we can now see that this effort was historically doomed, as moral conservatives proved just as likely (in fact, very much more likely) to be involved in conflicts between duty and desire as any sexual radical. Despite very real setbacks for a more humane and tolerant sexual order, on the whole the 1990s saw an increasing recognition of the importance of the freedom of individuals to choose their own ways of being.

But of course, by definition, individual autonomy means different things to different people. At its most extreme it can lead to an absolutist libertarianism that oddly now unites many people across the conventional political spectrum. To my mind it means something else: that individual autonomy can only be fully realized through mutual involvement, that you can only become fully free through chosen, equal relations with others (Weeks 1995). That is the challenge being confronted in efforts to shape 'created families' that is discussed in chapter 11 above. But there is also another possibility, a 'flight from freedom', which is best illustrated by the global rise of new fundamentalisms. In terms of the family/gender/sexuality nexus the various forms of fundamentalism generally have in common an obsession with the body, a hierarchical view of gender, and a desire to restore the traditional family as the essential building block of cultural reproduction (Bhatt 1997). The fact that this goes against the most basic direction of global change does not mean that the new fundamentalisms are not devastatingly effective in grabbing the political and cultural agenda. They in turn, however, can be seen as one manifestation of the third aspect of globalization I have picked out: identity creation.

For in a globalizing, detraditionalizing, individualistic world, who or what we are is itself up for grabs in a way which was generally impossible in earlier times. Identities can no longer be assumed or taken for granted. The stable social identities of earlier, pre-industrial periods, based on status, hierarchy, moral conformity and a sense of place, have long gone. But the sense of self and place shaped by twentieth-century industrial mass production and urbanization is now also crumbling. Identities have moved from being destinies to become the focus of resistance and in many cases to become choices. Now there are many identities that have salience for individuals and collectives: ethnic, national, gendered, consumerist, sexual, virtual. Identity politics became a defining characteristic of the new sexual movements from the early 1970s onwards, and the question of identity has been the central issue for lesbians and gays in both everyday life, collective self-assertion – and endless academic debate (see chapter 9). Increasingly we recognize that identities are like stories we tell ourselves about where we come from, what we are now, and where we are going. Through narratives we weave the web of meaning that restores ontological security, builds trust, and makes meaningful interaction with others possible (Plummer 1995).

This preoccupation with identity is not a strange obsession of sexual minorities or any other cultural fringe. It is a necessary effect of broader long-term tendencies. Castells (1997) has recently suggested that the assertion of identity is the logical complement of globalization. As the old certainties and loyalties are swept away people seek new belongings, in various ways. The assertion of long-suppressed or newly invented nationalisms is a reflex to the undermining of the grand sovereign nationalisms that have dominated modernity: in the half-lost symbolisms of a buried past people can seek meaning in a turbulent present. In the transnational truths of Islam or Hinduism, born-again Christianity or ultra-orthodox Judaism, scattered or disrupted peoples can find a meaning that offers hope of escape from the fragmented experience of their current life (Bhatt 1997). Globalization can give give rise to new particularisms, new identities, new belongings, which cannot be easily plotted along a scale of progressive–reactionary. Contemporary social movements, and the individual and collective identities they give rise to and are forged by, emerge as points of resistance and projects for social transformation in dialogue and dialectic with globalizing tendencies, in unpredictable, culturally specific ways.

The lesbian and gay politics of the past thirty years vividly illustrate this. On the one hand the internationalizing of experience has been profound. The American influence post-Stonewall has swept the world, giving rise to a hegemonic notion of what the modern homosexual is, or should be. Yet at the same time, we see the proliferation of differentiated identities, along the lines of gender, 'race' and ethnicity, sexual taste; and the settlement of a new sense of place as rundown parts of most western cities are reinvented as geographical sexual communities. A diasporic identity, transcending traditional cultural boundaries, marked by remarkably similar social facilities, organizations, styles, even domestic patterns, and more or less equally scarred by the threat of illness and death through the AIDS epidemic, co-exists with an ever growing diversification of specific identities, shaped by local cultures, social opportunities, legal systems, political choices and the like. The global and the particular feed off one another, changing what it means to be sexual.

The transformation of intimacy

This is the context for the second major tendency I identified, alongside globalization: the transformation of intimate life. The broad framework for this I have already mentioned: changes in the family and gender relations, and the diversification of sexualities. At the centre of these changes are several key, interlocking aspirations, which I would sum up as the ideal of the democratic relationship, based on equality, intimate disclosure and trust between partners (Giddens 1992; Jamieson 1998).

This is hardly a new dream. One of the elements that first drew me to the work of Havelock Ellis (chapter 1 above) was that he was closely linked to 'advanced' circles that were preoccupied with questioning marriage and the family, the relationship between men and women, and the 'problem' of homosexuality as part of the quest for a 'new life'. Ellis saw these issues as the defining ones of the twentieth century as the old problems of class and poverty and war faded. Of course he was hopelessly optimistic both about the disappearance of 'old' problems and about the ease with which the 'new life' could be achieved, but the search for more equal relations continued to be a strong undercurrent, and fed many individual struggles in everyday life. It became a defining characteristic of the revived feminist movement and the new gay movement from the late 1960s onwards. When Barrett and McIntosh in their critique of the 'anti-social family' spoke of the need for 'experiments in new ways of living' they were both evoking a post-1960s ideology and more or less consciously recalling a long radical tradition (Barrett and McIntosh 1982; see chapter 2 above).

But sociologists like Beck and Beck-Gernsheim (1995) and Giddens (1992) have gone further when they speak of the transformation of intimacy. They are not simply speaking for a dissident critical tradition. They are arguing that everyday life is already being transformed for everyone by the relentless onslaught of social change. The breakdown of traditional institutions and identities forces people to choose how they can live, and everyday life experiments are becoming increasingly the norm as individuals must reflexively decide what is best for them. As a result relationships become increasingly a matter of pragmatic decisions in which negotiation rather than ascription becomes the defining characteristic. 'Confluent love', based on equality between men and women, and the 'pure relationship', based on mutual trust and commitment, become increasingly the form of partnerships – which last only as long as the trust and commitment lasts.

Much of this argument has been severely challenged, particularly on the grounds that it ignores the continuing power of gender inequalities, in terms of disparities of economic power between men and women, the differential burden of emotional labour that falls on women, and the grinding impossibility of most people – even young people – living the egalitarian ideals that are now commonplace (Holland et al. 1998; Jamieson 1998). Many of these critiques are valid. But what is interesting from the point of view of my argument here is that many of the patterns that are claimed to be the norm for the culture as a whole are indeed – as Giddens readily admits – already the basis of everyday practice in same-sex relationships (see chapter 11 above). Lesbians and gays do not have institutional forms which define roles or status. Pragmatic choices do define same-sex arrangements. Trust and commitment have to be worked at in relationships that no one dictates should last unless individuals choose to make them last. If indeed global changes are working their way through into a transformation of intimacy on a broad scale, then it is lesbians and gays who are by necessity in the vanguard – which makes an understanding of the ways in which lesbians and gays have made their own history in recent years, albeit in circumstances not of their own choosing, not a peripheral interest but a key way of understanding sexual history as a whole.

The blues and beyond

As Susan Sontag (1989) put it in her essay on *AIDS and its Metaphors*, in the countdown to the millennium a rise in the apocalyptic may be inevitable. Apocalyptic thinking, Giddens (1991: 4) has suggested, is a characteristic of the late modern world because it generalizes a sense of risk which earlier generations have not had to face. Faced with the breakdown of old traditions which related trust and values to a strong sense of place and belonging, traditions which securely locked us into the certainties, or at least necessities, of family, gender and sexuality, individuals are increasingly thrown back on their own resources (see discussion in Weeks 1995). It is not surprising, therefore, that we are vulnerable to waves of anxiety highlighting our contingency. We respond in a variety of ways: assert our individual power, or retreat to the certainties of faith communities; slump into cynicism, or work out as part of the fetishization of fitness (or both). We live under the hegemony of epidemic, requiring us to avoid risk. We speak of epidemics of child sex abuse, teenage pregnancy, pornography. Governments worry about individual behaviour, seek new social moralities in communitarianism, the resurrection of the family and the like.

Yet I have a sense that something has changed in the past few years, that the apocalyptic tone of the 1980s and early 1990s is fading. We are gaining a new self-confidence in our own truths. There are resources for hope. Even the threat of AIDS, at least in the rich countries of the North, has been partially alleviated by the development of new combination therapies. The culture wars might continue, but so do forms of creativity in everyday life.

The principles of democratic autonomy suggest the need both for individual fulfilment and for mutual involvement, and there are many examples one could cite of this being worked through. In this book I have given two examples close to my own concerns over the past years, but examples which I think throw light on the whole transformation of relationships that is taking place: the HIV/AIDS crisis, and the construction of new families of choice (chapters 10 and 11 above).

The most striking feature of the response to the AIDS epidemic from the gay community was the way in which it brought out a new culture of responsibility, for the self and for others (Weeks 1995). The discourse of safer sex is precisely about balancing individual needs and responsibility to others in a community of identity whose organizing principle is the avoidance of infection and the provision of mutual support. The sexual ties of the new gay cultures of western society proved to be strongly imagined community ties which produced a massive effort of collective self-activity in developing community-based responses to HIV and AIDS, which showed the way forward for publicly funded services in Britain and elsewhere (see chapter 10 above).

Similarly, we can begin to understand the significance of the new stories about non-heterosexual 'families of choice' that are now circulating. The dominant belief in the non-heterosexual world is that lesbian and gay relationships offer unique possibilities for the construction of egalitarian relationships. This does not mean that the privileging of heterosexuality has somehow diminished, or that the achievement of equal relationships is easy and without scars. The point I would make is a wider one. Despite all the hazards, and the force and weight of institutionalized patterns, people do create relationships of mutual care, respect, responsibility and love (chapter 11 above). They provide realistic alternatives to traditional forms of life which are now facing unprecedented stress. They represent the emergence of new narratives of everyday life, and a genuine, if not easy, commitment to the democratization of relationships.

We are living in a new world already, even if we do not always realize it. In the 1970s we used to speak of prefigurative politics as if what we were doing was just in preparation for something better, in a revolution around the corner. Against that millenarianism, I would stress that we are in fact experiencing a social revolution, a transformation of everyday life in which millions are already engaged in everyday experiments in living. The traditional agencies of social and sexual regulation, states and churches, certainly recognize that, as their various confused and fumbling attempts to ignore, or repress, or constructively respond indicate. But whatever the forms of institutional action are, the real transformation is taking place elsewhere, in the nooks and crannies of everyday life.

It is impossible to tell where all this will go. But rather than despairing gloom or impossible dreams, both produced by a *fin de* millennium haze, we should concentrate more on recognizing and validating what is already going on. We live in very interesting times – and these interesting times are likely to continue well into the third millennium. We can negotiate the likely hazards and opportunities more skilfully if we recognize that sexual history is continuously being made and remade, year by year, in the intimacies of everyday life.

References

Barrett, Michèle and McIntosh, Mary (1982) *The Anti-Social Family*, London: Verso.

Beck, Ulrich and Beck-Gernsheim, Elisabeth (1995) *The Normal Chaos of Love*, Cambridge: Polity Press.

Bhatt, Chetan (1997) *Liberation and Purity: Race, New Religious Movements and the Ethics of Postmodernity*, London: UCL Press.

Castells, Manuel (1997) *The Information Age: Economy, Society and Culture*, Vol. 11, *The Power of Identity*, Oxford: Blackwell.

Durkheim, Emile (1974) *Sociology and Philosophy*, New York: Free Press.

Epstein, Steven (1996) *Impure Science: AIDS, Activism and the Politics of Knowledge*, Berkeley CA: University of California Press.

Giddens, Anthony (1991) *Modernity and Self-Identity: Self, Society and the Late Modern Age*, Cambridge: Polity Press.

Giddens, Anthony (1992) *The Transformation of Intimacy*, Cambridge: Polity Press.

Gould, Stephen Jay (1997) *Questioning the Millennium: A Rationalist's Guide to a Precisely Arbitrary Countdown*, London: Jonathan Cape.

Holland, Janet, Ramazanoglu, Caroline, Sharpe, Sue and Thomson, Rachel (1998) *The Male in the Head: Young People, Heterosexuality and Power*. London: Tufnell Press.

Jamieson, Lynn (1998) *Intimacy: Personal Relationships in Modern Societies*, Cambridge: Polity Press.

Plummer, Ken (1995) *Telling Sexual Stories: Power, Change and Social Worlds*, London: Routledge.

Showalter, Elaine (1991) *Sexual Anarchy: Gender and Sexuality at the Fin de Siècle*, London: Bloomsbury.

Silva, Elizabeth B. and Smart, Carol (eds) (1999) *The New Family?*, London: Sage.

Sontag, Susan (1989) *AIDS and its Metaphors*, London: Allen Lane.

Weeks, Jeffrey (1985) *Sexuality and its Discontents: Meanings, Myths and Modern Sexualities*, London: Routledge.

Weeks, Jeffrey (1995) *Invented Moralities: Sexual Values in an Age of Uncertainty*, Cambridge: Polity Press.

Weeks, Jeffrey (1998) 'The Sexual Citizen', *Theory, Culture and Society*, 15 (3–4), 35–52.

Index